Conversations
with **Seth**

ALSO BY SUSAN M. WATKINS

Conversations with Seth, Book 2

What a Coincidence!

Speaking of Jane Roberts

Dreaming Myself, Dreaming a Town

Garden Madness

Conversations *with* Seth

introduction by Jane Roberts

Susan M. Watkins

illustrations by George Rhoads

Moment Point Press

Needham, Massachusetts

25th Anniversary Edition, 2005
Copyright © 1980, 1999 by Susan M. Watkins
Preface to the 25th Anniversary Copyright © 2005 by Susan M. Watkins

Moment Point Press, Inc.
PO Box 920287
Needham, MA 02492
www.momentpoint.com

All illustrations, except figures 1–10, copyright © 1980 by George Rhoads, used by permission. "Song for Our Bones," "Small Rain—A Song," "Reincarnational," "The Green Man" copyright © 1980 by Dan Stimmerman, used by permission. "Intrinsic Artists" and "Ode on Sex and Religion" copyright © 1980 by Barrie Gellis, used by permission. "Follow Yourself," "Notes to a Young Man," Introduction, and all previously unpublished Seth material copyright © 1980 by Jane Roberts, used by permission.

Cover Design: Susan Ray and Metaglyph Design
Typesetting: Graphic Details
Printing: Transcontinental
Distribution: Red Wheel / Weiser

Library of Congress has cataloged the 1999 combined-volume edition as follows:
Watkins, Susan M., 1945–
Conversations with Seth: the story of Jane Roberts's ESP Class
by Susan M. Watkins; illustrations by George Rhoads.
        p. cm.
Originally published: Englewood Cliffs, NJ: Prentice-Hall, 1980–1981.
Includes bibliographical references and index.
ISBN 1-889828-04-1
        1. Spirit Writings. 2. Reincarnation—Miscellanea. I. Seth (Spirit), 1929– . II. Roberts, Jane, 1929–1984. III. Title.
BF1301.W226 1999
133.9'3—dc21   99-070189   CIP
ISBN: 0-9661327-2-6

2005 25th Anniversary Edition:
ISBN-13: 978-1-930491-05-2
ISBN-10: 1-930491-05-0
Printed in Canada on acid-free paper
10 9 8 7 6 5 4 3 2 1

for Sean, and now Dave,
who unknowing,
Know

Special thanks to:

Jane and Rob, for all the years of assistance and love;

Jeff and his statistics; HughW. and his photocopies and lists;
George R. and his comix; Richie and his exuberant phone calls;

Everyone who took the time and space (non-existent as these
might be) to answer my lengthy questionnaire;

And to:
The ghost of the old Nebene, who showed me the model for this
book, couched as it was inside several other books, all of them
distinct probabilities.
(Te jingjo le é bordujo—mayando.)

Contents

Illustrations

Drawings by George Rhoads

Figures

The world will take these ideas as it will. I give them play-fully, joyfully, and humbly, that they may fall as the seeds fall from a gigantic oak tree. I do not say that every man must pick up one of those seeds for himself and use it. I say merely, "I am." And to you, I say, "You Are."

Seth in Class
May 7, 1974

Preface to the 25th Anniversary Edition

AN INCREASINGLY UNPOPULAR WAR in a distant country. Struggles for gender and racial equality. Environmental degradation. A growing social and economic divide. Unfathomable natural disasters of epic proportions. These were some of the topics debated in Jane Roberts's ESP class a generation or so ago. Update this mix with 9/11, and you have yesterday's headlines come 'round again, in only somewhat different guise.

Of course much good has come to pass since the sixties and seventies (it's even possible we've learned a thing or two), but oh how outrageous Jane's ideas were back then, the notion that reality springs from the matrix of our own consciousness. At least as far as mainstream media were concerned, such things as dreams, ESP, and the so-called paranormal were suspect psychological anomalies or mere conjectures of science fiction and fantasy. Certainly no credence was given to a connection between individual belief and mass experience. Except for a few pods of original thinking, such as Jane's work and her ESP class, the culture was going nowhere but the same old place.

Sure, there were enormous pressures for social change in those years, but it was easy to feel outcast and alone. Technologically, the world in which Jane and Rob embarked on their journeys with Seth in 1963 was closer to the Civil War era than the one we know today. There were no home computers, no Internet or email, no satellite hookups, no cell phones or camcorders or VCRs; cable TV was in its infancy and the DVD unknown. "Reality" television was actually real—Vietnam, taped on-scene while it happened, a shocking innovation (and one that fed the war protests and helped end it). But nitty-gritty life issues didn't have the public forums we take for granted, like them or not. Talk TV and radio shows as we know them didn't exist. Dilemmas of sex and gender preference, divorce, affairs, babies out of wedlock, racial discrimination, domestic violence—all were forbidden territory in a way that's almost impossible to comprehend today, and required investment of personal energy to disguise, or suffer in silence. Today, most of this is so public as to be the subject of sitcoms and tell-alls (hooray for that), and permutations of law and compassion have freed us from many constraints; yet here we are squabbling over the basics once again, not to mention the specter of terrorism and its creeping impact on our social construct and habits.

In that, this 25th Anniversary Edition of *Conversations with Seth* is as relevant as if I'd written it yesterday. Jane's ESP class was diverse in age, background, and politics, but we were united by the feeling that none of the accepted definitions worked anymore, even when we wished they could. Reluctantly, with Seth's always wise, frequently exasperating prompting, we threw out the premise of cause and effect. We chose instead to behave as if the world were a result of individual and mass beliefs. Anguish, illness, disasters and joy, anything that happened to us: our creation. No accidents. Not even one. No excuses.

Daring ourselves along, we wrote belief papers, kept track of dreams, ranted and raved, laughed and cried while we wrestled with how these ideas mattered outside the walls of Jane and Rob's apartment. We didn't "study" the Seth material so much as we pummeled it. Gay and straight, we haggled our sex lives, told intimate secrets, swapped garb (or threw it off), argued love and war, draft dodging, fun and responsibility, drugs and religion; and all of terms of multidimensional existence and purpose, of infinite pasts and futures alive in the ever-expanding present.

In a way, what we did in class was conservative and ordinary, people trying to figure out the meaning of life. But in another way, the most important way, what we did there was magical and wild, more extraordinary than any of us imagined at the time. It wasn't merely that class included the presence of "a personality no longer focused in physical reality," as Seth described himself, a personality who gave original, beautifully written (and spoken) material for us to do with what we liked. No, the truly splendid, utterly scandalous thing about class was that we came to glimpse ourselves as personalities focused by choice in this reality, not here by accident or dint of inscrutable deity, with all the implications for consciousness, not to mention the nature of the universe, rippling out into the world.

But linear time does pass, and in our terms nothing lasts forever. ESP class ended in 1975 and Jane Roberts died in 1984, leaving this existence too soon and emptier for it. And so it goes, the sublime mix of past, present, and future in this rebirth of a tale that began so long ago—or was it just last Tuesday? I would hope that this anniversay edition of *Conversations* can spark a different kind of debate, one that recognizes the thread of consciousness that ultimately unites us all. As Seth would say—playfully, of course—"the experiment continues."

Susan M. Watkins
January 13, 2005

Preface to the 1980 Edition

I STARTED WRITING THIS BOOK IN October of 1978 with the idea that it would be a fairly safe project; that is, I could do a reporter's job—collect and record the memories of Jane Roberts's former class members—and leave myself out of it, as any proper reporter should do. I thought that I would be able to dodge the truly intimate stance taken by Jane and Rob in their books involving Seth, psychic revelation, and the search for a larger framework of identity. I'd read all of Jane's books and deeply admired her courage, especially with the publication of *The Afterdeath Journal of an American Philosopher* in 1978. Secretly, however, I began my own excursions into these realms feeling rather smug: I wouldn't be risking a thing.

Well, things didn't work out that way, of course. The fact is that I was a member of Jane Roberts's ESP class for nearly ten years, and there is no way that I could pretend to have been a dispassionate observer—and I wouldn't choose to be one now, if I lived that time all over again. I was a passionate participant, leaping into class events or retreating from them as my individual reactions so unobjectively decreed, involved in the unique give-and-take in my own particular way, as everyone was. And so as I wrote this book I came to understand that it was ridiculous for me to imagine that it could contain any kind of integrity at all without the fullness of my subjective input.

For in looking back on Jane's Tuesday night class, I see its effect on my own beliefs, intent, and purposes as an almost archetypal learning experience for the perspective that asks: How do people create—as we heard Seth say a thousand times—their own reality, and how does any group, or group of groups, or the sum of life upon the Earth, create the world we know? What are the inner equations of outer events? What migrations of desire lead us to perform the actions we later reflect upon, often in astonishment and pain? Do we, as individuals and as a species, in fact know a benevolent interior logic that, if understood, would show us the meaning of what looks like chaos and species insanity?

I believe that in its way, Jane's ESP class was a far-reaching revolutionary experience of the self, unlike anything that civilization has so far allowed its members. That is to say, the basic premise of class—even though we had to "learn" to believe it—was this: Personhood is innocent; and from that innocent personhood's beliefs and desires, you create the world you experience.

From that premise of multidimensional activity, class members began to understand and use the validity of subjective perception as perhaps no other group—religious, therapeutic, academic, or scientific—has done before. And I further believe that the effects of Jane's class, and its events, on the "students" and others who came there represent the kind of inner revolution that can begin to restructure personal and social reality along humankind's basically cooperative intent. This "un-organization," as Seth liked to call it, imposed no rules, dictated nothing, and strove only to recognize the artistry of the self; yet it touched and rearranged the assumptions and directions of all those who were part of it.

Through the years, Seth's class comments were preserved by two or three "regulars" who taped, transcribed, and duplicated the sessions as a favor to Jane and Rob and the rest of us. Although numerous members made tapes of class goings-on, the responsibility of transcribing Seth's remarks was usually taken on by one person, who somehow managed to have copies for us by the following Tuesday. In the early classes, Florence MacIntyre and Brad Lanton did the job; then Natalie Swing did so for several years, with occasional time off when I agreed to do it (it takes at least twice as long to transcribe and type up anything as it takes to record it in the first place). Finally, Harold Wiles, manager of a local shopping mall, made the tapes and written transcripts for the last four or five years, laboriously typing stencils and running them through an old handcranked mimeo so we'd all be sure to have copies.

"Without those people to depend on for session copies," Jane says, "I would never have let Seth come through in class."

Members often took notes, and nearly everybody kept dream records in some form.

Kernels of class, then, were already neatly preserved. But even though Jane had described class scenes in her books, a complete chronicle was a project that neither she nor Rob wanted to tackle.

Since I'd been a newspaper editor and reporter for about five years, and a close friend of Jane and Rob's for longer, I'd tossed the idea around for some time about doing a class book along the lines of Studs Terkel's *Working*, in which individual voices told the story. Both from my viewpoint and from the living mosaic of class itself, the interview vehicle seemed a natural. There were things that I recalled that I wanted people to describe from their own angles: two total strangers suddenly yelling at one another over a simultaneously-perceived incident that had apparently happened centuries before . . . half the class stripping bare-ass naked in response to a belief session on responsibility, of all things ("Your attitudes toward your bodies are like your attitudes toward responsibility," Seth commented that evening) . . . a girl with Hodgkin's disease seeing for the first time how much she'd been depending on her symptoms for her own identity . . . Seth carrying on an extensive dialogue on good and evil with a skeptical young man who believed that Hitler could have used Seth's ideas to justify his actions . . . class dreams, in which members would discover fascinating correlations among their dream records, sometimes even to the dream conversations and often involving the whole group, including Seth . . . the Halloween class in which we were "assigned" to dress up as the opposite sex . . . individuals who attended class and seemed to illustrate for us belief systems in microcosm . . . the sudden appearance of Sumari and the Sumari mini-dramas and songs . . . all of these memories, and countless others, were too good to leave alone. Then, at one of Jane and Rob's Friday night get-togethers, Robbie asked me what had happened to my book idea. "The interview-format thing you had in mind," he prodded. "When are you going to start doing it?" The next day, I happened to meet a former class member in a local restaurant. We hadn't seen each other in months, but the first words out of his mouth were, "Hi, Sue—when are you going to do that class book?"

I was hooked.

Subsequently, I made up a questionnaire to send out to as many class members as I could track down. Later, I interviewed some of these people by phone and in person. Consequently, members' comments in this book are a combination of the written and spoken word; but to simplify things, I've described their recollections as "said" rather than written, except where I've used passages from notes taken at the time of class itself.

Thus, with the extensive cooperation of former members, I assembled the story of Jane's class from those who composed it. In doing so, I am in no way implying that class solved all problems, gave perfect answers (or perfect questions), or tried to become the path for some kind of new religion, complete with its own mystical-priestess leader. In actuality, there was relatively little direct personal problem solving done in class. Instead, it was a flexible framework—or proving ground—where ideas embodied in the Seth material and in Jane's own books could be filtered through a multitude of daily realities. We accepted the context of Seth's ideas and dealt with the joys and sorrows of daily life from that level. And out of believing that "you create your own reality," we learned the personal power of the only true authority—the authority of the self.

I should add that all class members' names used herein are pseudonyms, with the exception of Dan Stimmerman, Richie Kendall, and artist George Rhoads, whose delightful drawings illuminate this book. Every Tuesday, George would fill dozens of notebook pages with everything from sketches of the abstract to line portraits of people around him—all inspired by the moment at hand. *Conversations'* illustrations are gleaned from those pages. (George appears in both volumes of *The "Unknown" Reality* as "Peter Smith.")

Original poetry appearing here was written by class members and is used with their permission, credited without alias.

Susan M. Watkins
January, 1980

Introduction by Jane Roberts

BY THE TIME THIS BOOK is in the stores [in 1980], it will be five years since my husband, Rob, and I moved from our apartments on West Water Street where I held the 400 or so ESP classes that Sue Watkins writes about in these pages. Now, Rob and I often drive past that old apartment house, and almost always I look up at those familiar second-floor bay windows, musing: Does some other self still sit in the Kennedy rocker in the living room, "turning into" Seth? Do those classes continue in some dimension of mind that never intrudes on the apartment's current tenant?

Though physical time has carried us "past" those classes, it often seems to me that they are still going on and still exist in some Spacious Present, even as the house still exists in space. As I read the class Seth sessions in Sue's book, however, I see that Seth's words aren't dated. They haven't deteriorated. They live, and in retrospect, they attain an even greater vitality than we may once have assigned to them.

Each time Seth spoke, I was in trance, and it was Seth who smiled out at students through my opened eyes. Sue Watkins attended most of those classes and she describes my "transformation" into Seth and Seth's interactions with the students very well—a considerable achievement, because of the psychological complexities involved. This wasn't just a class *about* the nature of the psyche, expanded consciousness, or the extraordinary abilities of human personality. This was a continuing demonstration, as I "turned into Seth" time and time again, taking off my own mental clothes and exchanging them for psychological Olympian garb; Olympian only in that Seth displays a superabundance of energy, compassion, wisdom, and exuberance—which, he assures us, are a part of our own human heritage.

These classes have been referred to in my own books, *Adventures in Consciousness* and *Psychic Politics,* and in Rob's notes in Seth's books; but nowhere have they been treated in any depth. Besides dictating *Seth Speaks, The Nature of Personal Reality* and nearly completing the two volumes of *The "Unknown" Reality,* Seth gave approximately 300 class sessions during the eight years covered in Sue's pages. He addressed the students, answered their questions, and participated in lively give-and-take discussions.

Rob and I wanted to make that material available to the public, but neither of us had time to do the work involved in such a project.

Conversations with Seth helps serve that purpose, including the "meatiest" excerpts from those sessions. People were free to tape whatever they wanted in class, but one student in particular taped the Seth sessions for the record, transcribed them, mimeographed copies, and distributed them to students for twenty-five cents apiece. Obviously the cost hardly compensated for the work involved, and I'd like to thank Harold Wiles publicly here for that service.

Sue also captures the exuberance, rambunctiousness, driving curiosity, and daring speculations that class shared. Besides that, however, as I read this book I went mind-sailing the two miles from our new house to the old one, seeing myself in a sudden series of images, caught up in my own situation at the time of my life that Sue describes so well.

First I saw myself watching from the small kitchen windows on some past midnight as my students emerged outside, downstairs, heading for their cars, my view partially blocked by the gracious terrace that later was ripped down to make room for a parking lot next door. Then, turning away, I went back into the living room to face the stacks of paper cups, ashtrays, and allied clutter, and to put away the assortment of porch folding chairs—quietly, so as not to disturb Rob, who slept in the back of the apartment. This mental image must have been from the earliest years of class because later we rented a second apartment across the hall; Rob quit his job in the art department of a local firm and, much later, began attending class himself.

I mention these points, though, to emphasize that the Seth sessions and the class's most "esoteric" adventures took place within the framework of normal living. Because if I was Seth in trance, when out of it, I was myself. Seth didn't make that room ready for thirty to forty people each Tuesday: I did. He didn't dress as quickly as possible and rush through dinner to wait the last few minutes before class, wondering, "What on earth am I doing, seeing all of these people? What is it really for?" For years I spent nearly half a day preparing the apartment for class, and half of the next day cleaning up afterward, though later Rob helped me a good deal, and frequently I reminded class that the finest flights of fancy must rest firmly in the framework of daily living.

Rob and I held some 375 private Seth sessions before I decided to have a class, and even then I didn't have a class session for some time. For one thing, our regular sessions were scheduled for 9 P.M. on Mondays and Wednesdays, and I wasn't used to the idea of having Seth come through spontaneously, even with the new class framework. Until then, I hadn't gone into trance without Rob in the room. In the early days of class it was a big step for me to have a session without Rob there, and before a group of relative strangers. I decided that I had to hold my own, though: I wasn't going to act like a swooning female with the strong male there to look out for me and my trances. I had to be able to trust myself and my abilities; and if I was going to have any consistent trouble in coming out of trances, then I had no business going into them to begin with. So I reasoned, anyway, but the problem never arose. In any case, as class members and I grew more comfortable with each other, I began to have frequent Seth sessions. Finally Seth spoke at almost each class, sometimes for hours at a time.

The sessions never became old hat to me, though. Even now in our private ones I'm newly struck by the wealth of Seth's knowledge and the extraordinary psychological organization that must be involved in the dictation of his books. Seth didn't dictate in class, however. He "came through" spontaneously, in response to a student's question, or to our discussion, or just as often to make a general contribution. He was quite aware of the "Seth baiting" that often went on, when some students made up leading questions that were supposed to rouse him into making an "appearance." I think Seth considered it a kind of children's game on their parts.

But through the class's largely supportive framework, I learned the fine nuances of trancelife and developed a dependable psychological poise: learning to navigate smoothly the many subtle subjective states that connected Seth's reality with mine; blinking off and on from one focus to the other, from mine to Seth's and back again. (Here again, there again, gone again, Finnegan.) In so doing, I learned to focus better *here* also. In class, I was "more me," while Seth was, as always, himself.

If I was "more me," the students were also more themselves in some strange fashion. Seth always seemed to bring out the best in them—not, as the transcripts show, the most pious, but the most creative, vital, and understanding portions of their personalities. Seth wasn't aloof, for one thing. He didn't just lecture, he also listened. He answered concrete questions concretely or explained his reasons for not doing so in any given instance. And—an important point to remember in reading this book—Seth was speaking to people who came back week after week, so he couched his sessions in terms of their backgrounds and culture, as any good teacher does. If he sometimes made a statement for its shock value, he knew that most of these same people would be back the following week when he or I could answer their questions. He tailored his discussions to their needs, and in so doing he provided an incredible learning environment. That itself is no small achievement.

Seth's humor comes through in these class sessions, more than it does in his dictated book material. Though he does speak each word aloud in our book sessions, he uses more of a "written English" geared for manuscripts, while in class he usually spoke in the vernacular.

Yet somehow there was always more going on in class than students could grasp. I felt like a psychic spendthrift sometimes, and sometimes it made me sad that so many implications were missed. But the psychic spendthrift in me doesn't care: We did what we did; we had what we had. And I guess I'd like to be a psychic spendthrift more often! But then another part of me takes over that wants to know exactly what we learned, how we're using that knowledge, and how we were different after class than we were before.

Again, the psychic spendthrift in me thinks, Who cares? Whatever we learned is so much a part of us now that it's impossible to separate that knowledge from what we are. The classes started and ended, following their own pattern. When we try to examine them now, they necessarily become something different than they were. Granting that, Sue Watkins has done an extraordinary job not only of reporting what happened in class, but in describing the larger psychological climate in which those events occurred.

On looking back, our unconventionality and our rambunctious swearing and hooting can be seen as their own conventions of a sort, and maybe they were. They were also healthy reminders that we wouldn't be cowed even by our own psychic experiences, even by Seth's unorthodox presence, and just maybe that's one of the reasons Seth enjoyed class so well. Because he did. He obviously enjoyed each person who came to class: the regular members, the occasional visitors, and the one-nighters.

And through the variety of people who attended the classes from all over the country, I was made aware of the differing, sometimes amusing and sometimes annoying, attitudes that people have about mediums or psychics in general. Sometimes I was considered a necessary but resented intermediary between Seth and the individual; someone to be complimented and kept happy so that I'd open up the golden gates to Instant Knowledge. Some people expected a holy woman, frightening and fascinating at once, with domineering electric presence, forever "turned on," eyes flashing, reading minds at will. Others wanted a vulnerable, passive female channel whose body was "possessed" in swooning psychological surrender. Others looked for a charming fraud, clever and calculating, an actress in a cunning psychic drama, playing a "cruel game" with gullible, hope-blinded followers, or involved in psychic manipulations in which she subconsciously conned herself as well as others. And a few came invigorated by the idea of "taking on Seth" or playing a game of wits with Seth or me. But most people came initially just to see what, if anything, was going on; and later they came to learn about themselves. They were more interested in discovering their own reality and worth; more concerned about how they could help themselves and others than in playing psychic games.

For one thing, I didn't play psychic games. I didn't make use of sexual overtones, either. If I swore and drank wine and if the air was sometimes thick with cigarette smoke, to me that atmosphere was a rambunctious, honest one. It didn't foster secret hopes that the Holy Ghost or Virgin Mary might be hovering in magic shadows. It didn't encourage other suggestions, either. If tables went thumping across the floor (and they did), then everyone in the room could see everyone else's position in relation to the table too, because all the lights were on. And if we saw odd gauzy figures in the night (and we did), then they had to appear in the illumination of several good sixty-watt bulbs.

Overall, the people who attended class were terrific. They were of all ages and from just about every area of endeavor. If any one attitude united us as a group, it was the certainty that there was more to life—and death—than our official fields of knowledge acknowledged, or cared to investigate; and that separately and together, we just might—just might—get an inkling of what was really involved. This gave us a sense of vital comradeship. I'd say that most of us, myself included, got more than we bargained for; and Sue Watkins's book describes our individual and joint experiences, experiments, "trial runs," and accomplishments with gusto and understanding. Since Sue is also a personal friend, she was able to draw upon other events in which Seth, Rob, or I were involved outside of class to shed further light on any given class event, or to explain our psychological attitudes at the time. Some class events splashed over into our private lives, for example, particularly into our Friday night gatherings with friends, affairs that Sue often attended.

Seth and I both used to joke with a particular student about his attempt to "spook out" the universe, but in a fashion, that's what we were all trying to do. We had the feeling that from that one second-floor apartment with its wide bay windows, we were spying out the universe, prowling restlessly around the edges of ordinary reality, poking around in the outskirts of time and space.

When Seth did his "energy thing," his (my) voice rumbled with power; the room and all of us seemed to quiver, ready to take off, riding heady gusts of energy that, Seth stressed, were our own. I don't think any of us would have been too surprised had we literally raised the roof. But each of us did "take off" in our own fashion. We grappled with our own beliefs about ourselves and the world in general and our place in it. The students asked pertinent, timeless, questions about the very timely events of their lives: about life, death, love, hate, war and peace, good and evil. And answering, Seth always treated each individual as a person of honor. He never built himself up at another's expense.

I didn't think in terms of teaching methods. Instead, I felt that each class innately contained its own drama: I merely sensed its dramatic shape and helped direct it. As Sue's book shows, classes involved far more than the Seth sessions themselves. There were our "reincarnational dramas," the acting out of beliefs, exchanges of sexual roles and garb, the assignments and various exercises with telepathy and clairvoyance and, always, the dream "work" that so held our interest.

We certainly seemed to meet in our dreams. Some of our out-of-body encounters with others in the dream state checked out, according to our records.

And there is little doubt in any of our minds that we operated and interacted at other levels of reality than the normally accepted one.

Sue Watkins has wound these various elements together so that they tell the story of what happened in class and to whom, but her words hint of the untold story of personality and identity that lies within each of us. She describes when and how the Sumari development suddenly emerged in class, for example, and does so in such a way that we must each question the nature of our own identities and the unofficial affiliations of our own consciousnesses.

Conversations with Seth contains some excellent poetry, and I had a small Creative Writing class during the period covered by this book. But Seth also stresses the even greater living art that we *can* make of our lives, and emphasizes that the creative abilities are devoted not just to specific arts and crafts, but to the entire framework of our lives. Certainly in those terms, class was as creative as any art form, and it was a kind of psychic theater of the mind with its own dramatic episodes.

And class kept changing, as Sue's book shows. People came and went through the years. Sometimes the one-nighters and people passing through outnumbered the regulars. We could fit only so many people comfortably in that one room, yet I tried to give as many people as possible the opportunity to hear Seth speak. For that reason I'm amazed when on occasion I hear that some scientist believes that "the whole thing is a fraud," that there is no Seth; or conversely, that I encourage blind belief on the part of my "followers." The fact is that Seth came through some 300 times over those eight years in full light, responding spontaneously to on-the-spot questions in a way impossible to prepare beforehand. Though I made a special effort to admit any scientists, very few contacted us. I think four or five psychologists visited class in that entire eight-year period, and two physicists. They were great people. But it's too bad that more of their colleagues didn't join them. Far more professionals contact us now, and we make an effort to see them when possible. Often Seth comes through during such visits, but between 1967 and 1975 the classes provided a ready-made platform and format for such activity.

Actually, most of the time we really didn't want anyone looking over our shoulders in class. But when anyone did, there was something worthwhile to observe. We were exploring the nature of consciousness, nudging aside its officially defined edges, and discovering that they gave way; they dissolved. The official barriers were artificial.

Sue Watkins is a highly gifted writer, and her words evocatively re-create the psychological atmosphere in which class existed. Her own psychic experiences are of a very high caliber, fascinating in themselves, and she possesses a fine blend of psychic receptivity and critical common sense, a combination that is far from common. And as I stress in my own yet-unfinished book, *The*

God of Jane: a Psychic Manifesto, we must somehow learn to blend our intel-
lects and intuitions. For if we believe that one is in opposition to the other,
then no matter which we choose, we lose.

Seth's own creativity was probably as much responsible as anything else
for my decision not to start class up again after we settled ourselves in our
new house. Rob and I have a hard time keeping up with Seth's seemingly
inexhaustible energy; he finished dictating volume 2 of *The "Unknown" Reality* right after our move, for example, and almost instantly launched into *The
Nature of the Psyche: Its Human Expression.* Since then he's completed *The
Individual and The Nature of Mass Events,* and has just begun another, *Dreams,
"Evolution," and Value Fulfillment.* So since class ended, Seth has been as busy
as ever. Through his books, of course, his "message" can reach far greater
numbers of people than could ever be handled in a class.

Rob has transcribed all of those Seth book sessions, added his own in-
valuable notes, and done just about all the work of preparing them for publication. He also devotes part of each day to his painting. I've written several
books of my own since class ended, and I've tried to keep up with the ever-
increasing correspondence from our readers. In a way I suppose I think of
them as a kind of extended family, friends in a quite vital dimension of mind.

In any case, I have no idea what I may do in the future; but for now it's
Rob and I and Seth alone again, except for a few occasional guests. We meet
our private appointments with the universe through the sessions, and when
Seth dictates his books, he speaks to a larger class, not dependent upon any
time or place, a "class" in which each reader is a welcome member.

January 22, 1980

CHAPTER 1

Who Said Truth Was Stranger Than Fiction? (That's How *The Bundu* Knew)

My Friend Is a Medium on Monday Nights
(to Jane)

Pinpointed yellow spaceship apartment,
Look in your grinning windows and see the universe fold up,
See tree-thoughts stand all charcoal and acorn,
Watch behind the air . . .

—SMW

When intuitive knowledge and understanding overflow,
then it overflows into all kinds of creativity and it is. It does
not form groups. Groups appear. There is a difference. There
is no need to form groups. Groups appear because there is no
need to form them.

—Seth in Class, June 11, 1974

IN THE INSCRUTABLE LOGIC OF NATURE, the summer days have turned brilliant and magical in the special light of autumn. Far above my hometown streets, the geese are following their ancient migration urge in its regular and obvious patterns, forming an equation so appropriate that no one in his right mind questions the seasons: What goose would fly south in July? What tree would turn red and gold in February?

In the equally inscrutable—and largely unacknowledged—logic of humankind, the people outside my window follow their own migrations of pattern and form, reacting and interacting in beautiful spontaneous appropriateness that no one in his "right" mind carries beyond certain accepted precepts of logic. And yet, what serendipity of selfhood peeks through our "logical" experience?

It was December of 1963. I was a freshman at Syracuse University's journalism school, one of 2,200 in the Class of '67; all of us still digesting the shock of JFK's death. We had watched it all: the funeral procession on TV interspersed with commercials for floor mops; the riderless horse augmented by ads for dog food. The campus magazine devoted its entire pre-Christmas issue to on-the-street interviews with students who described where they'd been and what they had been doing when they heard the news that Kennedy had been shot. The students' recollections were without exception precise, clear-cut stills of one moment in time and space; perhaps the first awe of history felt by our generation. Vaughn Bodé, that weirdo campus artist some few years away from the underground comics, illustrated the text of the student interviews with dreamlike clouds and bubbles outlined in black. The

Berlin Wall and Cuba had been terrifying, but was this not the death of poetry—of answers—in government?

Everyone taking Freshman Civics that semester was supposed to read Ralph Ellison's *Invisible Man*. I'd tried a few chapters and quit, bored. Though Ellison's book was considered the bravest, most searing social comment of the new decade, I was far more compelled by a science-fiction story in a paperback anthology I'd picked up in the campus bookstore. The story, called "The Chestnut Beads," dealt with college sororities and the Bomb. It told of a sorority's initiation rites that were actually a ritual of subliminal suggestion, given to the women on how to survive the coming holocaust—and, surviving it, take over the world so that men could never again have the chance to destroy it. The initiates consciously forgot the inner message embodied in the ritual, but carried it with them nonetheless, like an invisible mental fetus, through the rites of marriage and childbirth and house cleaning—until the Day came, and the Bomb fell, and the message was born again to the female survivors.

The story was powerful, brooding, and in those innocent pre-feminist days, defiant and deliciously revengeful; and I read it over and over, savoring it, surviving with the survivors, taking over the world's remnants with them. Later, I read an expanded version of the same story in a novel called *The Bundu*. The theme would haunt my mind for years, although I forgot the author's name until I met her five years later. And it would be more than a year after that before I would meet Ned Watkins, to whom I would be married for a brief time.

Yet so it was that as my eighteen-year-old self sat in my dorm room, far from my home in Elmira, New York, reading the story of "The Chestnut Beads" by Jane Roberts, she and her husband Rob Butts—perhaps at that precise jelly-cubed moment—were sitting in front of a Ouija board in their Elmira apartment, spelling out the first messages from a character calling himself Seth; while I, back at good old Syracuse U, was diligently skipping my civics assignment for a story that somehow began to answer the call of my tumultuous, assassination-raped feelings, in the tale of the chestnut beads' Olive and her somewhat disposable daughter—whose name was Sue Watkins!

And I wonder: What smooth, gleeful orchestra of logic, what migration of desire and intent—categorized "rationally" as coincidence—connected Jane and me five years before we met, through a fictional character whose name I would not have until six years after I read that story?

After graduation, I worked for a while on Elmira's daily newspaper, and then moved to Martha's Vineyard. For a few weeks I lived in a rooming house whose other tenants turned out to be undercover narcotics agents posing as

Sue Watkins

shoe salesmen. Given the bleakness of the island in winter without tourists, it was hard to imagine who would be buying shoes, let alone narcotics. But the agents plugged on, and eventually bagged the sons of some rich and famous people.

For two weeks I worked in the medical records section of the island hospital, having landed the job on the merits of a college education—never mind that I'd never been in a business office in my life. I was soon so mired in the mysteries of bookkeeping that I sent out bills to every name in the files—including people who hadn't been to the hospital in years. That was my last desk job, but I managed to support myself as the island's Western Union teletype operator and "social correspondent" for the Vineyard *Gazette*, contributing local tidbits on who ate Sunday dinner with whom. But I felt eternally lost at sea, doomed to extinction beneath a pile of rejection slips—and rightly so. Even my own desperate appraisal of the short stories my typewriter ground out foresaw a long apprenticeship with the written word.

So it was with portents of new directions one August night that I found myself standing in the streetlights' glow of my apartment kitchen, wide awake, trying to make the sink faucet work so I could get a glass of water. I struggled with the cold-water spigot. But no matter which way I turned the handle— and for some reason it spun around freely either way—no water came out into my waiting glass. The glass wasn't right either: it was shaped like a squash. *A squash?*

I stared at the glass, the faucet. I did not remember getting out of bed, or walking to the sink. I turned around and looked back into the bedroom— and there I was, sleeping soundly on my back, my mouth slightly open, the covers pushed away.

I walked to the bedside and stared down at myself, watching the breath moving in and out of my sleeping body. My consciousness was definitely not in that body—it was here, outside, standing and watching. I reached out and touched my body's arm, and leaped back, startled. The skin was warm and alive, but I had felt the touch on the arm of the body I was standing in—and I'd been aware of the touch on the arm of my sleeping, physical self. It was a strange duality, like endless mirror images. Affection for my physical being welled up inside of this aware, awake self that I was there, in the dark-light glow of my room. It was powerful and secure, my physical body, sleeping peacefully, refreshing itself in ways only dimly guessed at: was this projection of my consciousness part of that renewing process?

I turned away from the bed and walked out into the small living room, objects glowing with import, as alive and aware as I. The front windows opened up for me, and I looked out over the Vineyard. Sound, dark liquid velvet, the rhythmic clank of sailboat mastcleats chiming up through the damp sea fog surrounding the village. All the details of the night were clear to me; it was as though each physical thing called out separately, yearning to tell me its secret and its meaning. I leaped out the window, then, and flew into the night; down past the sailboats moored in the Sound; down through the dark water to the debris-strewn bottom; up out of the warm, thick sea into the air and past the gray-shingled houses lining the West Chop beaches; and my memory contains hours of this flight between the molecules of matter, soaring as a physical creature never could through the nighttime beauty of the physical land. Several times I passed others in the same state, flying in a kind of private rapture. At one point, I swept past a man in monk's garb who grinned and waved as we went our opposite ways. Throughout, I was as awake as I've ever been. And except for the ecstatic, perfect freedom of flight, I could have been walking the streets of Vineyard Haven on any fog-shrouded summer night.

Abruptly, I felt an urge to return to my body. I snapped awake, jolted almost violently with the feeling of slamming down on the bed. I stared at the room. The sun was streaming through the windows, but it was not my room. It appeared to be another room, in another place. I stared hard, forcing myself to find the "right" room—and with a sudden *snap!* behind my ears, my familiar bedroom fell into place. But that soaring, beautiful night flight of consciousness was still singing in my skull, and it stayed with me for days afterwards, calling up my childhood's secret dreams; a turning point in my awareness of how my own peculiar abilities bridged any gap that I might feel between my private self and the "real" world. ("There are no divisions to the self," Seth would tell us countless times, smiling gleefully.)

And so, a month later, pressed by an urgency I didn't understand and in fact resented (and still do, to some extent), I returned to Elmira, where my friend Dan Stimmerman took me that September of 1968 to one of Jane and Rob's Friday night parties; it was important that I tell my experiences to "that lady who speaks for the ghost of a dead man," Dan said. He'd dragged me, protesting, to a New Year's Eve bash at their place nine months before, though nothing had "clicked" then for a number of reasons. This time, things had . . . changed.

The living room was large, bright, cozy. Evening traffic noises mingled with the crisp autumn air that rushed in through the open bay windows of the second-floor apartment. Robbie's paintings filled the walls; the furniture was a comfortable conglomeration of castoffs; plants and books and writer's paraphernalia decorated the place. No dead men whispered through Jane's lips that evening, but the conversation turned inevitably to ESP and other such phenomena. As I described my vivid dreams and other "weird" experiences, I kept stealing glances at this handsome, lithe, dark-haired woman with this so-called spirit hanging somewhere behind her eyes. Could she see my past and future, perceive all my secrets, discover all there was to know? Such possibilities made me a little nervous, but then, Jane didn't really appear to give a damn about these typical "psychic" questions. She smoked constantly, drank several beers, swore and laughed and read her astounding poetry to us with delicious vigor. Rob, a dapple-gray-haired man with lean, athletic good looks, spoke with a kind of old-fashioned wit and charm; and between the two of them, you knew that no nuance of character play around them went unnoticed.

Finally, after several hours of conversation—with Jane's challenging, intimidating grin answering mine and that vivid, soaring night-flight through the Vineyard echoing in my bones—I said, "You know, I really would like to join that ESP class of yours."

"Sure," Jane said lightly. "There are two of them—the regular one on Tuesdays, and you can start in the one Thursday night, for beginners."

"Beginners?" I gulped, a little insulted.

"Yeeeah," she said, exhaling the last smoke cloud from her twentieth Pall Mall of the evening, "that's just so you can catch up with the others."

Catch up? My mind boggled. Catch up with what? For Chrissakes, what else was there?

What else, indeed!

I was never a true "group" person. Either I went to the one extreme of complete solitude, or I joined so many groups at once that I couldn't possibly be a member of any of them. I was suspicious of groupthink; disdained organization and ceremony as mindless; sneered at religion as the cruelest of idiocies; and adopted a stubborn contrariness that sometimes wanted to burst my own seams. But in spite of it all, in a strange parade of events, I found myself attending my first ESP class in October of 1968, and already the small group—a fiftyish woman named Rachael Clayton, seventeen-year-old Daniel MacIntyre, myself, and Jane—had leaped from the tacit assumption that death was not The End into a most contrary proposition: that an individual actually chooses the circumstances of that death. Strange. When I was four or five years old, my mother would often stop in our walks down Elmira's West Water Street to point out the huge red maple tree growing in front of this stately old three-story house. Now I was sitting in an apartment in that same yellow building, still shaded by that red maple, balancing in some footfall in time and space.

"What I don't understand about my husband's death is that it happened when we had grown so close," Rachael was saying. "I knew that he didn't want to grow old and feeble—but when he died, I was just devastated. I found myself hating him, almost, for dying . . ."

Rachael was struggling not to cry. Obviously, she was horrified by her feelings and yet relieved to be expressing them. It was a precise and delicate moment for her, so I was completely taken by surprise when suddenly, and for no apparent reason, Jane started yelling at Rachael—in a loud, vibrant, strangely accented voice. Rachael didn't even flinch, but to me, loud voices meant terrible anger (or something unimaginably worse). I cringed back into my chair with embarrassment and turned to see, with double surprise, that Jane was not only shouting at Rachael, but waving her glasses at the poor woman besides.

What the hell? I stammered mentally; and then, with a small shock, I realized that this was not Jane Roberts as I thought of her who was speaking—but Seth, whose appearance five years before had torn such a hole in the fabric of Jane and Rob's daily lives.

But . . . but there was no transition, no effort! From one minute to the next, this—*person* had just started being there. For sitting there as I was—feeling pinned to my chair like a moth in a display case, the terrors of noise and its connotations in my guts—there could be no doubt that Seth was very much a person in his own right.

"Your husband did indeed not want to grow old," Seth was telling Rachael. "He had a horror of old age, as you know, and had decided long before his physical death that he would not live to become decrepit. He believed that he would, you see. And so he took the steps to insure that he would not."

Rachael nodded, her eyes filling with tears. I felt tears of my own forming. In the first hour of this class, I had come to like Rachael a great deal. She was a warm, tender woman of grace and charm—"a great lady," Scarlett O'Hara would have said. "I understand that, Seth," Rachael said, after a pause. "It's just that . . ." now the tears spilled. "It's just that I can't let go. And then I dream about him all the time." She controlled her voice with effort.

"Now, my dear friend," Seth said, a huge grin crossing Jane's face, "I have seldom had so charming a person weep in my presence, and I have lived and died many times." He (or she) leaned forward in the Kennedy rocker and placed Jane's glasses on the long coffee table that someone had fashioned from a door. Having taken proper care of the glasses, Seth sat back in the rocker and placed one foot on the chair's front rung, exposing in the process a little more of Jane's leotard-covered thigh than I was entirely comfortable with. "Your husband does indeed communicate with you in the dream state," Seth said. "I will give you more information at another time. But he does not want you to get into too much trouble on your own, you see!" This last comment bellowed out of Jane's small body with such force that I was sure it must have blasted out across the Chemung River, a block away.

Rachael smiled and made some rejoinder about her and Seth being "old bar mates," and the two of them were off on a happy-go-lucky (but, sadly, unrecorded) contest of wits as to which of them had lived the seediest series of past lives—with both bragging happily about the nefarious details. I hardly listened to what they were saying (something I regretted many times while putting this chapter together), because what I was seeing there in that rumpled, brightly lit living room couldn't have been more astounding had the refrigerator walked out of the kitchen to ask if we wanted more ice cubes. In one fell swoop, this full-bodied, exuberant, and obviously self-aware presence had filled my universe with possibilities as infinite as the landscape of dreams.

"Thank you, Seth," Rachael was saying, their dialogue finished.

"Thank *you*, my dear lady, for your being and for your vitality; for that which is mine is also yours," Seth answered. They regarded one another briefly, affectionately; this lady and this—spirit? Ghost? Unfathomable Jane-self? And then without a second's warning, Seth turned Jane's wide, dark eyes on—oh Jee-zus!—me.

"And now, my dear young friend," Seth boomed—and I felt myself blushing fiery hot right up through my scalp—"we meet again!"

I could only gawk at this statement, its implications flying past me and out into the autumn night.

"You do not remember me now," Seth said, his eyes and gleeful grin piercing right down through me. "But I do not really mind. You have abilities now, abilities from other lives, and a responsibility to use them. And so you have come here to see that you shall."

"Really?" I croaked, giggling with embarrassment.

Seth nodded, a gesture I would soon recognize as a prelude to blocks of information. "I do have something to say to you at this time," Seth continued, "and it is this: There is no need to justify your existence, through writing or another means. Being is its own justification, and this is part of what you must learn. And I will say this to you again and again, until you understand what it is that I am trying to tell you!"

I couldn't respond. His words meant nothing—then.

"You will be married within three years," Seth added unexpectedly, and then he disappeared, closing Jane's eyes.

"Whoops—hold it," Jane mumbled, as swiftly herself again as Seth had been *him*self. She groped for her glasses, put them on, and finished focusing on the room. "Wow," she said, grinning at me. "What was that all about?"

The three of us looked at one another. "Uh," Rachael started. "Well, he mentioned my husband, Al." She paused, unable to explain what had just been said. And she was right: as pointed and as dramatic as Seth's appearance had been, it was a little like dream-talk. Unless you were in the framework of the dream itself, the words somehow began slipping away, just out of your grasp, like tiny minnows in a clear, green lake. "Oh, damn!" Rachael exclaimed.

"He told me that Al was contacting me in my dreams, all right. But he really dropped some kind of bombshell on Sue!"

Jane turned to me. "What was this?" she asked, lighting another cigarette. A heap of half-smoked ones already lurked in her large, pearly, abalone ashtray.

"Well, I think—uh, I *think*, anyway, that he told me I was sort of meant to come here all along, and—"

Crack! Like summer lightning, Jane's glasses flashed through the air. "You came here of your own free will," Seth interrupted loudly. "But you came here, nonetheless, because you knew what you would do here." A pause. "I just wanted you to understand that," Seth chortled, and again, like the flip of a switch, he was gone.

"Whoa—not so fast," Jane said, replacing those apparently indestructible glasses. "Sometimes I begin to feel like a yo-yo."

"But a loveable yo-yo," Rachael added, laughing.

Zip! "That is quite true," Seth burst in, "I am rather a lovable old ghost, if I do say so myself. And for your information, I am also watching out for you in the dream state. Between the two of us, we should be able to keep you on the right track!"

"Thanks, Seth," Rachael replied. "I really do appreciate that."

"That is very good, because I appreciate it also," Seth answered. "It gives me something to do in my off-hours!"

And so it went, for another hour—Seth appearing and reappearing, gesticulating, cracking elaborate jokes, bantering back and forth with us; advising Daniel to "use [his] mind, and not let it lie fallow, without harvest"; directing pertinent remarks to us all. But most of the words have vanished from my memory, sailing off into the ether with a thousand other strange class dialogues encountered over the years, in what quickly became, for me, a tumultuous, intriguing excursion into the unknown continents of the self, with endless discoveries tucked away inside this little group with its beckoning premise of ESP.

Seth appeared in Jane and Rob's lives on December 8, 1963, three years after they'd moved to Elmira from Sayre, Pennsylvania. Jane was thirty-four; Rob, ten years older. They'd been married nine years, working as writer and artist, paying the rent with odd jobs. At one point Jane sold Avon products and kitchen knives by bicycle and later worked in an Elmira art gallery and as an aide in a nursery school. Rob took a part-time position in an Elmira greeting card company and painted in the afternoons. Jane had published two science-fiction novels, *The Rebellers*, and *The Bundu*; she'd also had several stories accepted by *Fantasy and Science-Fiction Magazine* ("which paid us laundry money," she often remarked). Their lives were filled with their art, and with each other.

Perhaps appropriately, it was an artistic experience that launched Jane and Rob into the Seth material. In September of 1963, Jane settled down at her worktable for her afternoon's writing when (as she describes it in *The Seth Material*) it seemed to her that from one minute to the next, the universe ripped open and an avalanche of astounding ideas poured through the hole and into the very cells of her body. The notes she made of that experience, which she later called *The Physical Universe as Idea Construction*, were the beginning of a new set of perceptions for her and Rob, neither of whom had ever had what they thought of as a "psychic" happening in their lives. Both started to remember their dreams. They bought a few books on ESP at the local supermarket, but none of these satisfied their curiosity. And none of them even approached the originality of those startling notes that Jane had madly scribbled down.

So, at Rob's suggestion, Jane set up an outline for a do-it-yourself book on ESP.[1] The premise was that she and Rob would set up their own experiments, record the results, and develop the book from there, since neither of them had ever been to a seance, received telepathic messages, used a Ouija board, or been involved with any ESP type of venture. A publisher expressed interest in the proposed manuscript, and the two of them plunged ahead— starting with the Ouija board, which seemed the simplest "psychic" device.

In *The Seth Material*, Jane confesses, " . . . both of us were a little embarrassed the first few times we tried the board. My attitude was, 'Well, let's get this out of the way so we can really get down to the things we're interested in, like telepathy and clairvoyance.' No wonder our first attempts were failures."[2] After a few tries, however, the board actually began spelling out messages, and very lucid messages at that. YOU MAY CALL ME WHATEVER YOU CHOOSE, the board replied, letter by letter, when Rob asked whom they might be speaking with. I CALL MYSELF SETH. IT FITS THE ME OF ME, THE PERSONALITY MORE CLEARLY APPROXIMATING THE WHOLE SELF I AM, OR AM TRYING TO BE. JOSEPH IS YOUR WHOLE SELF, MORE OR LESS, THE IMAGE OF THE SUM OF YOUR VARIOUS PERSONALITIES IN THE PAST AND FUTURE.

A mouthful for a Ouija board—and the beginning of the Seth sessions. For Jane soon began to realize that she was hearing these responses in her head before the board spelled them out. An urge to speak for the cumbersome pointer pushed at her. "The pointer paused," Jane says in *The Seth Material*. "I felt as if I were standing, shivering, on the top of a high diving board, trying to make myself jump while all kinds of people were waiting impatiently behind me. Actually it was the words that pushed at me—they seemed to rush through my mind. In some crazy fashion I felt as if they'd back up, piles of nouns and verbs in my head until they closed everything else off if I didn't speak them. And without really knowing how or why, I opened up my mouth and let them out . . ."

Thus, Jane and Rob used the Ouija board a few more times and then dispensed with it altogether as they discovered how easily Jane could repeat the words she was hearing. As the weeks passed, this "inner listening" of hers gradually developed into deeper trance states until Jane was largely unaware of the specific words as they were being delivered. Rob carefully wrote everything down in his own form of shorthand and typed up his notes the next day. Soon, these pages would fill dozens of notebooks.

Eventually, Jane's voice deepened and acquired Seth's oddball "but cosmopolitan" (in his words) accent. The material ranged from the theoretical to the deeply personal; Rob segregated sessions dealing with their private lives into a separate "deleted" file, which would over the years include some of the private sessions given to others.

Many times, Jane and Rob nearly called the whole thing to a halt. But curiosity, the fascinating excellence of the material, and their basic faith in artistic expression urged them to keep going. In later years, when Jane and Rob would encounter the "official line of thought" and its attitude toward their work, it was, I think, this faith in the integrity of the self as a work of art that gave them the audacity to keep on going their own way.

Who or what Seth is in relation to Jane—and indeed to the concept of identity—has changed and enlarged in Jane's and Rob's minds as the sessions themselves grew through the years. Basically, Jane sees Seth, Ruburt (Jane's entity name, according to Seth), Sumari, and other such encounters (including the characters in the *Oversoul Seven* novels[3]) as aspects of her identity— aspects of herself existing in other dimensions, or realities, as she exists in this one, with Jane's abilities enabling her to express those aspects in physical time and space.[4] According to this concept, each of us also exists within a multidimensional identity and communicates constantly with its various portions, whether or not we consciously recognize it. In that context, Seth is like a "larger" version of Jane, speaking from the perspective of one who is no longer focused in the world as we understand it.

The idea for Jane's class was planted in 1966, less than three years after the emergence of the Seth sessions, when Elmira schoolteacher Florence MacIntyre arranged to meet Jane and Rob through a fellow teacher who lived in the apartment below them. It was Florence who suggested that Jane start a "psychic" class.

"I didn't go for it," Jane says dryly. She had published *How to Develop Your ESP Power* that year, but the Seth sessions were still private; and even though Seth later recommended the class idea as a good one, Jane nixed it—

at first. "I figured no damn ghost was going to tell me to start any 'ESP' class," Jane recalls. But again, her curiosity kept the idea alive. After a few more weeks of hesitation and deliberation, Jane decided to run an ad in the Elmira newspaper to see how many people would show up once a week, for $2.50 each, to explore the meaning of ESP. Florence MacIntyre and a few others arrived at the stroke of 7:00 that September evening in 1967, and Florence missed very few of those Tuesday nights from then on.

Initially, Jane held two classes—one for new members and one for those who had been attending for a while. Both of these were largely made up of area housewives and women students from nearby Elmira College. Florence's son, Daniel, and local banker Theodore Muldoon were among the first men to come to class regularly. In the beginning, class interest was mostly concerned with what you might call basics: discussions on the nature of identity, the "door" or envelope-test experiments, table-tipping, life after death, reincarnation, healing. Jane did occasional psychic readings, and she or Seth sometimes gave past-life impressions as they pertained to questions or remarks brought up in class—although Jane wouldn't allow Seth to come through in class for a long time: The first class session was Jane's 386th trance, in 1968, and was the first time she spoke for Seth without Rob there to take notes.

At first, class tended to be sedate and theoretical. Ideas implicit in the Seth material and in Jane's discoveries (and her students') were treated as fascinating possibility—but not quite as operational "fact." Somehow, that was a little scary. On the other hand, it was during these early years that class indulged in the exuberance of table-tipping—a noisy, hilarious pursuit—and was involved in "the Campfire," a group past-life recall that members participated in more than once.

"Watching Jane's growth was remarkable," says Jeany Krouse, one of Jane's first students. "I was majoring in psychology at Elmira College then. I saw Jane's ad in the paper, called her to talk, and ended up in class. We did envelope tests, book tests, impressions, etc. Jane was going through so many changes, like the Estabrooks experiments.[5] Now to compare her current books to the early books—watching all those qualifying statements drop away—has been terrific!"

Gradually, a sense of "quickening" began to whisper through class. More and more people were showing up in Jane's living room—sometimes packing it so full that it was a feat of ingenuity just to cross the room without stepping on somebody. From a group of five to a dozen people, class expanded by the mid-1970s to thirty or forty, with a record forty-seven people stuffed in that living room one hot summer night. Now the group included as many men as women—with a wide range of backgrounds. People in their twenties sat in jeans and sandals next to businessmen wearing suits and ties. Arnold Pearson, a brilliant engineer and inventor in a local electronics industry, brought his sons, who had hitchhiked around the country and were asking pointed questions about the military-industrial complex. Gert Barber, who had once been a nun and was now married and the mother of two daughters, brought her demanding, restless questions of sexual identity to the foreground—and clashed almost weekly with Bette Zahorian, a fiercely proud and assertive housewife and mother from a small Pennsylvania town. Faith and Lawrence Briggs were operating a goat and vegetable farm by the squeak of pennies, but they somehow eked out the time and money to drive into Elmira and add their earthy, practical outlook to the proceedings. Local radio announcer and occasional minister Joel Hess, who had worked briefly at Cornell with war protester Daniel Berrigan, started speaking for his own "personality" shortly after he came to class in late 1970.[6]

In 1971, a second phase of class began—initiated, I think, by the "secrets" sessions and carried through the reincarnational "dramas," mobility-of-consciousness exercises, the alpha healing experiments, and, for many of us, a heightened awareness in the dream state. Jane started speaking the Sumari songs and scenarios in November of that year; Seth II appeared on the scene and observed that the "experiment" was continuing; and events were rapidly moving out of the realm of theory.

The third stage of class—although all of these stages slid easily into one another and were not obvious at the time—probably had its beginnings in the aftermath of the Flood of 1972, when Hurricane Agnes washed through the Chemung-Susquehannah River Valley, dramatically affecting the lives of everyone in its path. That June 23, Jane and Rob stayed in their apartment with their paintings and manuscripts and the fifty notebooks of the Seth material,[7] alone in the neighborhood, as the swollen Chemung River crested ten feet deep on Water Street lawns. When class resumed a month later, we began using Seth's tricky "belief assignments," plunging in depth into our individual reality systems—and, by inference, into mass reality as we know it.

This third phase of class is probably earmarked in most members' minds by the arrival of the "Boys from New York," the lump label tacked on the dozen or so men and women in their early to mid-twenties who drove the 250 miles from New York to Elmira every Tuesday afternoon, stayed for the three-to four-hour class, and then drove all the way back the same night so they could get to their jobs on Wednesday. "Greater enthusiasm than that is hard to find," Jane often said as they'd burst through her apartment door. The "Boys" were a galumphing, boisterous, lovable, aggravating, charming collection of people who had grown up together in a New York suburb. Their happy, undisciplined energy served to shove class directly into the demands of the everyday world in a most immediate way—did Seth's ideas really work?

Throughout the class years, regular members were joined by one-time visitors, or by people who stayed for only a few weeks. After a while, material was repeated constantly, since newcomers always seemed to have the same basic questions about Seth, Jane, and class. Finally, Jane made Seth's published books a class prerequisite, but even that didn't cut down on the huge number of people asking to attend. Strangers also created a dilemma: Could we go on with a secrets session or some of the more intimate belief papers in front of them—especially when anyone who wanted to tape-record the goings-on was free to do so? Yet the influx of newcomers and characters did contain its own built-in appropriateness: the right people always seemed to show up at the right time. But it was a problem that was never really solved. (Class ended the debate by ending itself in 1975, when Jane and Rob moved to their new house in another section of Elmira.)

At all times, class was an earthy, warm, humor-filled experience. Jane distained the dour and the sour and reveled in the spirituality of fun—which never disregarded private agonies, either. When I recently read an unfavorable review of Jane's *Afterdeath Journal of an American Philosopher*, I was struck by the idiocy of the reviewer's harshest criticism of Seth and Jane: that the subject of sex was suspiciously missing from the Roberts books. Apparently, the reviewer came to that conclusion without reading any of them. Sex—and all of the other numerous body functions, for that matter—were discussed constantly in class, with no inhibition on Jane's part and with very little on anyone else's. Stewie Gould, for example, once read a five-and-a-half-page "body belief" paper that began with the statement, "I think my penis is cute," and thoroughly explained why he thought so. (You might balk at Stewie's narcissism, but you could never complain of a lack of rowdy creativity.) The "secrets" sessions also took us to the nitty-gritty of experience, if that is indeed a requirement of self-awareness; and Jane often read portions of her poetry or works in progress, none of which minced words. There was an exuberant honesty among us, and nobody who attended class ever seemed to disapprove of it.

What people occasionally did disapprove of were *Jane's* habits, particularly of cigarette smoking and wine drinking (wine, tea, coffee, and soft drinks were brought by students and made available to everyone). Sometimes complaints were registered toward the smoky atmosphere in the living room; but people who came to class with rigid ideas about what Jane (as Sethian vehicle) should or shouldn't be doing would react with shock when Jane lit up her first Pall Mall of the evening. "I just don't understand how you can impede the spiritual vibrations with your cigarettes and your alcohol," one woman said, pursing her lips in disapproval. Jane would answer with something along the lines of, "Look, I just don't think your spirituality is a thing you win or lose according to what you do or don't do." But underneath her reasoned response, these attitudes made her furious.

Above all, Jane was determined not to be trapped in someone else's ideas of what she ought to be. In fact, she admits that in the beginning, she often went overboard to prove how irreverent she was—which Jane naturally is anyway. But beneath Jane's charming, charismatic, and energetic earthiness hummed the real pivot point of her class: not only Seth and his unique perspective, but an unwavering sense of excellence that really piloted those Tuesday nights—and indeed, the body of the Seth material itself.

In holding those classes, Jane maintained a beautiful kind of inspired balance, with all of us and our varying emotions, beliefs, and expectations on one hand, and her own sensibilities on the other. Jane had an utterly dependable schlock detector, and an equally accurate stuffiness radar. She was at once completely spontaneous and completely in control. Her sense of the ridiculous was as surefooted as her sense of quality—and she had the grace and wit to perceive that quality could be hidden within the ridiculous. She had a quickness of mind and an acuity for ferreting out the heart of matters in whatever was going on. Jane was able to look at people as "classics of themselves," as she called it; as characters in their own right, whether or not she agreed with them or even liked them—since there were numerous people who came to class that Jane most assuredly did *not* like.

"The hell of *that* was that Seth would come through and say to the person, 'I like you!'" Jane says. "Then I'd come out of trance, and somebody would tell me Seth'd said that, and I'd have to smile and say, 'Heh, heh, oh, really?' or something . . . but the thing of that too was that when I was in trance and could feel Seth's larger—say, emotional range, I'd find that I *did* like the person!"

Jane and Rob's sense of excellence did more for us as individuals than we even marginally suspected while class was ongoing. For them, the old explanations and categories for many of our experiences weren't satisfactory— as indeed, the old explanations and categories for human experience as a whole had not been large enough for them, and thus had spawned the Seth development to begin with. When reincarnation reared its head(s) in class, for example, it would have been relatively easy—and probably fruitful in its own way—for Jane to have set up one reincarnational drama a week, with participating members going at it whole hog, just to record details of past-life events. These dramas did happen a few times in class, and they were certainly fascinating and valid in some realm or another. But what realm was it? Or could any known explanation contain what we were doing? And how long can people go on yelling at one another for those times back in the 1200s when everybody was being pillaged by the heathens?

Past-life information given by Seth or Jane, divined by others, or acted out in drama form was important for a certain phase of class—but even then, Jane refused to treat this as the latest donkey on which to pin our tails; and reincarnation's meaning changed for us and became a portion of identity's possibilities rather than its definition. It was also regarded as a source of viable personal information—because, quite simply, such information had an emotional validity about it that couldn't be denied, even without the "past-life" connotations. Similarly, although Seth did give personal information to a few students on deceased relatives and their attachments to the living, this was not where class left the issue of what happens after physical death. Most of the regular members wouldn't assume, for instance, that dead Aunt Mae would stay Aunt Mae (or dead) for the rest of eternity, or that Aunt Mae had even been what everyone (including the lady herself) had assumed she was while she lived. What *had* she been; and by inference, what *was* this personality that each of us contained somewhere inside our skin?

Nothing, in other words, stood still in class.

The most obvious difference, of course, between Jane's class and "self-help" groups—beyond the fact that class was not set up to "help selves" in those terms—was the participation of Seth himself. Jane went into trance and spoke for another, definitely independent, and psychologically astute personality. The dynamics of personality itself were dramatically redefined, right in front of us. That we saw, nearly every week, a dimension of personality not usually acknowledged in the fabric of everyday life, meant that in whatever terms we defined our beings, the reality of our individual consciousnesses contained far more than we'd supposed. And because Jane and Rob—and Seth himself—refused to place Seth in a neat, ready-made pigeonhole of "spirit guide," "split personality," "contact with the Beyond," or whatever, we as a class would never again place our own peculiar abilities or experiences in any ready-made category.

The mechanics of Seth automatically brought into our questions an element not generally granted to consciousness—or at least not with the qualities of intellect, intuition, good common sense, and freedom of "what if" that Jane's class provided. *Her* refusal to accept old terms was *our* basic lesson on all fronts: to discover the authority of our selves within the moment, and to trust its nature. Jane and Rob were embarked on their own sea of questions and doubts: Who was Seth? What did his personality mean in terms of human identity? And in her way, Jane expected no less from her students in this kind of embarkation than she did from herself.

"Now, Seth does not *dig* worship," Seth said to us one evening. "For one thing, Seth understands worshippers. And, when one understands worshippers, one does not dig worship!

"If you will think this sentence over, then you will realize that those who worship do no real honor to the object of their worship. For upon that object, they place all of their hopes, all of their dreams, all of their inadequacies, and all of the responsibility for their lives; and even a god—a sane god—would refuse to accept such a worship.

"The god would understand also the nature of the universe, and the nature of playful creativity, and would know that such a worship is—at its base now, at its base—a denial of the very vitality of life.

"For All That Is endows creatures with a latent capacity for the greatest kind of creativity. And a creature who says, 'Save me, Oh Lord, and hear my voice! Look upon my iniquity and save me from my sin, and rule Thou my life which Thou hast indeed given me,' says really, 'Oh, Lord, Thou hast given me no capacity for reason, no free will, no power, no authority, and no goodness; and since Thou hast wronged me of all the holy virtue, then Thou might as well protect me, for I have no abilities of my own, and Thou hast made me without honor. Therefore, it is Thy duty to preserve the poor world upon which indeed Thy mighty foot is placed!'

"So, Seth does not dig worship . . . but worshippers have to face the god that they believe they are worshipping. For they are saying, 'You have made an inferior product—a flawed image. I am despicable, and therefore, although I adore you and I *say*, 'Yea, though I travel through the valley of death, et cetera,' and though I *say*, 'I adore you, Oh Lord!' what I *mean is*, 'I hate you because you have created me an inferior creature, and therefore I will make you pay—for my iniquities, Oh Lord, are yours. How can I be good when Thou hast made me evil? How can I hold up my head in the universe, when Thou hast made me flawed? Therefore, do I crawl upon my knees to show you that I cannot stand upright before Thee, for Thou hast made me flawed!'

"Such worshippers take it for granted that the product of God is poor—from an inadequate factory—a poor cosmic assembly line. Ford calls back its products if they are flawed, and so such worshippers say, 'Oh, Lord, call back humanity, for we are flawed!' And, no one answers, so it seems . . .

"When the old answers and the old organizations no longer have any meaning to the individual; when he can find reflected in the official answers none of his own questions; then the individual rises up from within itself; and, as once this civilization was born, so shall others be born in the same way. And so always from within itself does the race then go within its psyche for newer revelations; newer in that they are fresher to the source of itself—they have not been worn away by distortions and so in-turned by organizations that their meaning has become lost.

"So you arise out of yourselves individually, and out of the heart of your psyche; and so shall the civilization also emerge out of its mass psyche."

"I met Jane in the early days of Seth," recalls Dan Stimmerman, "about 1965, in the table-tipping days before any of the [book] dictations. It was a new thing. Jane was excited about it, but I don't think she had any idea of what Seth would become in her and Rob's life.

"In the writing of her book, *How to Develop Your ESP Power*, she may have been preparing a channel for Seth. As a poet is essentially an intuit, it isn't surprising to me that her mediumship developed. As I see it, her mediumship is a natural step in her artistic development. Her gift as a poet combined with her eventual acceptance of Seth created a whole new dimension of creativity. Her decision to explore the Seth personality was a courageous one; and her genius, as a result, quite literally found a larger voice.

"But everything was there to begin with, and all the conditions were right. The sort of mediumship that developed was peculiar and special to Jane Roberts."

And by example, we were to discover that we were *ourselves* our own peculiar mediums.

CHAPTER 2

The Cast of Class and How It Grew

Song for Our Bones
(with Thanks to Richie K)

Steal me the heaving crust of the Earth,
steal me the fire and quench me my thirst.
Steal me the rhythms that gave the worlds their birth—
show me the secrets hiding in the Earth.

Steal me the anchors lost of the ships
that break on the shores of the strange continent.
Steal me the ruin and steal me the rust,
steal me the moth in the crown and the dust.

Whatever comes and goes,
my friends still at my side—
though centuries ago we died.
Minstrels so alive
with madrigals and rounds—
our bones stand up and listen
in the ground.

Steal me the song I can sing to the worm,
steal me the pipes that glisten and yearn.
Steal me the first golden day of the Sun,
steal me the sounds to the first song sung—

That first bright morning on the high mountain,
that first bright morning on the high mountain.

Steal me the heaving crust of the Earth,
steal me the fire and quench me my thirst.
Steal me the last copper days of the Sun,
steal me the words to the last song sung.

Whatever comes and goes,
my friends still at my side—
though centuries ago we died.
Minstrels so alive
with madrigals and rounds,
our bones stand up and listen
in the ground.

—Song by Dan Stimmerman, 1973

JANE ROBERTS'S ESP CLASS ATTRACTED a great diversity of people from every sort of background: teachers, ministers, housewives, psychologists,[1] engineers, scientists, artists, farmers, the unemployed and the retired, young and old, men and women, parents and children, liberals and conservatives. Some told of "psychic" or unexplained events in their lives; others came in search of answers for a family death, an illness, or other troubles. Most had never had any kind of paranormal experience and were simply interested in the content of the Seth material. All of this gave class a balance not often achieved in the lives of the class members themselves, since for every opinion, it seemed there was a counter-opinion; for every fear there was a hope; for every line of development there was its complementary face. And as it turned out, this balance was more than an accident of circumstance.

What everybody who came to Jane's class did have in common, whether they came once or for years, was a strong sense that the old answers were not fitting the new questions—that the old systems, in one way or another, were no longer working. Of course, this was the prevailing mood of the times, reflected everywhere, no matter who you were. But for those who were drawn to Jane's own experience and that of her ESP class, the new questions were being directed not toward the exterior social structures, necessarily, but toward the inner ones—toward the government of the inner self.

Again, this inner searching was a large part of the explosions of the 1960s, and, looking at it, you could surmise that humankind was either initiating a true revolution of the mind, or losing its collective sanity—or both. Certainly the massive popularity of the "occult" showed that an awful lot of people were accepting an awful lot of b.s. on their way down that long inner road. Old systems and dogma were replaced with new systems and dogma— new words with the same old trappings. If you no longer believed in Original Sin, you could still mortify the flesh for Buddha, or for Rolfian therapy, or health food dictates, or drugs, or even for beings from outer space who were naturally wiser and more advanced than us poor idiot earthfolks. And on the surface of it, how could you argue with the idiocy of a race that spent systematic centuries finding more efficient ways to destroy itself? Even our fantasy heroes agreed with our worst self-portraits—Mr. Spock showed us the stupidity of our emotions, while Captain Kirk delivered awesome eulogies on the virtues of struggle and self-torture.

Jane's class led away from these old assumptions with the truly radical premise, first of all, that humankind is basically good; and second, that everybody creates his own experience—right down the line. War, poverty, pollution, maniacal governments, disease, accidents—as well as love, joy, personal fruition, health and happiness—spring first of all from the individual: period. Anyone who came to class searching for a new spiritual dictator in

Seth (and I think that, to some extent, all of us hoped it would be that simple) quickly realized that not only was Seth not going to lead anybody anywhere (except back to our own authority), but that Jane wasn't going to become the latest priestess on the mountain, either. Some were disappointed in this, and they didn't stay long—not that they were asked to leave; class just didn't suit their needs. Others arrived every week in Jane and Rob's living room, through the developments and changes that class offered and experienced, in response not only to Jane and Rob's own expanding abilities, but to the development of alternate patterns of logic and perception in its members.[2]

Says Jeany Krouse, one of Jane's first students in 1967, "I had a normal, happy childhood growing up in New Jersey . . . remembered having vivid dreams, impressions, hearing voices, always. One of the first books I picked up and read as a kid was *archy & mehitabel*,[3] about transmigration and reincarnation. I always enjoyed being alone and getting into my own mind and thoughts . . . My dreams have always been very large-scale, very vivid and numerous. Specifically, I remember one night having thirteen dreams, remembering them and being amazed by their scope and variety. It was like thirteen petals of a flower, all . . . feeling independent of the whole." Jeany, now in her thirties, works in the personnel department of a New Jersey business.

Theodore Muldoon, a banker and early ESP student, grew up in "a religious environment . . . children were seen and not heard, especially when Dad was around and at suppertime," and remembers of his childhood "frequent repetition of a dream of a large person looking at [him] through a window, as though the window were a magnifying glass." Theodore and his wife were asked to come to class with friends, and shortly thereafter he began regular communication in dreams and during light meditative states with a character he dubbed "Bega"—who gave Theodore some excellent insights into the pattern of his daily life. (See *CWS*, book 2, appendix 2 for details on some of Theodore's sessions with Bega.) Many of Theodore's dreams took place in the setting of the "Great Hall," where a huge tapestry hung, its design filled with scenes that gave him, in symbols, inner information on his waking relationships, particularly with his son and his elderly parents. Of class itself, Theodore recalls, "Every [class] session was an evolution in deepening the participants' understanding and perceptions about reality, self, and beyond consciousness. I think 'ideas' evolved in an acceptable pace for the original regulars. Later—1971 on—there were some onlookers/curiosity seekers that on occasion handicapped the evolution."

Arnold Pearson is an engineer whose patents include space program technology. "Like many others," he says, "I was dissatisfied with conventional religion as presented in churches and was searching for something that I could believe. Independent reading of Watts, Hesse, Fromm, and others, plus a couple of books about Cayce convinced me that conventional religion was very limiting." Arnold, whose mother died in the 1918 flu epidemic when he was three months old, was brought up by "loving foster parents." He says of his childhood, "[I had] more appreciation of the power and beauty of nature than most people seem to have . . . this as a result of my foster father . . . a large, physically strong man but the kindest, most gentle person I've ever known.

"Curiosity probably is what brought me to class the first one or two times, but the logic and beauty of what Seth had to say is what got me involved. It made sense. Seth's discussions answered many questions that religion evaded."

Of his childhood years spent growing up with "sister, dog, parakeets, finches, turtles, snails," poet and songwriter Dan Stimmerman—one of the few gay class members—recalls as highlights: "(1) Flying downstairs once as a small child and landing soundly on my feet. I didn't think about this until years later. It must not have seemed remarkable at the time, but certainly pleasant. (2) Recurrent experiences of feeling unreal—short periods of time when I didn't know who I was. These continued throughout my growing up and still happen from time to time. (3) Hours in a Pennsylvania creek creating environments out of rocks, ferns, mosses, and lichen. HEAVEN! (4) A childhood dream in which I encounter a long line of people, spotlit, about twenty feet apart, all facing in one direction down a dark road. When I ask a man in line why they are not moving, he responds that they are, but they are going so slow I can't see them move. (5) Making out with Jimmie X in his bedroom.

"I began attending classes when I was living in New York in 1973 . . . I would travel up from New York City every Tuesday afternoon with some other members," Dan says. "What caused me to begin classes? What compels anybody to go about doing anything that might shed some light on who they are? Two forces—which are the same forces, ultimately—are at work. We want to find out, penetrate the mystery, find out why we hurt—and at the same time we can think of a million excuses not to look into ourselves . . . I attended for about five months. Dream content during that period was often exciting and vivid. Dreams involving music were very real, super-real . . . one in particular involved a tribe of aboriginal people playing marvelous horns through their noses . . .

"The flowers that Jane always had on her coffee table would often appear in my dreams. They were always very magical for me, and often captivated me in class sessions . . . During my class days, Richie [Kendall] and I were co-writing songs and George [Rhoads] was inventing new games. Sue

Watkins was working on a novel. There was an excitement that we all generated and inspiration we all drew out of class . . . The music I wrote in that period harkened back to my feeling of past lives and to my sense of identification with nature.

"It seems to me that once we can appreciate our own indefiniteness, then all the rich facets of mind can really begin to open," Dan says. "We don't cling; we can really enjoy the rich, deep identities that we are. We aren't trying to prove anything, really. We can experience and disown the many aspects of ourselves; and they lose none of their richness only because we are not setting out to place a stranglehold on them in order to 'secure' ourselves in an essentially mysterious universe."

Many of those who attended class had experienced some decidedly odd happenings during their early years. Jed Martz, one of the commuters from New York, also recalls vivid flying dreams. My college roommate, Bernice Zale, who attended class whenever she visited me from her home near Albany, New York, remembers a "house ghost" seen first by her mother as it wandered through their century-old home on the Hudson River. "I was under ten years old when I woke up in the night to see him pass by the foot of the bed and out through the wall," Bernice says. "I also had periodic 'perspective disturbances' wherein everything would appear very small and/or far away from me. Bouts of this would occur upon waking or in very relaxed states, would last five to fifteen minutes, and would frighten me." Bernice, an artist and craftswoman, has worked as a reporter for Albany area newspapers.

Nadine Renard, whose experiences show up elsewhere in this book, grew up in a homey middle-class environment with little money; consequently, she worked from age fourteen to pay her own way through nursing college. When she was nine, her grandfather—who lived next door to the family—died one night while Nadine was asleep. "I woke up as he appeared in my bedroom, about an hour after his death (as it turned out), to show me that he was cured [of cancer]," Nadine recalls. "He looked well and he could talk. I told my mother that he was better but that he'd died during the night, which at that point she didn't know.

"During college, I had many OOB [out-of-body] experiences: climbed over bunk bed . . . and saw myself in mirror still in bed . . . very frightened as I didn't know what I was doing . . . this happened on about five occasions in the same room. I had a boyfriend who had the ability to leave his body at will and describe what I was doing in Hornell [New York] while he was in Buffalo. I never questioned him too much about this, as I didn't know anything about OOBs at the time."

My own childhood dream life was also vivid, as were odd waking experiences. For example, I would see herds of animals romping through the room:

flocks of sheep would come out of one wall and disappear through another as I watched; dogs and cats would play on the living room rug, sometimes leaping up through the ceiling and diving down through the floor. Occasionally I would look up and catch glimpses of ponies with great liquid eyes, or lions and giraffes stalking among the jungle of household furniture. Their presence was comforting: they were real and not real, part of me and yet themselves. Sometimes as I lay in bed at night, drifting between waking and sleeping, bright circles of light would open in the dark and tiny figures would appear inside and act out scenes in pantomime. I would also see crowds of faces, holding conversations over my head. One night, I called to my mother because I needed to go to the bathroom. My bedroom door didn't open, but my mother came in. She was wearing a long white nightgown—and she had no feet. She came to the side of the bed and stared down at me, expressionless, stern, like a hole in the air. I screamed and snapped awake in my bed, but when I looked around the room, a door opened up in the wall.

I got out of bed and walked through the door. It led into our living room, where a lovely, smiling woman stood. "You can wake up any time you want to, you know," she told me.

I looked back at my bed and saw myself there, sleeping. "Sometimes I can't," I said. "Sometimes I'm scared."

"You are always in control," she said. "These are your dreams, and you can wake up if you want to. Try blinking your eyes very rapidly." I did so, and woke up instantly. It's a technique that I've used ever since to get away from nightmare situations.

By the time my parents and I moved in with my grandfather in his big country-gentleman's house when I was eleven, my dreams often included lengthy dialogues, sometimes in French, German, or Spanish—which I didn't speak while awake. A group of "regulars" and I would discuss the fact that we were dreaming; that all of these dreams as I perceived them were connected; and that some of us were not from the same awake world as I was. Occasionally there would be people in this group who had recently died—or so the group would tell me. I was then supposed to ask these newly deceased people questions: How had they died? Did they realize they were dead? (The people would usually register dismayed surprise.) Unfortunately, at the time, I never wrote down any of these dreams. But the dream that finally prompted me to start regular records happened when I was eighteen.

Two nights after my grandfather's death in 1963, I got up from my bed and walked out into the hallway. Grandpa shuffled out of his room, carrying his white-enameled chamber pot toward the bathroom. I was about to smile a cheerful good morning when I realized that, first of all, the wrong wallpaper was on the walls, and secondly, Grandpa was several days dead.

"Good morning, Mike," he said, using his pet name for me. I looked down the staircase. A parade of people was walking back and forth past the bottom of the steps, looking up at us as they passed by. I thought I could hear a line of people moving in a circle through the dining room, the kitchen, the living room—a circle of observers. Grandpa was standing in the door to the bathroom, staring at me.

"Grandpa," I said, "what are you doing here?"

"I'm getting out of bed," he answered, watching me closely.

"But don't you remember?" I said. "You're dead now. You died a couple of days ago. You don't have to do this any more."

He looked startled, and then followed my gaze down the stairs. "Is that right?" he said, in his old way.

"That's right," I said. "You had a couple of insulin shocks, and then your emphysema got to be too much, and you died. But that's all over now. Now you can be all right."

He only stared at me, his leaf-brown hands still clutching the chamber pot handle. "Now you're not old anymore," I added.

Tears swam in his eyes. "You know what else?" I said. The walls seemed to be fading out. "Your diabetes didn't get you after all. You fooled everybody." I woke up with a start, a thin shaft of light from my half-open door lying across the ceiling with unnatural brilliance. I got out of bed and went into the hall. A woman was sitting on the top step, face in hands. "Not bad, for a first try," she said, not looking up. I went back into my room and got in bed. I opened my eyes. Two chairs stood by my bed, talking to each other. "She can do it, you see," one said loudly. I froze, staring at them. They disappeared. I opened my eyes. It was morning. It was really morning. I lay there, thinking about the dream. Had I really talked to my grandfather? Was he alive, in his body's form, somewhere? What if I went out into the hall right now, remembering the dream? Would I be able to see him? I got out of bed and walked into the hall. The door to Grandpa's room was open, gaping, a geometrical mouth. The space near the bathroom door seemed thick, like a deck of cards. That was all.

Grandparents play a mystical role in most peoples' lives, of course. "My grandfather Harry died when I was about twelve," recalls Joy Mankowitz of the New York City group. "I was very attached to him. After his death, I gave him a rectangular spot on my ceiling. Each night I would talk to God and then politely ask Him to let me speak to my grandfather. I would then proceed to have conversations with him, directing my words toward that spot, hearing him speak as clearly as if he were there."

Joy, the child of second-generation Polish-Austrian immigrants, was raised in a home that stressed education and obedience. "I didn't trust people—

in my home, it was also stressed to remember that I was a Jew and to understand the history of the Jewish people and my part in it. I spent four years of Sundays in Shalom Aleichem school to be sure I learned about the culture of the Jewish people.

New York "Boy" Joy Mankowitz

"The most fascinating and oft-repeated fantasy I had as a child was imagining that no house existed where my house stood, then imagining there was no block, no neighbors, no New York, no planet Earth, no moon, no sun. Then I tried to imagine no air—a vacuum—the fantasy always stopped there. I could not imagine nothingness . . .

"I remember either a dream or a fantasy—in my grandmother Esther's house. I went on the back porch and saw a lovely woman in the backyard, down the steps from where I was. She spoke to me . . . this memory has been with me since I was a little child. My grandmother never lived in a house with a back porch and yard . . ."

Joy came to Jane's class as a result of her studies of Gnosticism.[4] "This study contained much faulty information, but it led me to the Seth books. Although since I was working, it was impossible for me to attend regularly, Seth's message to look within yourself for answers was a message that was priceless." Other members of the New York group had come upon the Seth books through this same class in Gnostic studies, taught in Manhattan by a man named Arturo. "I was a member of this philosophy cult which delved into the ancient mysteries of the various world religions and cultures to determine the Singular Path to enlightenment," Jed Martz notes with a touch of sarcasm. "One of the books Arturo recommended was *The Seth Material.* He had great respect for Seth, but was not in agreement with Jane. He had spoken to her on numerous occasions by telephone, and she had rejected the theories he presented to her about reality, and vice versa . . . Arturo died before I had a chance to tell him that I went up to [Jane's class] and discuss what went on there."

Jed, a New York State Employment Office clerk, attended class to the end in 1975, and feels that it "changed from a strong ESP format to a stronger focus on interpersonal beliefs, and I feel that my New York City contingent was integral to the change."

Another of the New York group, aspiring songwriter Richie Kendall, remembers a childhood peculiarly obsessed with death. "As a child, I had, as most children, my own private communion with nature," he says. "I remember the ritual I used to do every night before I went to bed. I must have been eight or ten years old. I would stand on my porch and say some kind of prayer to the stars—they were very important to me—and I believed they listened to me and could help me."

Growing up in a predominantly Jewish middle-class neighborhood in Bayside, Queens, Richie remembers his dreams as "very frightening. Dreams of the end of the world through some kind of nuclear destruction and dreams of death were very common in my childhood. Death became a complete obsession for me at a very early age. I went through phases of this but it was always a strong force behind and within many of my actions and attitudes . . . there weren't any outer circumstances that created this obsession, but it seemed always to be there.

"I did not have a particularly strong identification with nature, and actually for many years, including into my early teens, I rejected psychic things as a lot of bullshit. My main focus was sports, and I excelled there and received much attention, approval, and delight for my abilities. At about fifteen, sports became secondary for me and feelings of death and questions of the universe began haunting this tired skull once again. Drugs seemed the most interesting avenue to find answers. Having gone to Hebrew school didn't answer shit, and neither did public school.

"More than anything, my experience with drugs was rather inclusive—pot, Seconal, Tuinols, cough medicine with codeine, speed, hash, heroin, and acid. The LSD experiences were the strongest mind experiences I ever had, and one trip—in which I 'flipped out' and went through a lot of agony for some time to come; where psychedelic stuff just seemed to keep happening without my control—was probably the strongest impetus for me to explore the dimensions of the mind because I was living in my own private hell of experience that terrified me, with no one, it seemed, who could help me. Someone later turned me on to the Seth books, and I wrote Jane a letter expressing my desire to come to class—she said I could come by any time. January 4, 1972 was the first time I came by, and I have come by ever since.

"Through growth from class," Richie concludes, "I got involved in music; it's interesting that before I flipped out on acid, I'd been playing music, but then I stopped playing and sold my guitar and just became a listener for some seven years. During Seth class I got re-involved, like taking up a self I'd left off, or an aspect of myself I'd let go and brought it back into my experience."

Charlene Pine was eighteen years old when she had emergency surgery for extensive ileitis, and nineteen when a case of hepatitis was diagnosed as incurable. After years of medical tests and procedures, Charlene decided that her body's condition was beyond science's ability to help. Through a friend, Charlene heard of British healer Harry Edwards (now deceased) "who healed

Charlene Pine

people clear across the ocean," Charlene says. "I was sure then it was all bunk." Nevertheless, she wrote a letter to Edwards describing her medical condition, and it was hand-delivered to the healer's group by friends in England. "The next night [after the letter's delivery], I had so much energy that it was overwhelming, and then on Monday I received a letter saying that there would be no guarantees, but that I should look for a slow, progressive heal-ing. This really blew me away, as if magic really could exist. I continued to feel bet-ter and my blood tests began to show improvement. By December of that year, a mere six months later, my blood tests were normal and I began to start cutting out all medications (against my doctors' advice)—this from a situa-tion where a liver biopsy had said that it was curtains!"

Soon after Charlene's recovery, she and her husband bought a horse farm near Elmira and discovered Jane's books in a local store. In Charlene's first class, she says, "I was really surprised; I expected candles and levitation, and Seth scared me to death. I barely opened my mouth and [since] I had not even read *The Nature of Personal Reality*, I had no idea what everyone was talking about when they spoke of their beliefs. I thought Sumari was crazy, [but] I returned because I felt I would make 'valuable friends'! Finally I started making my way through *Personal Reality* and was amazed that somehow I'd managed to find my way to this group, without understanding consciously how right it was for me.

"I was most affected by the New York Boys. They scared me, and because I felt my connections to them, they intrigued me, [though] I thought they were loud, obnoxious, and buttering up the teacher. It wasn't until classes stopped that I had class dreams, and by following the impulse to do so, I ended up at the 'un-classes' in Jane's new house. It wasn't until then that I realized what some of my beliefs were, and how scared I'd always been, and how much approval I'd always wanted, and how all these things had affected my past."

Priscilla Lantini, an Elmira housewife and waitress in her early forties, remembers a childhood filled with philosophical diversity. "I was brought up in two religions," she says. "One was Presbyterian because it was my parents' religion, and the other was Catholic because my mother believed in strict discipline, and believed Catholic schools best for that. She got special permis-sion from the priest, and there I was—the only non-Catholic in a Catholic school. Incidentally, I had the highest grades in catechism, which I think is funny. So there I was with all kinds of philosophy thrown at me, marching in Catholic processions with some of my friends and singing in the Presbyterian Church with my other friends.

"From Catholic school I went into public high school . . . I really hated it, so much so that I began to skip school all the time. My mother caught me one day and asked me where I was going. I said that I was sick, and she took me home. I spent the rest of the day in my room munching candy bars and reading funny books. That night after I'd gone to bed I got a terrible headache, so bad that I went crying to my mom and dad's room. They took me to the hospital . . . the doctor told me I had polio.

"Now this in itself was strange, my skipping school and then getting sick, and that it was cold weather and not the polio season, and I was the only case of polio in Elmira and no one came down with it until later. I spent the next two years in bed, out of school. When I did go back, it was only for a couple of months until I graduated. I realized after I went to Seth classes that what I suspected for years was true: You create your own reality!

"I also had an eccentric grandmother who lived alone," Priscilla recalls. "She chose me above all her grandchildren as her favorite. She was a self-taught woman, as she only went to the third grade. She dealt in antiques. It was great fun when she would open her big trunk and let me play in hoop skirts and Chinese Mandarin kimonos. She had beautiful fans with plumes and spangles and the shield, hat, and sword from suits of armor, some of which I couldn't even pick up. Mostly she dealt in glassware. She loved nudes and Madonnas; they hung all over her two-room apartment. She taught me how beautiful the human body was.

"Sometimes she would read to me; other times we would listen to her Caruso records. Her favorite people were show people and she knew lots of celebrities. Once in a while when they were in town,[5] I would get to meet them backstage or in her apartment. Once when I was in bed with polio, Blackstone the Magician came in with her to see me, and I still have the charm bracelet he brought me . . .

"She loved to playact with me. I remember mornings at her apartment at the small breakfast table. We would pretend to be great socialites: she, Mrs. Asterbelt and me, Mrs. Gotrocks. It was expected of me to start things by saying, 'My dear Mrs. Asterbelt, how are you and your pet horse?' and then she would expound on all the funny things her horse did, and if the groom

Priscilla Lantini

got mad she would always fire him . . . sometimes when she would walk to my house I would be playing and I would spot her a block away. She kind of reminded me of Queen Elizabeth's mother, the old Queen Mary. She was kind of chubby and wore a princess-style coat and walked in great dignity with a gold cane and always wore a hat and gloves. She had dozens of pairs of gloves and once told me that a lady never leaves the house without them. She died when I was about seventeen. She was quite an old girl, and I loved her so . . .

"I guess I called Jane out of curiosity because for many years I had been searching for my own philosophy," Priscilla says. "I had run through other folks' ideas: Yoga, Buddhism, Ekankar, Wicca . . . then one day my neighbor gave me *The Seth Material* to read, and what Seth said made more sense to me than all the others rolled together. I just had to go to class. I'm a very stubborn person!"

Betty DiAngelo, a thirty-four-year-old housewife and librarian who attended Jane's class during its last year or two, grew up in an Italian neighborhood in Endicott, New York, living with her parents and siblings above her uncle's bakery. "I think of this as a magical era for me," Betty says. "There was the security of an extended family, a host of aunts, uncles, cousins, and in general people who enjoyed children . . . I had much freedom of movement, even as a young child, with school, library, and park nearby, and many small shops that were quite fascinating to a child: a shoemaker's, a candy shop whose owner could be heard practicing her arias for a local opera company, the usual delis, and of course the bakery with its delicious aromas . . .

"Best of all were the times when my father and his friends would go serenading, as we called it, with their instruments, and end up at our place for the rest of the evening—with all the singing and din and no one mentioning that children should be in bed. The feeling of camaraderie stayed with me, and sometimes I can't believe this really happened—it is so seldom now that I see adults having spontaneous fun for the pure sake of it."

Betty's paternal grandmother often talked to her of communications with people who had "passed on," and of a white dove that visited her on momentous occasions, it seemed.

"When I was six years old I had a special experience," Betty says. "I was leaving the library and when I stepped outside the large double doors, I saw a girl seated on the stone railing of the steps. For some reason I stopped, very curious, and sat on the ledge opposite her. I asked her what her name was and she finally replied, 'Elizabeth.' I was astounded that we had the same name. I don't think she ever looked directly at me; but about this time I'd had a fantasy about meeting a little girl with the same name as mine, as if it would give us some secret connection. This girl looked the way I would have liked to look, the physical opposite of me, with long blonde hair (I was scrawny with short dark hair). Somehow, she just seemed to disappear. I think I went back into the library to see if she popped back in without my noticing . . .

"I never saw her again and the reason it was unusual to me was that I knew all the children in our section and in our school. I would go over and over in my mind trying to determine where she disappeared to, as I could have sworn I didn't leave my spot on the ledge opposite her . . .

"At age seven or eight, I read a book about a pussy willow bush that came alive with kittens. The idea delighted me and led me to try my first mind experiment. I went behind our garage where there were several pussy willow bushes, closed my eyes, and concentrated. I felt what can only be described as a mind expansion. It frightened me, and I closed off the experience, although I had the feeling that I could do things with my mind but wasn't sure what.

"When I was ten I had a scary experience," Betty remembers. "I woke as it was just starting to become light and I was enjoying listening to the birds singing. It was very pleasant. I turned over on my stomach and . . . realized that someone was walking down the bedroom hallway. It sounded like my mother's taffeta robe, but I knew it wasn't her. I became very still when I realized whoever it was had walked into my room. The next moment, there was a finger jab on my left shoulder. I whirled around, extremely frightened, and saw a strange man—he had on a wraparound maroon robe of some shiny material, long white tangled hair, and white fang-eye teeth! His overall appearance was menacing . . . I ducked under the covers and screamed until my parents both came running. When I explained what had happened, my parents searched the house to make me feel better. For years this experience haunted me and I would be frightened of going to sleep for fear I would have a repeat of it.

"[In later years] something happened that made me curious concerning a word that I would think of now and then: "Moloch." I looked this word up, and this was an Egyptian god that children were sacrificed to. Weird—my sister had this very same experience when she was nine, and it crossed my mind that we have both lost a child [in infancy] . . .

"I remember being fascinated with the idea of little people and vaguely recall a dream of my bedroom being filled with a crowd of them—they chattered quietly. Not long ago my sister told me that she wouldn't go near my room at night when we were children because she thought she saw little people marching in there on several occasions . . .

"I started having out-of-bodies, or remembering them anyway, when I was sixteen . . . at first I was quite frightened of them, particularly by the noise, a huge whirring sound that seemed to come from inside my head. Once I was just about to get out of bed, as the smell of bacon cooking downstairs was quite enticing, when the noise started and some feathery brown stuff slithered all over my body. It wasn't entirely unpleasant, just rather suffocating. Imagine my surprise upon taking an art history course in college and seeing this same experience of mine in a painting by William Blake!"

Betty and her husband, Tim, came to class after Betty read an article on Jane and Seth in *Inner Space* magazine. "The ideas in the article seemed to come alive and leap right off the page, and I ordered *The Seth Material* that day," Betty says. "The ideas, while new, were in a sense also familiar, as if they found a home in myself. After reading the book, I called Jane—a letter just wouldn't suffice—her book meant so much to me, and I wanted to tell her that fact personally. I was so nervous I took the phone into the bathroom and shut the door so Tim wouldn't hear me stammer all over the place."

Matt Adams, an editor and aspiring writer, reports that "Oddly, my childhood was relatively barren of the weird and paranormal," in spite of his adult experiences with trances and altered states of consciousness. Matt says, "[I had] strange, brilliant waking dream visions before falling asleep that persisted, over and over, until a light was turned on. I mean, my eyelids were closed, but the pictures—of vast space, broiling water, an array of ceramic dolls—would repeat and repeat . . .

"Once, I recall reaching out my hand at night to a small kiddie-chair beside my bed and feeling my hand grasped, briefly but warmly, by something invisible. Following Dr. Doolittle's example, I tried to talk to flowers, but they didn't reply. Whenever a warmhearted relative died, though, I'd see them about a month after death in a dream. The best example I recall was of my great aunt 'Olie,' who died about a year before, when I was eight. In the dream, she—who in life had been extremely religious—handed me one of the potted hyacinths that Episcopal churches used to give to kids at Easter in celebration of the Resurrection. 'But Olie,' quoth I, 'you can't be here (in my upstairs hallway)! You're dead!' She just smiled—looking quite a bit younger than I'd ever seen her in life—and faded away.

"In the eighth grade, I did start a gang of sorts—we used to direct telepathic commands at teachers. Now I shudder at the thought: five or six kids all silently commanding their teacher to drop the chalk or scratch his head— with success after a few minutes' concentration . . . I did enjoy nature—was a nature counselor at camp and have written a garden book—but never had to go into trance to enjoy the outdoors. Ordinary, bookish, rational kid."

George Rhoads, a professional artist in his forties during class years, grew up in the Midwest, lived for many years in Europe, and had practiced yoga and meditation for most of his life. "My earliest memory of this life is being in a stroller on a wide street, vaulted over with tall elms," George recalls. "I felt drawn to the long, graceful branches, and I found myself up among them, surrounded by leaves and sky. I examined the texture of the leaves, the bark; listened to the rustling of the leaves in the wind; then I was back in the stroller. I resolved at that time to somehow celebrate the beauties of this event and of nature in general. This would now be described as an out-of-body experience. To me then, being up among the leaves was not remarkable, just another event in the new events of a life of eight months.

"My father, a doctor and a dedicated Presbyterian, sent me to Sunday school. The church dogma made no sense to me. The idea that one was supposed to lead as pure a life as Jesus did might have been all right. But it seemed that nobody was really expected to do that. People were weak sinners, evil by nature, and the best we could do was try to be good—and failing, go to church, ask forgiveness of sins, repent, and in general, go around tail-between-legs in fear and guilt.

"Since my idealism could not be directed into religion, I pinned it as best I could on science," George says. "This was pre-atom bomb, before science fell into disrepute. America was all behind science and the 'rational' approach to life. Fundamentalists opposed the scientific view of the evolution of man, but their inner conviction was that American know-how would solve all problems and answer all questions . . .

"My main interest was in art, which for me was of the inner secret life. Yet I was fascinated with science and did my best school work in math, physics, and chemistry . . . In college, philosophy absorbed me. I hoped to find here revelations about the inner life and existence generally. I soon realized that the Western philosophies are interested mainly in creating 'systems' with special terminology and categories into which all human experience could be filed away neatly and rationalized. I felt betrayed and insulted. If the greatest minds of my civilization dealt in irrelevancies, where did that leave me? I did discover Lao-tzu. He made sense, as did Zen later . . .

"In college, I also discovered Freud. His theories still seem silly to me, but his techniques of dream analysis were intriguing. I began to record my dreams and analyze them. This produced useful results and affirmed my reliance on the inner life. I have recorded outstanding dreams ever since that time, and since the class years I remember and record dreams nearly every night . . . As a teenager I was electrified when I saw photographs of yogis practicing asanas [postures]. I had been doing yoga postures since I was a small child. I often sat in the full lotus, and stood on my head for long periods . . .

"When I first came to class, I was living in a small house in the country about an hour from Elmira. I was painting, sculpting, and making fountains [on commission for Hammacher Schlemmer Company in New York] and making a meager, unreliable living at these things . . . I came to class persuaded by Sue W.'s enthusiasm. Jane was impressive. She showed no signs of being a phony. At this time, I had an uneasy glimmering that the course of my life was taking me into rough country . . . I had many dreams about riding in various unmanageable vehicles, controlling them badly."

"Why did I come to class in the first place?" asks Geoffrey Beam, who works as a clerk in Elmira's prison facility. "I half hoped that Seth would kindly explain to me why such a nutty geek as myself was permitted to go on breathing in an otherwise sensible world; but at the same time, I was afraid he might tell me more than I wanted to hear. I was absolutely terrified at that first class. When Seth first began to speak that evening, I seeped unobtrusively into the wall plaster.

"I was raised by a protective mother and grandmother—could not have felt more secure in a Mosler safe . . . As a result of these intensely protective years, I now see myself as a middle-aged gentleman [of forty] in a black business suit, black shoes, black tie, mercilessly starched white shirt, and a poorly concealed teddy bear in a back pocket. Though apparently in despotic control of myself, I virtually reek with feelings of worthlessness.

"Even though I was brought up on the Old Testament stories of fire and brimstone, of terrible punishment far out of proportion to the offense," Geoffrey says, "I could not help having a strong feeling of belonging in the world of nature. I felt at home with the Universe . . . My feeling of being in complete harmony with nature has never left me. God must truly be much nicer than his public relations people have painted him.

"[In class], it was refreshing to be in a group of people who were interested in extrasensory perception and who could freely admit being interested in such matters," Geoffrey concludes.

Concurring in many members' disillusionments with conventional religion is Faith Briggs, who now works for the Army Corps of Engineers in Arizona. "Except for Dad, we all went to church regularly . . . often four times on a Sunday . . . ," Faith says. "However, I admit to being taken aback by an experience when I was twelve. In full view of the Sunday morning congregation, I was baptized. Now, I figured, all my sins would be washed away and I would immediately become a vastly better person, once and for all! Imagine my dismay, to emerge dripping and still holding my breath, to find that I was exactly the same! I thought about that for a long time . . ."

"Never since my teenage years could I accept beliefs about religion and beliefs connected with it—couldn't understand why," Fred Lorton, an Elmira contractor, writes. "Started in 1951 trying to find out about life after death; pounded my way through many books. In Aruba on vacation in 1973, read first Seth book suggested to me by 'Our Lady of Florence.' Very excited about it as I read deeply when the personality never told me what to do and how I should be—such as Eastern writings [did].

"Asked Florence to ask Jane if I could attend, she said yes, with reservations. Later she told me that she'd wondered if a middle-aged building contractor might be fixed in my beliefs!" Mostly, Fred remembers being impressed with Jane's "ability to run class and her delicacy—and if necessary, her *shotgun*, in dealing with so many people of such diversified backgrounds!"

"You come from many backgrounds, and [in class] some of you have your own ideas thrown back at you," Seth told us once. "What I have to say to you has nothing to do with the age that you imagine you are in this particular existence; for as I have said often, the old man or woman that you will be and the young girl or boy that you were, and the person that you imagine you are, exist now . . .

"And everyone does not learn with age, and all the young are not innocent. You cannot deal in this class in terms of generations. You will deal with the selves that you are, and as they emerge, so shall you know your selves: the selves that you think you are, the selves that you think you have been, and the selves that you think you shall be. [Here] you cannot relate in terms of male or female; as a mother, daughter, child, son, or father . . ."

"I have always felt that the people who are attracted to Seth are looking for ways to un-tap their creative potentials," says Dan Stimmerman. "In Seth, there is plenty of encouragement to do that. I regard Seth's teaching as an unofficial religion of poets."

CHAPTER 3

Experiments: In Which Tables Tipped and Doors Revealed Their Symbols

in a time when
men's minds cannot
see thru walls,
surfaces have a flirtatious
role

our sensuous eyes serve
visions as a
filet of form into which
our thoughts
slice

with invisible ideas we
bite and mold land-
scapes, then
live on our creations as
proud artists showing off
their masterpieces

—Barrie Gellis, 1974

I DOUBT THAT ANYONE CONNECTED with the scientific community would have called Jane's ESP class "scientific" in any contemporary sense of the word. For that matter, I doubt that anyone from the spiritualist establishment would have attributed to Jane's class a whole lot of conventional "spirituality," either.

Nonetheless, class did set up several ongoing ESP experiments, but not so much for scientific proof (as the term is thought of) as for exploring the subjective nature of the objectified world. Some, like the envelope-on-the-door test, had precise directions to follow; others—like predictions, table-tipping, or mobility of consciousness "trips"—just seemed to grow out of themselves for the fun of it and led in all kinds of directions.

Soon after class began, Florence MacIntyre told Jane about a group of people who met weekly in a nearby town to hear messages tapped out by a spirit communicating through a tipping table. "Florence suggested we try doing this, but I objected *strenuously*," Jane recalls. "It just smacked too much of all the stuff I wanted to avoid. I said, 'Florence—honestly! We've got better things to do in class than try to move a stupid table!'" But when Jane's reporter friend Maggie Granger was assigned to do a story on the table-tipping group, she and her husband Bill asked Jane and Rob to accompany them on the investigative venture.

"There were about twenty-five people sitting around this big round table, and they turned out all the lights," Jane says. Everybody was then instructed to rest their fingertips lightly on the tabletop. Eventually, they said, the table would start rocking back and forth, picking its legs a few inches off the floor and thumping them down again. "They had a code—one tap meant yes, two taps meant no, that sort of thing," Jane recalls. "I don't know, I didn't think they got much of anything, but the lights-out thing really drove me up the wall."

With misgivings, Jane finally decided to try table-tipping in her class, "just for the hell of it, to see what we'd get. I thought, who am I to bitch? Why not at least try it?" She and Rob had originally made the Seth contact on a Ouija board, after all—so *some* kind of energy was behind this sort of phenomenon.

"The next Tuesday, we were all at Rachael Clayton's house, where we held class sometimes, for a change," Jane says. "All the lights were on, of course. I remember I put some people on the couch, some at Rachael's fancy little scalloped-edged table with me. Everybody was supposed to make sure we didn't touch it with our knees or under the top with our hands!

"I got all ready and said the sort of thing I thought I should say," Jane recalls, rolling her eyes humorously at the memory. "I said, 'Spirits—move this table. Spirits, move this goddamn table!' And it really took off! It danced all around the room, our fingers sliding all over the top of it. So then we knew enough to get a code system going, one tap for A, two taps for B, and so on. Right away, it tapped out the initials A. A.—going all the way through the alphabet for that second A, and claiming it was somebody for Florence. So then for a long time, whenever we did this table thing, we'd ask for Florence's A. A. and ask it to do a jig for her—which it would do."

Attending this first table-tipping session was a nineteen-year-old girl who'd never been to class before, Jane recalls. "The table started giving messages to people, you know, on the one-tap-for-A scale, with somebody writing these all down . . . The thing gave your usual messages to people around the room, like 'I'm watching over you,' and 'I love you,' and stuff. But when it came to this girl, it said there was a message for her from a Mildred Sullivan. Well, I'd known a Mildred Sullivan in town who had died, and so I thought, 'Sure, that's it! Big deal!' As it turned out—and nobody in the room knew any of this—the girl's deceased *mother* was *also* named Mildred Sullivan; the girl had a different last name, you see. The table gave specific information to her, including initials, dates, and facts that nobody else in that room could have known about. And the girl never came back to class after that!"

At the time, Jane was holding a creative writing class in her home on Wednesdays, and decided to try the table-tipping stunt with her two writing students. "We sat around my green work table, trying to make it move—but it wouldn't budge," Jane remembers. "It wouldn't do a thing! So finally—and this was the only time I ever said this—I said, 'Seth, will you *please* make this goddamned table move!' It skidded across the floor, zoom, as we ran with it. I yelled to Rob, who was working in his studio, and he came out to take a look. As he was standing there by the bathroom door, I yelled, 'Go, table! Go get Robbie!' And it skidded right over and pinned him right up against the wall!

"Actually," Jane says of those early table ventures, "I was terrified! What, for God's sake, did this kind of thing mean? Where were those messages *coming* from? And it still just seemed so sleazy, the old seance bit in new clothes—even though the validity of the information to that girl, for instance, couldn't be denied.

"Sometimes we'd have two or three tables going at once up there—*Whump! Whump! Whump!* and we'd be yelling, 'Go! Go! Go, table, go!' at the top of our lungs, and then the next day I'd see poor Leon, the guy who lived below us, and he never said a word, not even, 'Uh, hi Jane, uh, what *was* that noise up there last night, you know, the footsteps and all?' "

One Friday night, this vigorous sense of table-tipping fun had an unexpected surprise. Jane and Rob and some friends decided to try out the experiment, "particularly because a couple of them wanted to prove that it was all a bunch of garbage," Jane says. The table—one of those Victorian models with a single fat spool in the middle—started rotating around on its three legs as soon as the five volunteers (including Jane and Rob) placed their fingers on its top. As usual, Jane started yelling, "Go, table, go! Go, table, go!" But instead of dancing all around the room, the table began rocking ponderously, back and forth, back and forth, slowly, like a family patriarch in his rocking chair. After about twenty minutes of whumping back and forth, the table finally stopped—balanced neatly on two of its legs, everybody still dutifully touching it.

"Push down," Jane suggested on impulse.

Everybody pushed down on the raised side. The table wouldn't be pushed.

"You know how things feel when they're on a spring, and you push down on them?" Rob asks. "That's just how this felt—it was the weirdest sensation you can imagine."

They pushed, grunted, and pushed. And the table stayed put, one leg hanging a few defiant inches above the rug.

"Go in and get the bathroom scale!" Jane shouted. One of the fellows ran into the john and brought out the floor scale while everyone else stood there, fingers on table. The scale was put on top of the table's raised side and several people, in turn, pushed down on *that*.

The scale registered more than fifty pounds of pressure. And still the table hung there in the air.

"I'll show this goddamn thing," one of the men growled between his teeth, and he practically lunged on the tabletop.

Crack!

The tabletop shattered—broke right off on the raised side. The scale crashed to the floor. Everybody jumped back and the table fell over with a crash.

"Great!" Jane moaned. "Just great! I borrowed this table from a neighbor! How in hell am I going to explain how I broke it?"

Rob adroitly glued the table back together, but this "building up pressure" escapade was done several times in class, with varying degrees of success. Joel Hess reported a similar table-smashing incident during a group experiment in his home—using, however, a heavy plastic table.

"It was always great fun," says Betty DiAngelo. "I was surprised—yet not surprised. It was not a little interesting that three strong men could not force the table to keep all of its legs on the floor!"

"It was all just freewheeling fun," Jane says. "It just showed you what you could do with energy, that's all. I liked the fun—but I steered away from the message bit."

Messages in another context, however, provided class with the basis of the "door" experiment—a simple test that anyone can set up. Every weekday morning at 9:00 A.M., Jane would tack up a different *something* on the inside of her apartment door: a sketch, a page from a magazine, or perhaps an object inside an envelope. This object would stay on the door until 9:00 A.M. the following morning. During that twenty-four-hour period, class members would try to "pick up" what might be on the door, and either draw their impressions of it or write down a description. Then during that week's class, everyone's results would be checked out against the five objects themselves. Class members rarely visited Jane and Rob except on occasional Friday nights, and thus before Tuesday, had few chances to see the five door objects—in the usual sense.

The "hits" that occurred were often surprising, and not only for their correlation with the actual door objects. Some weeks there would be people who had every single object right; other weeks, nobody had anything right—and then sometimes there would be a weird combination of the two, in which everyone's incorrect guesses would match!

Once, I scored five direct hits in one week—my personal "door" record. Most people drew pictures of their impressions; I usually wrote a description of the object, since I'm more word oriented. From my notebook, dated from the class of November 5, 1968:

1. Guess for Wednesday, October 30: Page with writing on it; small, lined, from loose-leaf notebook, or out of something like that—this remembers a time when the owner had a lot of fun. Object: Library book index card, filled with names, for the book, *Golden Book of Guns.*

2. Guess for Thursday, October 31: A daisy or long-stemmed flower. Object: A button with a large, long-stemmed flower on it.

3. Guess for Friday, November 1: A fish—a drawing or a photo. Object: A fishing license.

4. Guess for Monday, November 4: Something from a gun, or from a metal footlocker. Object: A metal serial number plaque from a gunstock.

5. Guess for Tuesday, November 5: An article about fashion, or maybe the "best-dressed" list. Object: An advertisement from the local newspaper illustrating ladies' winter coats, jackets, and dress suits.

Betty DiAngelo reports one hit that was shared by herself and her husband. "The thing was Jane's father's nail clippers," she says. "Tim had gotten the impression of a pair of tweezers—I had seen a small rectangle of old metal." Priscilla Lantini remembers but one hit: ". . . the one I got right, which I picked up as a crooked letter, like a letter envelope lying on its side. At the time there was a piece of paper on the door with the letter S on it. Jane said that a 'crooked letter' was my interpretation of an S. That was good; it gave me a little insight on things—it was great fun."

Exploring another "angle" of the door, Harold Wiles says that he had several direct hits. "Though I no longer have my records to check," he says, "I believe the thing that impressed me during these experiments was the fact that I intentionally did not do them daily. At some time during the week, usually just before class on Tuesday, I would make my sketches of what I felt had been on the door each day during the week. In other words, I did it all at once! After all, if time is simultaneous, the objects were there all at once—correct? My hits reinforced my understanding of the nature of simultaneous time."

Geoffrey Beam, who struggled to relax in class (and everywhere else) and who, in his words, was left "completely cold" by much of what went on those Tuesdays, had "very good luck with the door experiment." "I scored an exact direct hit once when the picture on the door was that of a comb," he says. For him, the door gave him a seldom-sensed feeling of participation and inner accomplishment.

Not everyone made hits, of course, and some members didn't even like this particular experiment—it just didn't turn them on. "I remember the time there was this big letter S up on the door," says Joel Hess, somewhat ruefully. "The next week, somebody came in with the letter S on a piece of paper. Someone else had drawn a bird with a big, curved neck. Still another person had come up with a snake curved on the ground, sort of like an S. I think I had drawn a breast."

"I really liked that part of class," Betty says. "It gave me an outline or format to try picking [things] up in an altered state, and also it felt like it brought class members close together, in that during the week we were working on something together in waking reality—something conscious and tangible. And it was fun to compare later on."

Particularly evocative in this door series were the sketches drawn in late 1967 by Marion Chalmers, then a music teacher in the Elmira school system, and by Pat Klein (see figure 1). Pat's drawing (on top) is nearly identical to Marion's drawing (see figure 3). Attempting to pick up the target for Wednesday, November 29, Pat drew this bird at 7:00 A.M. on a Thursday, November 30, two hours *before* Jane pinned up her Thursday drawing (middle, figure 2) of the bird-shaped incense burner that sat on her coffee table. Marion drew her bird at about 11 A.M. on that Thursday, during a free period in school. "Did I 'pick up' my bird from Pat, who drew hers at 7 A.M.?" Jane wonders in her notes. "If so, then did Marion receive her impression from my drawing, or from Pat's?

"Marion, incidentally, taught Pat music several years ago, but the two had not met again until they did so at my classes . . . Pat and Marion had no idea that their sketches were hits. They are not even in the same classes [Pat attended the Thursday beginners class at that point], but met when one of them came to a makeup class. Marion was particularly discouraged the night we scored hits. 'All I could think of was an old bird!' she said. How quickly her expression changed when I showed her the target picture!"

Jane adds in her notes that "the students have no idea whether or not they had picked up the target sketch when they did their own drawings. This lack of conscious awareness has been characteristic as a rule . . . To this point, no student when notified of a hit has said, triumphantly, 'I knew at the time that I was right!'"

Figure 5 shows another hit made by Marion Chalmers—this time with variations on the theme! Jane had drawn a graceful swan (see figure 4), with curving neck and head. Marion drew a picture of a coiled snake, complete with arched head—but this time, Marion's snake (figure 5) was facing in the same direction as Jane's swan. (In the two student drawings, figure 1 and figure 3, Marion's bird and Pat's are both facing in the opposite direction from Jane's sketch.)

In another example of a miss turning out to be the strangest kind of hit, Jane's target object was an ad from *Esquire* magazine for Pierre Cardin boots

Figure 1. Attempting to "pick up" Jane's target drawing for November 29, Pat Klein sketched this bird at 7 A.M. on November 30. Jane would not change the door object until 9 A.M. on November 30.

Figure 2. Two hours after Pat sketched the bird in figure 1, Jane drew this sketch as the door target for the day. Did Jane know, telepathically, of the sketch Pat had already drawn?

Figure 3. At approximately 11 A.M. on November 30, Marion Chalmers made this sketch. Note the great similarity to Pat's drawing (both birds face in the same direction).

(figure 6). One student's drawing for that day of an ear (figure 7) appears to be a complete dud.

Yet, when you hold the ad for the boots up to the light, something happens to the dimensions of this student's guess. On the other side of the boot ad is a four-color fashion photograph showing three men and two women posed in the typical postures of modern clothing display (figure 8). But all of these five models' heads are in three-quarter profile and display a prominent feature in common: their ears. The men's heads are posed in such a way, and the women's hair is fashionably yanked back, so that everybody's ears are exposed to the evening breeze. Seen in this position, through the boots ad, the shape and direction of the ESP student's drawing coincides remarkably with the ear on the model standing with his foot on the deck railing—and incidentally, this man is the one figure in the fashion photograph whose feet (although in blue suede loafers) are prominently displayed!

In particular, this door hit reminds me of the advertising techniques discussed by Dr. Wilson Bryan Key in his books, *Subliminal Seduction* and *Media Sexploitation.*[1] It is Dr. Key's contention that advertising art and design are purposely embedded with certain charged symbols that are capable of directing, on an unconscious level, the buying habits of consumers, even if they glance at such ads for only a few seconds. Several of Dr. Key's examples of sensory imbeds show the kind of bleed-through perceptual pickup from one page to another as displayed in this class member's hit sketch. While I would add that nobody is manipulated on any level unless he or she concedes to it, the student's sketch represents the exact process that Dr. Key charges advertisers with using to sell their products. On an unconscious level, for example, the Pierre Cardin boots might be lent more romantic and virile meaning through their bleed-through relationship with the five obviously rich and sexually available people in Esquire's four-color ad. And does the student's hit indicate that he had, in fact, unconsciously reacted in the intended manner?

In her notes on the door experiment in 1968, Jane wrote, "I am convinced that we constantly receive extrasensory information and act on it, without ever knowing it consciously. The implications are staggering. It will be difficult to prove such a statement, since the very fact of conscious ignorance would prevent us from receiving the necessary proof in usual cases. Experiments such as [the door] could, however, over a period of time, provide strong evidence supporting just such a contention . . . Until we learn to be alert, to recognize ESP when it does emerge, we will not learn its true nature. We will not discover how we receive and interpret it.

"If we think we do not have psychic ability, then we inhibit its use in our daily lives. If we honestly believe that we are merely physical creatures,

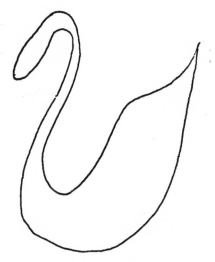

Figure 4. Jane's swan outline.

Figure 5. Marion Chalmers's drawing made the same day.

Figure 6

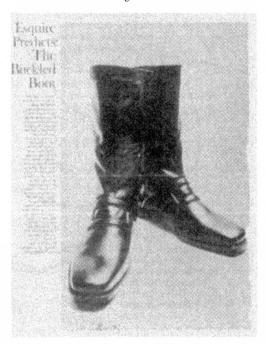

Figure 7

Figure 8

then we will inhibit any nonphysical manifestations that may otherwise occur through us or to us. Then it is easy to say, 'But we have no proof,' since we make very sure, subjectively, that no proof will appear.

"Instead we must realize that the physical world would have no meaning at all for us were it not for our subjectivity; that this inner consciousness is precisely what does make the physical universe meaningful; and accept the possibility that this consciousness may indeed exist independently of the physical world that it allows us to perceive."

In September of 1974, class had again been trying out the door targets for several weeks, and Seth had this to say of our efforts:

"You are involved in more than you realize. These experiments will lead you to other areas—not only into the lands of your own symbolism, but into the realization of a different kind of communication. You *can* learn the ways in which you communicate *always* beneath language. You can, if you are curious and astute, discover the very patterns behind language through studying what you are doing.

"Become alert to your own symbolism as you decipher it here in class with your [door guesses]; as it appears to you in the dream state; and as it appears to you through free association. You will find correlations.

"You will also, if you are astute and curious, find in those symbols, the patterns behind the objects in the physical universe. You have a shorthand kind of symbol for those.

"There will be symbols, in other words, that you will use as you try to approach the target on the door. The methods that you use to approach that target are important; and yet, those methods will vary with each of you. In discovering your own methods, you can, again *if you are astute*, discover the way in which you personally perceive, create, and interpret the physical world that you know, and communicate with others.

"Now at other levels of actuality, you are doing this all the time. But the more you learn—in your terms, on a conscious level—then again, in your terms, the more you will remember after death, and the more self-conscious you will be, and the more capable of carrying on new endeavors . . . You will open up avenues that exist within your own experience. You will find the symbols and the abilities that are uniquely yours, and belong to no other.

"I bid you then, and now, a welcome into the threshold of your own being; and you *are* ready to take steps into those lands that are your own. And the work that you are doing here, and just beginning, will show benefits in all other areas of your life and of your experience."

Within this threshold, class also did many different kinds of altered-consciousness experiments (which Jane has described in several of her own books, including *Adventures in Consciousness* and *Psychic Politics*) using the alpha trance state[2] to imaginatively "travel" away from the usual apartment setting, later comparing what we had "seen." These mental gymnastics were, I think, like physical training, in that they toned us up in certain ways: heightened our inner alertness and helped us distinguish the levels of validity within subjective experience.

One of Jane's favorite consciousness "trips" sent us playfully journeying into other living things, like a squirrel outside the living room windows, or the leaves of her many houseplants. "[I was] told to select a leaf from Jane's philodendron and project to it," Theodore Muldoon recorded in his class notes on September 1, 1970. "I select one by a green, long-necked bottle containing water. As I concentrated on being part of that leaf's consciousness, I felt a great desire to enter the cooling, refreshing water in the bottle (the room was quite smoky). Suddenly, the cork in the bottle was not an obstacle, and I did enter the water. A good feeling! In return for the favor, I in turn (imaginatively) wiped off the outside of the bottle so it too looked and felt better . . .

"After everyone completed telling class their experience, I noted . . . we could learn something about ourselves by it. For example, I noted my first feelings were for my own comfort, and second a repayment for the favor.

"In experiment 2 [we were to] allow ourselves to project outside the window. While all other members of class did do this according to their reports, and with a number of explanations of astonishment and happiness, instead I had a strong draw to gain a better understanding of Being versus Non-Being. So I was aware I could not really experience the full depth of Non-Being as physically I was not equipped to handle it, but there was a little experiment that I could try [during class] that would illustrate.

"I was suddenly holding my violin in playing position, but could not finger it or draw the bow. But even worse, I could not even imagine the sounds or feel of playing. I knew: this is Non-Being—to know but not be able to imagine, or feel, or do. Then suddenly—I was released and could play. Such joy at Being!"[3]

Class tried consciousness expansions in nearly every phase of class—to explore probabilities, past-life information, alternate realities, or in healing experiments; and often the results were electrifying and filled with great personal import for the individuals involved. While in alpha, we would occasionally try to see each other's auras—bands of colored energy that seem to emanate from physical bodies (and which have been recorded through Kirlian photography), visible to some while in mild trance states. We'd try changing our auras' colors, for example, to see if the others could detect this. Some could—and described great multicolored bands of light broiling around fellow classmates' heads and shoulders. I rarely saw or cared much about auras;

but then, that's a measure of the impact of personal preference: what you feel a subjective affinity for is generally what you best perceive.

On the other hand, sometimes you get surprised.

In one of the first Thursday beginner's classes, Jane suggested that we try lowering the lights and relaxing while she played a Moog synthesizer recording on her stereo—"just to see where the music takes you," she said. That night, Daniel MacIntyre and I were the only students there. As the Moog's somewhat annoying *ooorghs* and *squeeps* emerged from the stereo, I leaned back in my chair and let my mind wander, and I soon felt sleepy. Nothing out of the ordinary seemed to be happening. I straightened up and looked dreamily across the room at Jane, who was sitting in her rocker near a small, bright table lamp. She was wearing a black ankle-length dress and was resting, chin in hand, eyes closed. The sounds droned on and on, like the audible chewing and twisting of bubblegum. But as I stared at Jane, I suddenly realized I was seeing—mentally at first, but then quite plainly—flames leaping up around Jane from the floor by her chair.

Utterly flabbergasted by what I was seeing, I somehow managed to hold onto whatever state of consciousness I was in—and the flames continued. They were dark red—almost black—and somehow seemed cold: frozen fire, not hot at all. They would die down, then flare back up above Jane's head, at times nearly obliterating her from my sight. (She was apparently unaware of anything going on.)

Oh, fine! my mind chattered. Talk about crappy occult images! I glanced over at Daniel. To my surprise, he was staring open-mouthed at Jane's corner of the room—and then to my double surprise and shock, he whispered, "Flames!"

"Yes, yes," I whispered back, "I see them too!" We spoke beneath the sounds of the Moog record—from across the room, I'm sure that Jane couldn't have heard us.

We both looked back toward her. It took a minute of relaxation, but once again, I saw the curiously livid, cold flames leap back up around her. I looked back at Daniel. He nodded—he'd seen them too, at the same time. This continued for several more minutes, until the Moog record shut off and Jane opened her eyes.

When the three of us compared notes, we were astounded all over again to discover that while Daniel and I were perceiving flames, Jane had mentally sensed something that she'd described as being "like flames" rushing from the floorboards up around her chair.

Suggestion? An unconscious relating of the weird Moog sounds to some long-forgotten nightmare visions? Or a mutual recognition of our mutual abilities, using Jane's leadership position as a symbol base? Probably all of these—our consciousness had certainly fallen into a sideways state in response to Jane's suggestion that we "get" something, and get *something* we did—even though Jane and I wrinkled our noses at each other and grumbled, "Flames? Eeeeyukk!"

Another good example of an extrasensory apparition that appeared in class during one of these consciousness expansions is recorded in my own notes from the night of September 1, 1970. There were fourteen people in class that night, arranged in the room according to figure 9 (my drawing). Three table lamps held the room in a pleasant glow. Just as the evening was drawing to a close, Jane had us try throwing our consciousness out the bay windows, "out over the city."

"Almost immediately," my notes state, "I had an intense, vivid image of flying out the window and tumbling among the trees, until I landed in an apple orchard. I walked under the trees, touching the apples and feeling the grass under my feet. I picked up an apple and threw it over a tree—whereupon, I flew after it until I came to a forest.

"Vividly, I could see myself floating down under the trees. When I touched the ground, I spread out like a large puddle. Suddenly, I was a long floor of grass, feeling each individual blade and the oneness of the field at once. It seemed that the seasons passed by in a few seconds' time: I felt deer walk on me in the summer and leaves touch me in the fall; snow felt like a warm muffler of vibration; I felt a human foot step on my snow-covered edges here; and spring was a grand rush of energy and feeling.

"I could have stayed for much longer," my notes continue, "but at this point Jane touched my arm, and I opened my eyes. It seemed that the living room returned before me in pieces, like the putting-together of a jigsaw puzzle, filling in over the forest floor of my vision. I was very dissociated, in other words.

Figure 9

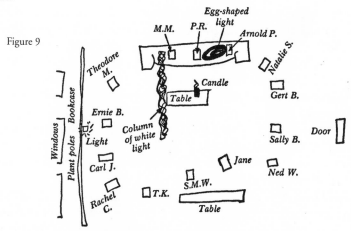

"While the class was discussing their experiences, I was gazing hazily in the direction of the couch, on which sat Arnold Pearson, Pat Reynolds and his date, Margaret. Suddenly I began to notice shards of filmy lines, curving in toward themselves, in the space between Pat and Arnold; these somewhat overlapped Pat's crossed leg. I let it go on for a few minutes, until the filmy white shape had attained a definite egg shape, concentrated near (but definitely not part of) Pat's leg. At this point I told Jane what I was seeing and she lit the small, fat candle on the table between us and the couch. She suggested that whatever energy there was [should] give some effects with the candle. But nothing happened.

"However, Jane began to see this shape also, and we both remarked on the black or opaque appearance of part of it. Pat put out his hand and said that he felt 'heaviness' in the area, but could see nothing. I cracked a joke at this point and the class laughed—and instantly, the shape became larger and more solid.

"Then I got the definite impression that there was another, 'probable' ESP class sitting around in its own universe, experimenting with consciousness as we were, and that this white shape was like a UFO, so to speak, appearing between the probabilities, perhaps like a materialization of the connection we were intuitively feeling between this class and the probable one (knowing that the probable class would consider us the 'other' reality). I said this, while shrugging the impression off at the same time. Natalie Swing said that she could see the thing also.

"The shape gradually faded and the class began to leave, although Jane and I still 'felt something around.' Margaret leaned forward to pick some matches up off the table. As she moved, I saw a huge column of brilliant white light *zing!* down from her outstretched arm to the floor and then soar somehow up and down from ceiling to rug. At that same instant, Jane whirled around from the door, where her back had been turned, and cried out, 'Oh!'—just as I said, 'Look!'

"We had both exclaimed on it at the same time. Our descriptions matched, and this time the perception had been quite simultaneous. Jane said that she had turned around because she had 'felt' something enter the room.

"The tingle of energy stayed in that spot for quite a while, but nothing else happened. I definitely felt that my perception of the thing was connected with the way I had 'rearranged' my consciousness in the earlier expansion experiment, in which I had felt the sensations of a different kind of creaturehood—that of a field of grass."

Interestingly, it was soon after this event that we started to record frequent class dreams (which will be explained in later chapters), with some of those dreams and Seth's comments apparently probing the reality of probable, or parallel, classes. (See also chapter 6 for Seth's comments on UFOs.)

There was a sense of play and freedom about these consciousness experiments, and an emotional validity, that were unmeasurable in laboratory terms; yet ironically, it was this playful approach that gave us the most "measurable" results. When we yelled at the table in great roaring fun, it would practically hop out the window. When we treated the door targets like a game, the guess was very often a hit. Perhaps one reason for this is that in our earnest search for "proof" of ESP, the requirements of our logical approach simply become too narrow to accept the kind of data that can in fact check out— according to our usual specifications. It may be that we have yet to understand the range and fullness of *true* logic.

For example, as an adjunct to the door test, class was supposed to keep records of daily predictions. During the day, each of us would take a few minutes, sit quietly, clear our minds, and quickly write down a list of ten to twelve words or phrases as they came into our heads—no matter how silly these sounded. Then we'd keep track of whatever happened during the next twenty-four hours or so and check events against this original list. Basically, these predictions were asking such questions as: How much data do we constantly perceive beneath our usual perceptions? How much do we actually know about what our personal future holds? How do we consciously and unconsciously connect the myriad details of our lives?

The hit rate in class predictions was surprisingly good, although sadly, most members didn't preserve these records. Jane describes some of her prediction results in chapter 12 of *Psychic Politics*, however; and for a while, when my interest in predictions was keen, I made some humorously accurate scores myself. On Monday, July 7, 1969, I wrote the following in my notebook for the next day, July 8:

1. Cataracts.

2. An old friend will call you—you haven't seen him in a long time.

3. Salamanders.

On the next day, according to my notes, the following events occurred in this order:

1. I received the weekly Martha's Vineyard *Gazette* in the mail and read in it that a woman who used to help me write the social news for our village had been operated on for cataracts.

2. Dan Stimmerman, whom I had not heard from for more than a year, called me at 6 P.M. from California.

3. Later in the evening, I drove to a local shopping mall and saw snakes and chameleons in the pet shop there. I like reptiles, but

like many people, I confuse the orders within these classes: salamanders are amphibians, chameleons are reptiles.

Similarly, in July of 1970, I recorded the following:

1. Traveling salesmen.

2. Saddle or something about leather or saddle soap—a barn that has saddle shops and belts.

3. Daemon [*sic*] Runyon dies.

4. Daniel DeFoe too.

5. Purebred information.

6. Hide in the bannisters—they're coming! Hide!

The next day, my notes describe the following incidents:

1. A group of Mormons came to the house while I was gone and attempted to convert my husband.

2. On the afternoon TV show, *Sale of the Century*, a girl won a pure-bred cocker spaniel. The dog's pedigree was given.

3. Also that afternoon, an eye-stopping TV public-service commercial showed a man running frantically away from polluted air—the background music was "No Hiding Place."

4. At my in-laws' house that evening, a discussion arose on oiling baseball gloves after Ned [my husband then] said that he might take his old catcher's mitt to a saddle shop for repairs. His father suggested a nearby tack shop, located in an old barn. [Ned and I were always careful not to show our predictions to each other or to talk about them before we'd had a chance to write down daily correlations.] It turned out that this place also carried leather belts.

5. Later, a character named Daemon in an old TV movie was eaten by an alligator.

6. The last thing I read before going to sleep that night was the current *Time* magazine book review section, which included an analysis of Daniel Defoe's *Robinson Crusoe*.

Of course, there were plenty of days when none of the things I scribbled down connected with anything—or when only one or two predictions were even vaguely related to events. But with hits like the above, the implications are awesome: Does extrasensory data include everything that will or could happen to us, right down to the magazine articles we might read and the television programs we might watch? How is it that our inner perceptions can skewer through massive nuances of circumstance and record that data which will touch upon us? And what of the predictions that don't happen—is this data false, or from directions that we just didn't take?

And what of inner knowledge itself? Why don't we accept our layered perceptions more readily? Or, when we do have such experiences, why are they so often greeted with dread, or total loss of common sense, or—as happened one night in class—snuffed out by merciless "critical" demands?

It was a warm summer evening. All the windows were open in Jane's living room, and from the streets and sidewalks below came traffic noise, sirens, and the voices of children running by. Seth had been talking about black holes in space, reincarnation, and a number of other subjects—at one point remarking that "you each possess in miniature all properties of the universe as you conceive of it at this present time . . . so what seems to you or to your scientists [to occur] outside of you, occurs within you, and now."

Suddenly, Ron—a humorless fellow with an expressionless face and large innocent eyes—leaned forward in his chair and dropped a deck of playing cards, face down, on the coffee table in front of Jane's rocker. "I want to throw something out," he stated in a flat voice. "Several sessions ago, we got into a conversation about the nature of the way you perceive this reality—"

"The ways in which I *can* perceive this reality," Seth interrupted, with an amused air.

"—And you were saying that if you wanted, that you could perceive it just as clearly in the same terms that we ourselves perceive it," Ron continued.

"*In* as limited terms," Seth replied. "The trouble with you is that you have no sense of humor!"

"Well, let's see how yours is," Ron said coolly. "I would like to suggest an experiment, and I am suggesting it to you to see your reaction. I was really undecided whether to suggest it to Jane or to you, but you see—like, I'm kind of at an impasse because there are a lot of words and a lot of concepts and philosophies bandied about. But when you make a claim that you know things in specific and nonconfusable terms . . . well, it would be very simple to demonstrate," Ron gestured at the cards on the table.

Class held its collective breath.

"Now, my dear love," Seth said, his voice low and soft. "Jane may or may not look into your playing cards; that is up to her—or to Ruburt. As far as I am concerned, I will not bother.

"Now, we have been through this with keener minds than your own," Seth went on. "The claims I make, I make not only for myself, but for you and for each person in this room. You can perceive those playing cards as clearly as I can—and if you will not believe *me*, you will not believe yourself.

"When I follow through with such demonstrations, I will do so not in the confines of this room and not under conditions set by you, but in a situation in which the claims are clearly recorded with the results [so that] there is no possibility that anyone will say suggestion is involved. You can, however, prove it to yourself by reading the cards. I do not have the doubts—you do!"

"Well, you give me the impression—I mean, that's an easy way out," Ron said.

"What is important are emotional realities, not symbols upon cards," Seth answered. "Until you realize that, and until you are willing to open up emotionally to the atmosphere of the class . . . then no proofs will be proofs to you."

"Well, I would disagree very much with that," Ron said, still in that same flat voice. "If you are able to do even to a limited extent what you claim that you are able to do, I would be completely dumbfounded. However, I don't think—"

"You are setting forth challenges in terms that you do not understand," Seth interrupted, "and until you understand that, that is the position at which you will remain."

"You could be equivocating."

"I could be indeed, and you can interpret what I am saying in any way you choose. The fact remains that it is you, not I, who are worried about my perceptions. The fact remains that what we have done has been clearly set forth in the book that Ruburt has written.[4] You can accept it or deny it, and as far as Seth or Ruburt are concerned, that is your right."

"We never read the results [of the Estabrooks tests], though," Ron said slyly.

"You are speaking of one specific group of tests—and the doubt exists, you see, in your mind; and while that particular kind of doubt exists, nothing will convince you. And any work that is done, is done with Ruburt's consent . . . If I were you, I would tiptoe out the door before someone tells him [Ruburt] what you have come up with, for I am also dependent to some extent upon his receptivity and ideas—AND THAT IS EXACTLY AS IT SHOULD BE!"

Seth's voice suddenly boomed out, making us all jump, but now he stared intently at Ron.

"You see," Seth said quietly, "you come here with demands. Now, those who have come open-mindedly to class have found their proofs—and proofs that were not dependent upon cards or showy tricks. But strong proof, in that the nature of their reality changed! They understood themselves better. They could relate to the experience that they know. They had experiences that they did not have before; and their mental, psychological, and spiritual worlds expanded. And to them—and me—card reading is an entirely different and inferior product. But while that is what you are looking for, you will find yourself at the level that you are now."

"So your answer in essence is that you yourself would not be interested in this because you don't consider it relevant," Ron concluded.

"I do not consider it *at this time* relevant," Seth answered patiently. "I did when Ruburt was so concerned."

"It isn't relevant to the rest of the class, either," Arnold Pearson broke in. "Nobody else in the class is interested in wasting time on this. Can't you get that through your head?"

"I fear," Seth added, "that like our friend Dr. Estabrooks, unless you change, you will be looking for proofs that mean nothing . . . ignoring the inner reality that is all-important and closing your mind to inner validity that alone would give you the kind of proof that you require.

"For example, had your attitude been different, and had you in a mood of fun and free giving thrown cards upon the table when I was speaking and said, 'Seth, what is on the other side of the cards?' you may have gotten an answer. But not in the framework in which you asked the question, nor in the framework in which you proposed the experiment."

"Well, I don't know," Ron said, undaunted. "I kind of doubt it, but as for looking inward, *you* know that there has to be a balance between the inwardness and the outwardness."

"Three years ago we went through all of this, and it's in Jane's book!" Sally Benson exploded.

"Now, before I let my friends very sweetly and nicely rush to my defense, let me mention that Ruburt, also, when classes began, made an effort . . . to give spontaneous readings, which worked out very well," Seth pointed out. "This means that they 'checked out.' He [Ruburt] quickly found, however, that [giving readings] was not the answer; that people merely said, 'He has the answers and I have none'; that they projected upon him abilities that they thought *they* did not possess. And therefore he has changed that policy. Whenever evidential material has been given, my dear friend—and it has been given—to help others deal with a problem of vital interest, it has not been given as a demonstration, and it has not been given to prove anything to anyone."

Seth withdrew. A small smile of triumph passed across Ron's lips. To him, all that Seth's words meant was that the tough scientist had prevailed.

"I had a lot of trouble with that kid," Jane said, years later. "I was trying to be gracious—I mean, after all, he was in *my* house! As far as the card thing went, I remember thinking at the time, 'Oh, for crying out loud, Seth! If you can read the damn cards, why didn't you just read them?' " But the directions that class was about to take would soon cut through this burden of "proof" in a crafty, far-reaching, and quite practical way.

CHAPTER 4

Who Hasn't Got a Secret? (Said the Selves We Loved to Hate)

Small Rain—A Song

Small rain in the evening falls,
smoothing down the mind;
letting images well up—
unhurried rain to fill your cup.

Let small rain down in the evening,
let it chill your prescient skin;
let it dance upon the fallen leaves
and stir your ancient memory in—

And say you are, you are;
and you have been.

—Dan Stimmerman, 1973

NADINE RENARD SAT ON JANE'S blue-covered couch looking pixie-like and bashful, her slender legs curled up underneath her. She was holding Robert Heinlein's novel, *Stranger in a Strange Land,*[1] which by that March of 1971 had become the fantasy gospel of the new consciousness; a post-1960s achievement handbook. The hero, Valentine Michael Smith, is brought to Earth from his native Mars with completely innocent beliefs in goodness and peace, and establishes a community of sensuality and joy, based on the communication of "grok." To grok, in Heinlein's world, was to achieve a oneness with another, or "to understand so thoroughly that the observer becomes part of the observed."[2]

"It's a beautiful book," Nadine was saying. "In it, people drop all their barriers, and they're completely open and honest and they really *love* each other . . ." She smiled at Jane. "I'd like to see us all try something like this," Nadine said. "I mean, in the book everybody has sex together all the time, and I don't mean anything like *that.* But Heinlein really had something there—he really did."

"Well," Jane said. "Well, well." She looked around at us. Most of us had read the book and were listening to Nadine with interest. Something was in the wind; you could tell. What were we daring ourselves to do now? "Grokking" sounded a lot like those experiments in which we'd imagined ourselves as part of a leaf or a cat or something . . .

"We *could* establish something like this between us," Jane said, holding the book in her hands. "But it would mean a kind of commitment we just haven't made up to now, and we'd have to do it without reservation, or it wouldn't work."

"What wouldn't work?" I croaked, my stomach suddenly jangling with stage fright. "What is it we're going to do?"

Jane looked at me with a mixture of impatience and amusement. "Well, if you're afraid that I'm going to have us all groping around on the floor, *that's* not it," she said smoothly. "It's just—well, it's as though we've reached a certain stage in this class, and unless something happens—and I'm not even sure what that something is—class just won't go on." Her face was solemn. "It just won't go on," she repeated.

"You mean you'd stop having class?" Gert Barber said in a hurt voice.

"I don't know, Gert—no, I'd probably still have class," Jane said. "But what I mean is, in a funny way, class just wouldn't go on, like it could, in some other crazy fashion."

Holy jumping shit, I thought, what is Jane onto now? I felt a huge anticipation—of what, I did not know. I did know that Heinlein's goal of losing individual identity to a group experience was utterly unacceptable to Jane and the class and represented the worst of what we were developing away from. No, we were talking about something else here—something brand-new that had just leaped from our contemplation of Heinlein's ten-year-old fantasy.

"But—" Gert began, and then Seth was there, interrupting her in his most vigorous, animated manner.

"Now, you are all out of touch with your emotions," he stated, tossing Jane's glasses into the air and grinning at Ned, who reached out and grabbed them on the fly. "It is not so much that you put up barriers between yourself and others, but that you put up barriers between yourself and yourself, and each of you in class [has] put up paper people that sit in front of you, and you hope that the others relate to those paper people!

"You all have your roles in class, as you have elsewhere, and you are afraid of disturbing the balance of the class. You have a good thing going, and you do not want to lose it! You have various gradations of intellectuals; you have various gradations of those who are willing to express some emotions; and I am looking at no one in particular! *I* am the only one who expresses my emotions, and I am supposed to be dead!"

"I think the society we live in is expressed around the fact that you don't show emotion," Ned remarked from his position on the floor.

"Well, we are starting a new one, and you had better get used to it," Seth retorted. Ned and several others giggled nervously.

"Now, our friend Ruburt is not about to go for all this sexual hanky-panky that is described in this precious book," Seth went on. "But the man who wrote the book picked up his information from the inner self and then he made a story about it. And when you come to class from now on, I will expect to find you *all here*, not just the physical self, not just the intellectual self, not just the portion of yourself that you term psychically inclined, but the emotional self! And I will expect to see it showing!

"Now, you must admit that I have set you some example. I *laugh* more than you do. It is true that I have not cried, but if things continue as they are, I may be about to, for I want your entire self here, and expressive! Now you show somewhat more of yourselves in class than you do in your usual life situations. Some one percent more. But to come truly alive, and to come truly alive in this room, you must show far more. It ill behooves me to have to tell you that it takes someone as long dead as I have been to tell you how to become truly alive!"

"You've never been happy until you've been sad," Ned sighed dramatically.

"I did not say that—you did," Seth admonished. "Sadness does not make you happy automatically. Happiness makes you happy."

Ned shook his head. "You don't realize how happy you are until you've been sad," he repeated.

Seth turned in Jane's rocker, staring down at Ned with wide, dark eyes. What was Seth leading up to, with all this talk about showing your "real" self in class? Something was going on, and we were all scuttling around in our minds trying to guess what it was.

"You do not need to be sad, though," Seth said to Ned, "any more than your big toe has to be a little toe before it understands what it is to be a big toe." Leaning forward, Seth reached out and tapped Ned's open-sandaled big toe with Jane's fingernail. "Your big toe is smarter than you are," Seth grinned. "Listen to it."

"But for the majority, the people who aren't that sensitive, they have to be sad before they are happy," Ned pursued.

"*Everyone* is that sensitive—you do not realize that they realize it," Seth responded, flashing the old 1960s peace sign at Ned, who smiled his radiant, irresistible smile and returned the gesture.

"Now, many of you still do not realize what I say," Seth said to the rest of us. "You listen to the words and that is all, but the power behind the words, and the power behind the voice, is emotional power and emotional energy, and it represents—again—energy that is within each of you, and there is no need to be afraid of it. I am not worried about being dignified and adult— why should you be? And why should you try to be psychically educated while closing yourself off emotionally from the others who come to class?—for you all have put up barriers between yourselves. You must learn to recognize and use and pool your emotional energy. You do not lose, but gain.

"I have not told you to be decorous or quiet. I have spoken to you of direct experience, and by direct experience, I mean also emotional experience. You cannot divorce it from your own sense of reality; and I use, there-fore, the word love, without the embarrassment that some of you, quite pri-vately, ascribe to it. You can love a flower [and] you do not hate it because it has one brown petal; and yet when you find another individual with a sym-bolic brown petal, you immediately latch upon that.

"Now!" Seth's voice rang out, impossibly loud and full, from Jane's small frame. "Now, when I conduct a sensitivity session, you will know you have been to one! And if you do not all let down some barriers on your own, then that will be what you are faced with!"

Abruptly, Seth turned back to Ned. Ned grinned up at Jane's Sethian features; Ned had been closed off and uncommunicative lately, but tonight his smile was handsome and charming. But Seth shook his head in reply. "Behind all your ostentatious openness there are closed doors," he told Ned. "They are simply not as obvious as other peoples' closed doors. There is one certain way to avoid detection by others, and it is to appear so open that it will not occur to them that there is anything you are hiding—but you do not fool me.

"You may all take your break."

Jane came out of trance to a class chattering madly away, ignoring her. What was this all about? What was this "sensitivity session" Seth was cooking up? "I feel like I've been stuck with a pin," Ned mourned.

Jane hardly had a chance to hear even part of an explanation of what had been said, however, before Seth was back, his wide eyes staring at each of us in turn. "You will shortly learn, here at least, to be honest with your own self, to free your own emotional energy and then learn to direct it. You have all been afraid of feeling it; you have, therefore, been unable to direct it. To some extent this applies to Ruburt also, for he realizes its strength. But the time has come for you all to learn to recognize, feel, and direct your own emotional reality.

"Now we have spoken in terms that you'd understand—the nature of your world and reality as you know it. But you have not taken the stuff of reality into your hearts and understood it, and this is what you must now begin to learn to do. In other words, you must accept the emotional self, not superficially, not idealistically, but as it now exists: the reality of what you are *now*—and then you can begin to work with what you are and what you have.

"You cannot project psychic reality elsewhere. It is one thing to project a God outward into another universe and then try to find it. You realize by now that this is a futile attempt, but it is also futile to try to reach yourself by imagining that your self is somewhere else in another universe—you are doing the same thing.

"The self is immediate as All That Is is immediate, and your quickest entry point is at the point of your present feelings, and there is no other way. The door to your feelings [is] open *by* accepting your feelings, at this moment or at any moment as they apply to yourselves and to others in the room.

"I suggest now that when I am finished, for a preliminary starter, each of you tell a secret.*"*

A little shock wave seemed to ripple through the class. We looked at one another uneasily.

"Now," Seth continued, after a brief pause for effect, "you may have told this secret to your mate or to those closest to you, or you may not have, but [choose] one that is not known to the world at large. And in a preliminary step in expressing honesty in this room, and in expressing your own experience and feeling, each of you, therefore, tell a secret and put your beliefs into action. Some of you will doubtlessly choose secrets that are meaningless, but even this is a beginning. I suggest, however, that you choose meaningful secrets, for you will benefit. And when I run sensitivity sessions, I do not fool around!"

"Oh, brother!" Gert moaned as Jane came out of trance. Gert quickly explained to Jane what Seth had asked us to do.

"Oh, yeah?" Jane said brightly. "A secrets session, huh? Great. Ha-ha, ha, ha-ha," she added mirthlessly.

We all sat there stupidly, like frogs blinking under a flashlight. I was hastily going through my mental list of awful things I'd done; terrible things I'd said; disgusting things I'd thought of; guilt-ridden things I'd gotten out of doing. Oh, God, there was the time I'd hit my dog; the time I'd left that insulting note on my father's office desk; the time I'd—it was all too awful.

You could tell that everybody was doing the same thing: each digging up all the garbage of a lifetime.

"Well," Jane said in a singsong voice, "who's-a gonna go first, my loves? After all, this is *my* class—*I* don't have to go first!" She lit a cigarette and waited.

"All right, I'll start," Lloyd Fredericks volunteered defiantly. "I might as well, it's no big thing. I stole some candy from a store once when I was a teenager. I never told anybody about it. I don't even know why I did it. So there."

That's his idea of a secret? I thought. Why, that's nothing! Who cares about a thing like that?

"All right," a woman stated with a determined air, her teeth clenched. "I'll tell you this: I used to go with a married man!" She glanced around the room, waiting for the expected gasps.

"Oh, hell," Lawrence Briggs laughed, "who didn't?" But the woman didn't seem amused.

I was sort of next, by default—I was sitting third in line. "Well," I stammered. I felt horrible, worthless, deserving of death by fire. "I . . ." I couldn't meet Jane's eyes. "I once hit my dog with a stick," I gulped, biting back tears.

Silence. Jane shrugged. "I guess I'd have to say I'm surprised, Sue, but if that's what's got you so upset . . ." She looked to the next person, who gave a long, agonized confession of hating his elderly father, whom he had taken into his home. I nearly sneered at him. Big deal—at least you never hit your dog!

Once again, silence fell on the room. People coughed and blew their noses. Nobody looked at anybody. The class member in the next place said that she "wanted to pass for now." Someone else made the remark that he was "sitting in hell."

"You can get out in a twinkling!" Seth bellowed, coming through Jane so suddenly that Sally Benson let out a startled yelp. "You have only to realize that you created it yourself! Now, I know your secrets, and I will be interested in how long it takes for each of you to get to them! No pressure is being exerted, however."

Nobody said a word.

"Now, you can feel free to pass at this time, but you cannot always pass," Seth said. "What I want you to do is to admit here the things that are *important* to you that you have not told. That is, important to you, not to me, and not to anyone else in the room—but highly important to you.

"You all have more than one secret, and there will be plenty of time for the rest of them and then you will dance through the grasses, and I will lead you with a merry flute, indeed . . ."

"Okay, I'll tell mine," Gert announced dramatically, not even waiting for Jane to put her glasses back on. Gert then launched into a description of a clandestine affair she'd had with another nun during her convent years, before she'd left the order. Everybody listened in fascination; but knowing Gert, who had hinted many times in class that she struggled with lesbian yearnings, this whole story surprised nobody. (Years later, Gert wrote a manuscript—as yet unpublished—about her convent experiences and her emergence into the Gay Rights battlefront; it's quite probable that this class "confession" was the beginning of Gert's acceptance of her true feelings.)

"A-hem, well," Jane said, clearing her throat. "I guess that makes me next." She then told a simple fact of her childhood—that she and her invalid mother had existed for a time on welfare. Her voice was a near whisper as she spoke, and she was obviously very ashamed of this. I had known about this (to me insignificant) piece of her past, but what shocked me now about it was that Jane held it as such a secret. *That* was Jane's deep, dark, hidden skeleton? My God, I thought, at least she never would have hit her dog . . .

"Now, my sensitivity session with you has barely begun, but we will continue at another time," Seth interjected, cutting Jane off in mid-reach for a cigarette. "I will not be satisfied with these tidbits that you have thrown out for me! You are so negatively oriented that you automatically think your secrets must be negative ones, you see, and you think of them in negative terms where they are not negative. This has to do with the charge that you have built up around them. They are not negative. You hide them because you think they are. When you feel free to realize they are creative, you will feel free to release them. And until you feel free, you may keep your silence. I bid you all a hearty good evening and an emotional and a joyful and a loud and a spontaneous good evening!"

Class broke up quietly. During the week, I thought about the secret I had revealed to the others. I felt ashamed of myself all over again. But when I tried to remember what the others had said, I discovered that it took some effort to do so; and when I did recall those secrets, it seemed obvious that nobody had told anything of any magnitude at all—except for me. (In fact, when I put this book together eight years later, I found it extremely difficult to reconstruct the secrets classes, since mine were the only ones I could recall clearly, and many of the people who had participated in these sessions didn't answer my questionnaire. The implications of this facet of memory was, of course, the main point of the whole experiment.)

The next week, those of us who had spilled the beans came to class feeling pretty smug—after all, we were off the hook, so to speak, on the secrets stuff. But Seth was, as usual, trickier than we were: he wanted each of us to explain why we were "afraid of the implications of the word 'love,' or of showing it here," and why we found it "far safer to show love to an animal than a person."

"Some of you would almost rather stand up in this class and say, 'I killed an animal in hatred,' or 'I knocked a man's guts out,' or 'I shot my neighbor,' than express a simple statement of love or acceptance to another person in the class wholeheartedly . . . The secrets do not bother you half so much as you imagine that they do," Seth told us.

So around the class we went again. "I'd rather love my cat than another person because the cat needs me and doesn't hurt me, frankly," one woman said. "Everybody's afraid of love, and why not? It's something that can humiliate you worse than—worse than telling secrets!"

"Well, I can genuinely tell Jane and Sue and Ned and all the rest of you that I love you," Rachael Clayton said. "I feel that I'm a loving person, and it's easy to do. But I'm not sure I could really feel too secure if you all said you loved me back! I guess I'd feel like you were flattering me, 'cause I'd say, 'Why me?'"

Class actually took a couple of weeks to go through these love confessions—but when we did get back to telling secrets, Seth's directions added another dimension: we were supposed to explain why we "did not tell the secrets that [we] glossed over [that first time] . . . and why instead, [we] chose the particular secrets that [we] did!"

"Now, each of you went over very thoroughly in your mind your charged list of secrets," Seth said that night. "Some of you found to your amazement that you did not seem to have any; others found such a list that you made up priorities. Now, I want to know two things: why you chose to divulge the particular secret that you did, and why you did not choose to divulge another; why you used one secret to cover up for another. I want *you* to know the answers to the questions. And those of you who were not present at that session may then divulge their initial secrets.

"Now, regardless of those who come and go within this class, we shall achieve a state of trust, and this is one of the ways that we shall achieve it. And we shall begin with our friend, brother Joel!"

"Um, well, I really can't think of a thing," Joel mumbled as Jane came out of trance. "I guess maybe if I had to think of something, it would have to be, like—oh, one time when I was little, maybe I stole something from a store. But I don't even remember that clearly and now I'm not really sure if it happened the way I'm thinking it might have—" He stopped, mid-sentence.

Immediately, someone else said, "This reminds me of the time when . . . " and class spun off onto other subjects—much to Joel's obvious relief.

Perhaps because of his reactions, Jane reassured everybody that no one had to tell any secrets if they didn't want to. "It's your own choice," she shrugged.

But Seth was undaunted.

"I am even more amused by Ruburt's statement [than by the course of class conversation]," Seth broke in, waving Jane's glasses in Joel's direction. "And if we are going to have trust, by God, we are going to take it tippy-toe at a time!"

"I don't have a list of priorities, I really, really don't," Joel protested. "I feel that I told you a secret."

"As you know and I know, and with no accusations involved one way or another," Seth said to him, "the answer is facile. It is too easy. Now ask yourself some further questions about the answer that you have given and whether or not you truly accept it, using the knowledge from the whole self that is now becoming available to you."

"I still get answer number one," Joel said quickly.

"Do not answer so quickly—feel it through."

Joel licked his lips, not looking at his wife, Alison, who was sitting next to him. "My other secrets might hurt someone else," Joel finally said.

"Now you are being more honest," Seth said. "I would give you a medal, but I do not have one available! To establish the overall position of trust between yourself and the group, if you want to establish it, then the answer was important. And to everyone else in the room, so will your own answers be important."

"That," Joel said, "is my most honest answer: I don't want to hurt anybody."

"That is much better than number one," Seth concluded jovially. Several people then went on to tell secrets, and it seemed to me that for some, at least, it was a little easier this time around. Even Florence MacIntyre, who had missed the first secrets class and who held her private life sacrosanct,[3] decided to tell at least part of a long-buried fact of her childhood—and wept in doing so, one of the few times Florence expressed her emotions in class.

"I not only support you, I congratulate you," Seth said to Florence on that occasion. "In trying to deny these early facts of your existence, you have shut off strong portions of your own energy and creative strength so that they could not operate for you in your life. You used, literally, a half of your energy . . . repressing these memories and ideas, building up a [barrier] between yourself and the rest of the world in terror [lest] they should discover this secret, and so you could not use this energy constructively. And you built up about your physical image a fortress of flesh to protect you. The image that you have has been built around you from these fears so that you would be so secure that none could find out the secret . . .

"Now, we have done several things . . . the inner gestalt of the group has been opened, for one thing, and a better group unity will result," Seth told the rest of us. "For another thing, through listening to what others have said, you should realize the vitality that is distorted in these deep charges that you often carry within you, for these deny you the use of your own energy. They literally tie you up in knots.

"I have a book of secrets. In each life I had secrets. Now I have no secrets, but I will see to it that some of my favorite secrets are written down so that you may read them. Now your secrets leave me completely untouched, since I was an illegitimate mother seven times, and as a father I sired many that I did not know![4] That was in many of my youths. I was quite a pious old man and woman in many of those lives and completely forgot or justified the errors in the course of my youth."

"I do not come to you as someone who does not know what it is like to be human," Seth would tell us in later classes. And as class moved into areas of more direct experience with Seth's ideas, it was these secrets sessions that seemed to be the wellspring of our intuitional—and humanistic—growth. Other secrets classes took place now and then, like initiation rites of sorts, as new members appeared and the group's core of regulars changed.

"In that class it was not so hard to tell secrets, because it didn't matter," recalls Priscilla Lantini. "It didn't matter how awful you thought it was. No one else thought so. I think once it's out, it's easy to forget about it. Any hang-ups I had before are sure gone now."

"My secret was a joke on me, and telling it to Jane in a letter constituted grand revelation," says Mary Strand, who couldn't bring herself to mention it in class. "My secret was pinworms, which I was periodically plagued with.

Arnold Pearson

I think now that fear of pregnancy drew them. Now with a little distance between us, I can laugh at them." Jed Martz, one of the New York group, also did not reveal his secret in class, but told it to the others who shared his van on the long drive home after class. "It was no big deal to them, and the stigma I attached to it dissipated," he says.

Several class members, including Arnold Pearson and his wife, Molly, and Harold Wiles, could never think of anything that they considered secretive enough to qualify. "Perhaps I have led a particularly sheltered life," Harold conjectures.

"I'm sorry, I just can't think of a thing," Arnold said in class after listening to tales of affairs, cruelties, ambiguous sexual preferences, and other confessions. "Maybe I took some penny candy from a store when I was a child, but I don't—"

"Then how do you expect the rest of us to be honest?" Ron Labadee interrupted suddenly, with the nearest show of anger we ever saw from him.

"I just told you, I can't think of one to tell," Arnold snapped back. "What do you want me to do, make one up?"

"It's just that I don't think that *anybody* has to make one up," Ron answered. He obviously could not believe that Arnold and Molly weren't holding out.

"Ron, nobody has to say anything, including you," Jane admonished.

Ron pursed his lips and sat stiffly, regarding us stubbornly. "I will not take part in an inquisition." Clearly, he was sitting on a secret more horrible to him than we could imagine, and I felt sorry for his pain, as I know the others did.

"Now," Seth's voice cut in, "there are—and I do not mean to shock you [to Ron]—individuals who quite humbly and sincerely do the best that they can. There are married couples who meet in their daily lives with a good measure of honesty, compassion, and understanding . . . Of all the others in this room, [these] two [the Pearsons], in their relationship, have a simplicity and an integrity that speaks for itself and it is, indeed, highly unusual. The biggest secret that this one [Arnold] has, if you will forgive me, is a deep feeling of inferiority that is disguised sometimes as humbleness. This I know and this, intuitively, the other members of the group know, but you [Ron] question; and the fact that you question it . . . is good, here or in any other group. But do not question yourself out of feeling or emotion, and do not build up a barrier in your own mind, for there are no barriers there."

But Ron would not budge.

The levels of personal participation, then, were purely voluntary; and sometimes the results of these secrets sessions were immediate, revelatory turn-arounds in members' lives, both for the individual telling and for those listening.

For example, Richie Kendall told a secret that resulted in some remarks from Seth that literally revolutionized the course of his thinking. "I purposely picked a secret [one class night in May of 1972] that was no big deal to me, but I knew would affect class members enough to rate me as being revealing," Richie says. "The secret was that I once got into shooting heroin—no big deal, really, since most everyone in my neighborhood was shooting something." That night, Richie described the drives behind the drug's use in more detail than most class members had probably ever heard before. "When you pump it in and out of your vein, the feeling is—it's like—it becomes a lover," Richie said. "At the time, when I did it, when I was using it, it made everything okay, and I guess I've just spent all of my life in some way or other—this is absurd, I know, but it's like I've just been trying to capture forever the 'lost joys of youth.'" (Richie was twenty-three.)

At this point, Seth came through with an exuberant sweep of Jane's glasses and spoke to Richie in a loud, amused voice. "Now, we will see that you do, so that *you* will see that there are many ways to break an egg and also so that you will not have to look back for the rest of your life with envy toward the ecstasies of your youth."

"That really blew me away," Richie says. "That paragraph meant so much to me. First of all, it gave me hope that to get out of the suffering I was still feeling—[that] there were many ways, and therefore to me it meant that I didn't have to suffer more to get out of the suffering I was already in . . . that there was a way out of all the negative shit I was creating for myself, without having to go through hell to get some peace of mind—a belief I had previously accepted and never really questioned.

"The other statement about 'WE' will see that you recapture those ecstasies, etcetera, had—has—an even more profound effect on me. Seth was not only telling me that I could get out of the pain I was in, but even though I was past twenty-one, I could actually look forward to joy, to fun—to life as free and joyful as when I was a child. He wasn't saying 'maybe'—he was saying, 'WE will see that you do' and I felt exhilarated. For the first time in many years I felt that someone, or some-ones, actually gave a shit whether I found joy again, and actually were freely willing to help me. It was like a burst of sunlight in a room so dark and dank it had forgotten there was even a sun to shine. Many other comments affected me a lot, but that one really got to me."

A few weeks later, Richie "rehearsed" another secret by telling it first to Jane, Rob, and me before class: that he had been raped by a man when he was fifteen years old. A few hours later, he repeated this information to class. "Jane had just all of a sudden said, very intently, without looking at me, that 'someone in the room' had a secret that if he would tell, would help someone else out very much," Richie recalls. "She was very insistent in her tone and repeated the statement several times . . . I began to feel this inner pressure to tell my secret, somehow instinctively knowing that . . . [another member's] secret had to do with being molested by a person in her family.

"So—despite the fact I inwardly trembled at my male friends' reactions— I told all [and in gruesome detail] and it felt damn good," Richie says.

As Richie finished his narrative, another class member suddenly burst into great racking sobs—something this person had never done before—and told us that as a child she had been raped by someone in her immediate family. We listened sympathetically, but as she finished her story and began to dry her eyes, someone else spoke up: "That's nothing," the woman said. "I was raped when I was eight years old by a gang of boys . . . " She went on to describe the incident, her voice shaking with a child's terrors long suppressed, since she had never told anyone, not even her parents, about the rape. "I felt that I would be blamed for 'causing' it," she whispered. Imbued in her story was forty years of resentment toward her unknowing parents, and guilt for feeling the resentment in the first place.

"It was like secrets running wild and no one reacting strongly to the secret except the teller," Richie says, "and that was one of the main points of it all. Being accepted, with all the truths of our experience naked, and realizing the shame and confusion we felt could literally be let go as easily as— telling a secret.

"This particular event had further repercussions on the ride home," Richie remembers. "[Will] Petrosky bared his soul more than he ever had; I received a lot of affirmation from friends, and went one step further in accepting my being as GOOD and WORTHY, regardless of whatever my experience had been."

* * *

"There is no division except the division that you make when you close off your own thoughts from yourself," Seth commented during this "secrets series" in which Richie, and others, told all. "You have been speaking about secrets, secrets that you have kept from each other. You have not spoken about those secrets that you keep from yourself: those thoughts with which you are quite familiar and yet you pretend not to hear them; those feelings that are yours that you ignore; those impulses that you stop just before they reach your consciousness.

"The stream of consciousness—you look down into it, and you say, 'Aha, there is a nice [thought],' and you pick it up. The rest of it, you say, 'Aha, subconscious matter! It is no good!' and you let it go by.

"You each know yourselves. It is simply a matter of how much knowledge you are willing to assimilate. There is no division—you keep secrets from yourselves. Those are the only kind of secrets you really have to worry about. Some of you have learned some of your own secrets, not through what you have said but through what others have said."

And during some reminiscing in class in 1974 on the secrets sessions, Seth remarked, "You have been told, often, to know yourself. But usually, behind that request was a very definite idea that the self was not really that worth knowing. You were told to know yourself but behind that was the idea that the self was not, after all, very good. To know yourself, then, did not become anything like a joyful pursuit—[instead] to know yourself meant, know how sinful you are—know thine iniquities!

"Look around, even at the creatures of the earth—they are more innocent; they are closer to God; and they can run faster! Look within yourself, you were told—know yourself. And when you know yourself, you will realize your poverty, your lack of spirituality, and you will come face to face with your guilt. And why were you so guilty? Because you existed in the flesh, and so you learned to try to escape the flesh, and consider it like a poor relative; so that you felt that you were in tatters, when you should, indeed, instead wear robes."

Although the technique was not original with Seth, the secrets sessions did serve to clear away the emotional furtiveness from our class experience; and to give us, even if sparingly, enough of a faith in the goodness of ourselves to risk the true understanding of what "you create your own reality" is all about. "What I feel this is good for is not to dredge up 'evil' in a person, but to dredge up what people have hypnotized themselves with to *believe* that they are evil," said a clinical social worker of Seth's "secrets," adding, "then you can show people how they've done this and can try to redirect their self-hypnosis in a positive manner—toward positive goals."

CHAPTER 5

Belief Box: Seth Assigns Us To Hear Ourselves Think

Belief Box

Like the good laser that cuts steel
your questions dear
Savage through my mind to where
idea memory impression mist dreams
are stored and
I have no facts to send back to you and
Like a curious stumbling minstrel
my questions dear
Brush against your mind where
factsmethodsdataformulaequationsrealities
are stored and your dreams cry out to me but
Like two silly grinning robots dear
we shut our eyes and blink on and off
on and off

—SMW

If I Believe I'm an Apple

If I believe I'm an apple and you believe
I'm an orange, is there something I really
am besides what we believe I am?

—Inquiry to class by Stewie Gould, 1972

HOW MANY TIMES A DAY DO you do it? More than you're consciously aware of—
I guarantee it.

Think about it: You get up in the morning. "Yuk, I'm a fat pig," you tell
the mirror. You sit down to eat breakfast. Bacon and eggs? Bacon's loaded with
cancer-causing chemicals—eggs will clog up your arteries. Death on a platter.
But if you don't eat something, you won't have enough energy to catch the
bus, let alone slog through another depressing day at the office with all those
boring, backbiting people you work with.

And look at the newspaper! The world's a mess. Every time you read the
headlines, you get more proof that people are just animals. If the Bomb doesn't
finish us off, food riots will. After all, history repeats itself; human nature stays
the same—right? Everybody's out to get you. More discipline, that's what's
needed . . . get tough . . . bring back the death penalty . . .

Well, better run for the bus . . . gotta keep in shape; pushing forty, after
all . . . things are all downhill after you hit twenty-five . . . harder to lose weight

. . . never used to get sick in flu season . . . getting to the age where you hafta worry . . . better have a checkup . . . sure miss the good old days . . .

Practical acceptance of the way life is? Hardheaded realism? The logic of the obvious?

"You create your own reality," Seth told us a thousand times. "You create the world that you know, individually and en masse." In all of Seth's books, class sessions, and explanations of the workings of the physical universe, this statement is at the center; it is, in fact, the basic proposition of "truth," as such, in Seth's philosophies. ("You get what you concentrate on," reads a Seth quote hanging on the wall opposite the toilet in the Butts bathroom, "there is no other rule.") Indeed, "you create your own reality" was a class catchphrase, used for many years without much practical understanding, as a sort of Band-Aid for misery. "Oh, well," somebody would sigh after describing a grim experience, "I guess I created my own reality, didn't I?" And while Jane or Seth or class might deduce the *why* of an experience, the *how* of creating your own reality was largely unseen and unaddressed.

But in September of 1972, Band-Aid application was ripped away, exposing the underlying structure of circumstance: beliefs.

During 1972, Seth had been dictating his latest book, *The Nature of Personal Reality*, in Jane and Rob's private Monday and Wednesday night sessions. "It's utterly fantastic," she told us at one point. "I keep wondering though, if—my God, Seth, you're going to really get the medical establishment p.o.'d." The book, Jane said, was proving to be a fascinating practical guide for changing unsatisfactory aspects of private life. "I don't know what he's up to yet, but this material is getting tricky as hell," she said. We all laughed. "*Seth Sneaks!*" someone joked.

"It was always exciting to be let in on the production of one of Seth's or Jane's books and to get to hear portions of the manuscripts as they developed," commented Lisa, a student for several years during this time. "This always made the book material more lively for me later on; I could read along and 'hear' Seth's voice and it would bring back what we'd been doing in class all that while."

One Tuesday night, Jane returned from class break with a portion of the *Personal Reality* manuscript, which she began reading to us in a quiet, steady voice—intense excitement humming just beneath her words. One-way traffic lurched and screeched along the streets below, jockeying for position toward Elmira's one good bridge, several blocks away, left after the June flood had destroyed or weakened all the others. Familiar autumn smells mingled through the windows with wafts of flood-mud stink, which would be noticeable for months to come whenever it rained. In the ruined downstairs apartments, carpenters were working late, trying to paste floors, walls, and ceilings back together after the Chemung River had drowned everything in ten feet of muddy water—including my own first-floor apartment, along with all my belongings and manuscripts. In this, the aftermath of the forces of nature, we first heard the premise that was to lead us out of sedate theorizing and into the reality of our own actions.[1]

Jane looked up from her reading. "It's all right here, people," she said. "This means that whatever it is—Sue, if you think you're too fat; or somebody else, if they think they're too easily hurt, or that the world stinks, or that you're doing a great job as a mother, or whatever it is—your personal beliefs reflect outward and make that experience."

"*Anything* you experience?" someone asked. "But it can't mean everything, because there are certain facts that you can't—"

"According to this," Jane interrupted, in that light, quick voice that so often presaged new material, "anything that you see as a 'fact' is an invisible belief!" She grinned. "An invisible belief, folks!"

Jane quoted from the manuscript: "'You take your beliefs *about* reality as truth, and often do not question them. They seem self-explanatory. They appear in your mind as statements of fact, far too obvious for examination . . . They are not recognized as belief *about* reality, but are instead considered characteristics of reality itself.'"[2]

Then Jane had us do a simple exercise: Each of us got out a paper and pen and wrote down a few beliefs that we held to be true about ourselves. "I am a twenty-seven-year-old writer; I need to lose twenty pounds," I wrote, rather carelessly. "I have great dream recall, but I can't balance my checkbook." But, I thought, how can you deny certain facts of existence—like being twenty-seven years old, or forty, or fifty, or five, or male or female, or even thin, fat, or anywhere else in physical terms?

"I am a twenty-three-year-old male and I haven't held a job for more than two days in a row," Richie Kendall read. Another member wrote, "My parents hated me—they beat me up on schedule until I was fourteen years old. Once my old man beat me with a piece of drainpipe." He looked up from his paper. "I mean, how can this be a belief?" he asked. "It happened, right?" Several others read their mini-essays. "I'm a good housewife and nurse, but I would also like to develop my writing abilities," Mary Strand announced.

At this point, Seth came through.

"Your own consciousness—it is realizing that you form your reality, and if you do not like it, then you must change your beliefs and thoughts and expectations," Seth said. "Each individual does, and you can do it. If you were not meant to assess your physical reality with a conscious mind, you would not need a conscious mind. If you did not need a physical reality as a counterpoint, and for feedback, then you could do it all mentally.

"But your conscious mind is meant to assess physical reality clearly and concisely. Your conscious mind is meant to be conscious. You have only to be aware of the contents of your own conscious mind. There is no mystery there. *Your thoughts are not you.* You are the self that has the thoughts! Your beliefs are not you. You are the self that entertains them—and you can change them!

"You have only to understand the truth to change those areas of existence, quite practically, that bother you. But you must begin with yourselves and with your conscious mind—quite joyfully!"

After emphasizing to us the importance of "feeling [the] energy that pervades you when you are pleased with your experience, [and] then [translating] that energy and those feelings into those other, [unpleasant] areas," Seth gave us the first of his "belief assignments": to clear up in our minds the beliefs we held about ourselves, and write these down during the week. "You know what you believe," he said. "I am not talking about buried desires, but of conscious ideas that you hold. You are making it too difficult."

For the next couple of years, Seth would assign these belief papers in such specific areas as *"the* body, *my* body"; "children, parents; men, women; sex and love"; "health, wealth, and color"; "ceremony and ritual"; "responsibility and fun." Needless to say, most of our papers were searingly personal. Sometimes we'd read our own; sometimes we'd put the papers in a pile, shuffle them around, and take turns picking papers out to read aloud. Then class would try to guess which one of us had written it.

Sometimes this was obvious; sometimes it was anything but. What was immediately obvious was the connection between these belief assignments and the secrets sessions: we had prepared ourselves for intimacy, both before our fellows and, most importantly, with ourselves. For most of us, it was the first time we'd listened to the noise of our conscious minds as meaning anything at all.

For example, there was a unanimous difference in our minds between *the* body (upheld in most essays as a biological miracle of physical function) and the *individual's* body (mourned as being out of shape, sick, getting old and flabby, or otherwise inadequate). On my own belief paper, I discovered myself writing that I considered the female body (mine or any other woman's) to be vulnerable to overweight, disease, and decay—in contrast to the male body, which in my estimation was easy to maintain and aged gracefully besides. These were quite conscious thoughts that I accepted as truth. However, I also noted my belief that I'm a healthy and vigorous person—probably a fortunate counterbalance, since after reading my own essay, it was with a considerable shock of recognition that I made the connection between these beliefs and the stubbornly recurring "female problems" (my words) I'd had troubles with for several years. Up until then, these symptoms seemed normal to me—problems that besieged women as a matter of course. And my beliefs in that area were quite invisible—and conscious.

Geoffrey Beam read a hilarious essay on his own body beliefs, in which he'd forced a rigid, expressionless mannerism upon himself to ensure that his physical reactions would never betray his emotions, of which he was deeply ashamed. Unfortunately, Geoffrey acknowledged, this stance had backfired; not only did he yearn underneath it all to break out of this pattern, but he'd failed to reckon with a group of children on his block who persisted in yelling, "Hey! Cannister Man! There goes Cannister Man!" whenever he walked by in his severe, robot-like way.

"I tore into the belief exercises with all stops pulled out," Geoffrey says. "I have discovered much about myself, have come to terms with much of it, have changed some of it, would like to change some more, but have not found the right key. Am still searching. I can see the problem, and the cause of the problem, but the means to remove it elude me . . . Now, though, I can discuss extrasensory matters with friends without feeling like a freak. That has been quite a big step for me."

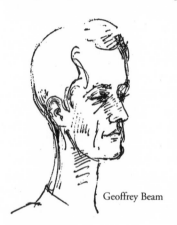

Geoffrey Beam

Enlarging on his original belief statement, Richie Kendall's impassioned composition revolved around his hassles with the workaday world and what he saw as its detrimental effect on the creative spirit. "Of course I wouldn't be able to keep a job," he stated, "since I believe that a nine-to-five routine would destroy my creativity and any joys of youth I had." Along with this, Richie said, he believed that the world's expectations of manhood would also destroy his freedom: the freedom to play endless hours of paddleball, his favorite pastime; the freedom to relate to his "happy childhood self"; the freedom to find his own way on his own terms, write songs, and play music. On the other hand, Mary Strand offered up a funny and well-written paper on the fears of being creatively buried *unless* you held some kind of regular job.

"Oh, God," Richie groaned when Mary finished reading. "I guess that's all right for you, but I just can't see some eight-hour day turning on my creativity. I mean, how can I bury myself in some bullshit job, like you see so many people do? Why should I let that happen to me?"

With that, Seth entered the conversation.

"Now, I have a word for you—tonight, when you did not ask for my advice," Seth said to Richie. "Now, play paddleball with the universe. Play paddleball with the universe!"

"Aaawwwl riiiight!" Richie agreed happily, clapping his hands.

"In more mundane terms—in *much* more mundane terms—get out!" Seth continued. "Go into the world! Seek your own sustenance! You have the energy. You have the creativity. There is no job that you need fear, no contest before which you need to cower. You will not *lose* your creativity in honest work but *find* it, for it will add a new source to the creativity that is within you. But, you need more feedback.

"And there is nothing that you need to fear. You are not a Junior Self. There is no need for you to put yourself in that position. You are not a kid, you are a young man. Then go with that young manhood, out into the universe, and find yourself and the universe. Play paddleball with it!

"And I tell you again, because I am such a grand old eccentric uncle—or because I allow myself to seem to be such a grand old eccentric uncle—that you can indeed triumph, and a nine-to-five job is not going to destroy you. How fragile you must think that you are! What a trap you must consider it, that it would gobble your manhood and you could never escape!

"When you work with your beliefs, you will find that you have inhibited yourself, and your natural curiosity about the world, out of fear that you are inferior and you are not 'ready.' And so, you hide. But the great corporeal reality of the body, and your blessed curiosity, keep at you to get out into the world that is, and to do your thing.

"And while it seems strange to you now, if you allowed yourself your full spontaneity, you *would* be out in the world, mixing with people, having jobs, leaving them, putting yourself with the world that is, using your abilities, having a give-and-take with the universe; and then, from that give-and-take, writing your songs, even from anguish and exaltation. But you deny the reality of your emotions and your feelings."

"So," Richie said, "if I follow you: in some crazy way, just sitting around writing songs is another crafty cop-out, like playing paddleball?"

"The songs are not a cop-out, but your beliefs about the songs are," Seth answered. "The songs are creative and good, and going out into the world is creative and good.

"Now," Seth said to the rest of us, "I want each of you to look at your beliefs in the same clear light. For I used our friend [Richie], and also gave him some good advice, so that each of you could see how you handle your own invisible beliefs!"[3]

Seth often cautioned us to treat beliefs playfully, to understand that limiting beliefs were not weighty, impossible barriers. "Children deal quite joyfully with blocks," he told us, "and if they erect structures that do not please them, then without an instant of remorse, they knock them aside, and make new ones . . .

"Your thoughts have an electromagnetic reality. Now, you must realize that this is true or the rest of what I am saying [about beliefs] will indeed sound like Pollyanna nonsense. [But] when you think in terms of abundance and plenty, for example, then those thoughts draw to you abundance and plenty as a magnet does.

"There will be a while, while you are changing your beliefs, [when] you will find yourself in a period where you feel quite self-deceptive, as you are saying, 'I am surrounded by wealth and abundance,' and you look around you, and you are poor. And you think, 'This is a lot of bull!'

"But it took you time to build up your beliefs to the point of your present experience, and so in your terms, there *may* be some physical lag before your new beliefs draw to you abundance. But your physical experience follows your thought. And you cannot change the experience without first changing your thought!

"Now, it does no good to believe two things at the same time. So what you do is this: You say, 'I will play around with this idea. I will admit that it might be possible that my own thoughts about money are causing a lack of it. And so, for the hell of it, I will, several times a day, pretend that I am surrounded by abundance, and in my mind I will imagine the things that I want. If it does not work, I have not lost a thing; but if it works, I'll have gained a lot.'"

One of the belief papers read during these exercises was by Carl Jones, an airplane pilot, science teacher, and sailor who yearned, he said, for conscious recall of his inner journeys—he rarely remembered his dreams or out-of-bodies. "I really, really believe that I want to remember my dreams," Carl said passionately. "But if there's such a thing as beliefs, then maybe I don't really believe that I believe that! That's the trouble with all of this for me—I don't know! I mean, maybe it's just wistful thinking on my part about my dreams. It's hard to tell the difference!"

Seth came through abruptly, still holding Jane's wine glass in her hand. "It's about time—now you are beginning to recognize the difference!" he boomed. "Think of this: 'First of all, I am matter of fact. I trust the real Earth. I am a physical creature and I trust my body.'"

Carl hesitated a moment and then grinned. "Yep, right," he agreed. These were, apparently, beliefs that he held about himself.

"But! These may become core beliefs," Seth continued, "and if you hold too strongly to them, then they connect [with] other beliefs. And these beliefs, subsidiary but hanging on, say, 'To be matter-of-fact is to stay in my body and be related to the earth. To leave my body is to leave my common sense behind.'

"This is but one example," Seth told Carl. "Your beliefs connect other ones about them: 'I am in my body and I am alive therefore, to leave my body is to die.'"

"Well . . . ," Carl scowled, puzzled.

"Now, these beliefs are not unconscious!" Seth said. "You need only to assimilate them, and to realize that you hold them, and then you bring up other conscious material that is also present, to combat them. You *can* say, 'Old Ruburt over there is quite alive and has been out of his body many times. So, there is nothing to fear! He did not die when he was out!' But when you bring up your ideas, then you can realize those that fight each other, and deal with them. While you do not recognize your beliefs, then you become power-less to work and play with them.

"Your body, for example, is quite able to take care of itself while you are gone," Seth emphasized to Carl. "Assure yourself of that. That is important to you, you see, because you are vigorous in a physical manner. You are afraid when you leave your body, it will become less physical—weak—with you out of it. This is not true."

Seth withdrew. As usual, we took a few minutes to relate his words to Jane, but in the midst of the explanation, Richie suddenly said, "All right, but if I believed strongly enough that every person I met would give me a dollar, and I stood out on the street corner believing it, would they do it?"

Seth returned immediately, still waving the untouched wine glass. "I am saying that your beliefs form reality!" he said, bending toward Richie, who sat on the floor by Jane's chair. "Your individual beliefs and your joint beliefs. Now, the intensity of a belief is extremely important—and there are some root assumptions that you share, and it is more difficult for you to go counter to these assumptions. But you can go counter to those assumptions as this class goes counter to those assumptions!

"And, if you believe, in very simple terms, that people bid you well and will treat you kindly, they will. And if you believe that the world is against you, so it will be in your experience. And, if you believe"—Seth's voice rang out loud and clear—"IF YOU BELIEVE THAT YOU WILL BEGIN TO DETERIORATE AT TWENTY-TWO, THEN SO YOU SHALL!"

"Heaaa-vy!" Richie responded, nearly nose to nose with Seth now.

"When I speak to you about beliefs, you think of *negative* beliefs, you see," Seth admonished mildly.

That was true—few of the belief papers thus far had mentioned anything other than bad experiences and their accompanying pessimistic thoughts. "But! You are all sitting here, quite physical, in front of me. Your eyes move, your heads nod, your blood thunders through your veins. You quite obviously all of you believe that you are alive, and the belief serves you well! You believe that it is autumn, and so it is. So do not neces-sarily think in terms of negative beliefs . . . I did not mean you to concentrate on the negative beliefs that you have . . . I want you to see where your beliefs conflict with each other. I want you to examine, for the first time in this life, your *conscious* mind, and its contents.

"The hobble-goblins are not down deep in the unconscious. You do not have to play hide-and-seek with psychologists to find them. They are not buried in your past in this life or any other life. You are not bound by promises given. You are not bound by false beliefs. You are free, conscious beings. And so, hopefully, you will learn how to be joyful, conscious beings."

"Well—yeah, okay," Richie answered, his face lit up by a Cheshire cat grin. "Okay, I believe in beliefs, but what if—let's say, if I believe, let's say, that I can go up to a lonely purple mountain that nobody inhabits, and that in ten years a beautiful woman with purple hair and purple eyes is going to walk by and fall madly in love with me—if I believe it strong enough, is it going to happen?"

Screams of laughter tore through the living room. "I don't *believe* you asked that question!" someone yelled. Seth sat patiently, he and Richie smiling at one another, while pandemonium rose and fell in blasts. (Years later, long after class was over, you could bring back the fun and outrageousness of it all with "the girl on the purple mountain" analogy; yet it was typical of a certain kind of derring-do that we'd achieved; a certain kind of exaggerated love and fear that maybe, *maybe* these ideas Seth was telling us were possible; *maybe* we really did create our reality; and if it could only be proved to work in any gross, ridiculous situation, then maybe, just possibly, we might dare believe that it worked on our personal hopes and dreams.)

Finally, when the racket died down a little, Seth said to Richie, "If you believed it strongly enough"—whoops of laughter broke in again—"and if you did not find it easier to accept a woman with a different color hair," Seth continued, "and if there were not a reason why you could not simply accept a normal love on a normal street corner, and if you are willing to offset all the other connections, and believed it deeply enough, THEN GO WITH MY BLESSINGS!"

And Seth withdrew. "When Jane came to," Matt recalls, "the class was utterly rolling on the floor. That was one of the few times I recall Jane actually being disappointed that she's out when Seth is in. I think she felt like a crasher at her own party."

In the ensuing explanations to Jane, Richie started to rephrase his purple-mountain question. "It is a long time to wait besides!" Seth interjected suddenly.

"Whoops—hold it!" Jane gulped, rolling her eyes. She looked down at her wine glass, still in her hand, the ice cube now melted away in the warm chianti. "Shit," she mused, "I lose a lot of cigarettes that way, too! What is this *about*, Richard?"

"Well, it's a good question," said Rudy Storch, one of the New York bunch. "Let's say, for example, that you really get it together with your beliefs and you really convince yourself that if you step out in front of a train that's going 100 miles an hour, it won't hurt you at all," Rudy laughed along with the class—"and you work and work on this and you really get so you *believe* this!" he shouted above the noise. "I mean, you got your whole self to believe it! Could you go out and stand on the railroad tracks in front of a train, and . . . "

Shrieks of laughter drowned out Rudy's voice—but not Seth's. "All of these mythological questions protect us from dealing with the beliefs that we have now in our normal daily lives, and instead we project fantastic beliefs that we do not have so we will not have to face the one that is in our head right now—the quite ordinary beliefs by which we form our reality" he roared. "And they are clever tricks that you use often to yourself! They are cute rejections. They allow you to hide yourself from the beliefs that you do have.

"And what's more, you know it!" Seth told Rudy. "All of you, however, are apt to do the same thing. Why is it that you will so hide from your own conscious beliefs? Because you still want to assign to other causes the nature of your own daily reality—and you want some out! You want some contradiction. You go for it! You say, 'everything works for everyone else. They form their beliefs and their own reality. But not me—because!'"

Seth tapped Richie's knee with Jane's glasses. "I expect this one over here to begin concentrating upon his purple woman, knowing ahead of time, as he shakes his head, that he does not really believe he will meet her, and then be able to say, 'AH HA!' after ten years, 'It does not work!' and then come back to me!

"You always play games with beliefs. That is why I want you to become aware of what your beliefs are, so you can know what your games are—and the rules! That is what I am trying to get you to see.

"Listen to what you tell yourself every hour of the day. *Those* are your beliefs. They are clear. Listen to them!"

As the weeks passed and the belief assignments continued, it appeared that more of us were indeed starting to listen to what we were constantly telling ourselves. In fact, some of us started to construct a whole new vale of tears out of what we thought we were hearing. Diana, for example, read a belief essay filled with self-recrimination for what she saw as endless areas of "lousy beliefs." It seemed to her that all of her beliefs contradicted themselves! "I can't seem to get it together no matter what I do," she read. "I'm just doing a rotten job of projecting my beliefs, I guess. I've got a pretty inferior reality!"

To this, Seth responded with great good humor. "For all of you, on your papers, or the papers in your head, write down what I hope will be your prime belief—and it is hardly original, you have heard me say this often!" he joked. "[It is]: 'I am a worthy, deserving person. I have a right to my life in this universe. I have a right to be because I AM!'

"Now, as you examine your own beliefs, any beliefs that contradict that one, scratch them out," he told Diana. "If you do that, you will have no difficulties. And do not compare yourselves with the idea of perfection! You are perfect as you are. You are happening!

"When you believe that you are unworthy, and when you interpret this particular belief, for example, to mean that you are fat, or that you are lonely, or that you are poor, you are following through with your beliefs perfectly! There is nothing inferior about such a reality that you have created! It is a beautiful example of your beliefs in action, in your terms!

"If you believe that you are inferior, Diana, and you find before you the result of your belief, then you have done an excellent job of projecting the belief outward! Pat yourself on the back! But if you do not like the results, then change your beliefs. There is nothing wrong with *you*. You did a good job of projecting your beliefs.

"There is nothing wrong with any of you, with your being, and with what you are. And do not ever let anyone tell you that there is! You are simply using your abilities and learning how to do it. And continue to learn. But there is nothing wrong with the self that is learning, and that is what I want you to know.

"There is nothing wrong with the selves that you are. Do not identify beliefs that you do not like with the self that you are. And now I am ready to listen to some essays!"

Carl Jones then re-read portions of a lengthy theme that he'd been presenting in pieces for several weeks. In it, Carl bemoaned the fact that he felt in deep conflict between his desire to travel around the world by sailboat, and with his attachment to his four children, who lived with his ex-wife. "It must be that I'm faced with a conflict in my belief system," Carl mused. "Otherwise, I don't think I'd feel this way, but I don't know what to do about it. I want to do both!"

Immediately—and somewhat predictably—Seth entered the conversation.

"Why are you faced with your own beliefs?" Seth asked Carl, who threw up his hands good-naturedly. "If you really *believed* in your role as world bum and hitchhiker, you would not have *had* that many children!" Seth said jovially. "You purposely, therefore, saw to it that you would navigate between your beliefs and give yourself an excuse for doing what you want to do, while making sure that you were securely anchored, because you need strongly those feelings of security with other earthy beings. And you believe that it is better to navigate in between, and to feel those yearnings, and to satisfy them within certain strict boundaries that you have set by your beliefs!

"You have created your reality. You want to be free, but you are afraid of being *too* free! You want to feel close family ties, but not *that* close! And so, you set yourself up in a situation in which you have a certain amount of operating space, and it is up to you to take advantage of the space that you have created. Therefore, change your beliefs, and realize that you have freedom within what seems to you to be the limitations of your existence. The limitations do not exist, and as soon as you realize you can do what you want to do, and fulfill your obligations at the same time, then you will do so."

"Well, but . . . ," Carl mumbled. "What is an obligation, then?"

"What do *you* think an obligation is?" Seth answered. "My idea of an obligation has nothing to do with your beliefs!"

Carl thought for a moment. "An obligation is a belief—an imposed belief," he finally said, rather halfheartedly.

Rudy, from his slouched position in his chair, quickly added, "The word 'obligation' implies responsibility, and if you don't fulfill that responsibility, you'd better watch out!"

"You have the freedom to do what you want," Seth replied, "and also fulfill the ideas you have about responsibility. As long as you believe that you are caught between two conflicting beliefs, then so you are.

"Your beliefs are invisible to you only if you believe that . . . your own thought processes are hidden from you, and that your own values and ideas are unconscious; and if you believe that it is difficult to understand what you are, and who you are. Your beliefs about yourself are quite clear to your conscious mind and can be discovered there, if you only understand that the information is available."

"Well . . . ," Carl continued, wrinkling his brow in concentrated perplexity as Jane came out of trance. "Well, then, what about another situation of mine? Underneath the keel of my sailboat are a set of tiller bolts that hold the steering mechanism together. Since it's a secondhand boat, I don't really know if these bolts are okay, or half-rusted out, or what. It's a real chore to get to them to check—you have to take half the tiller assembly apart—but if they should fall apart in the middle of the ocean, I'd be done for! My question is, if I really create my own reality and really have good beliefs about myself and my ocean voyage, then should I just assume that the tiller bolts are okay and go on from there?" He looked toward Jane, expectantly.

"C-A-A-A-R-L-L-L!" Jane screamed at the top of her lungs. "My God! I mean—you create your reality, right, but if your life depends on the condition of those tiller bolts, Carl, then for Chrissakes, it only makes good common sense to check the goddamned tiller bolts!"

"Oh," Carl said. "Oh, oh, well, okay. I just figured . . . ," he shrugged.

"People, listen," Jane said to the class. "Please! Your reality exists in a practical universe!" She smiled back at Carl. *"Especially* when you're going sailing in a physical boat out onto the great big physical ocean!"[4]

Philosophical knots such as Carl's were some of the tangles that Seth warned us about; in addition, he'd caution us not to emphasize negative beliefs and limiting ideas as another form of "reality." A good example of this emphasis operating in a more familiar context is a belief paper written by a friend of mine. Carmen never attended class, although she's read some of Jane's books. When I suggested that Carmen try writing down her beliefs about men and women, this was the result:

"A man takes charge, gives orders, is obeyed, commands rather than seduces, calls the shots, is decisive, makes a lot of money generally, is direct, active, often unintuitive and scornful of emotional issues and intuition; is likely to make fun of me," Carmen wrote. "A man is boorish, stupid and uncaring; insensitive, demanding and selfish; wants all women to conform to a certain standard of beauty (American magazines). Doesn't want a woman to be strong; is supercilious and superior, opinionated, doesn't listen or care to listen. Wants things his own way. A man makes fun of how you do things and wants you to do things his way.

"A woman is internal, intuitive, sensitive, secretive, has a lot of power, the more if she doesn't show it," Carmen continued. "She keeps to herself, works as a man's assistant but gets all the work done and none of the glory. She is kind, patient and sensitive, hides men's faults from themselves. Takes a lot of shit. Is alone in her feelings and beliefs, is often lonely.

"Men watch and listen while women talk to women. Then a man will say something to his woman and she will laugh with him in collusion against the other woman (her friend)."

Carmen's social life, choice of men, and troubles in her office faithfully reflect these beliefs. Her men friends, for instance, are often exact replicas of the "man" she describes here. Curiously, however, while Carmen understands the relationship between beliefs and experience, she's let these particular ones remain fairly static—almost as though their existence gives her a strength and insight that she trusts, even while they cause her misery. Would changing her beliefs leave her vulnerable to something she fears more than selfish men?

"Now, sometimes you craftily and joyfully trick yourself," Seth said of this kind of emphasis on negative beliefs. "For example, if you believe that you are unworthy, that there is something wrong with you, and that your life is flawed, then you can pick up a very good book—like mine [*The Nature of Personal Reality*]—and use it to reinforce that belief by concentration upon your negative thoughts, or those thoughts that appear negative to you, so that you end up picking yourselves apart, saying, 'Ah-hah, there is another bad, dirty old belief—I was right all along! I do not believe in Original Sin any longer—I realize I am not at the mercy of my karma, but there are those nasty lice—those beliefs that crawl around in my head; and I can only look at them, I cannot get rid of them, and what am I to do, and woe is me!'

"And so you forget your own vitality, and when you are asked what good beliefs you have, you have to stop and think!

"Now, good beliefs can also be invisible to you. You may not allow yourself to see how well you are doing in certain areas, because if you realized that you were doing well in one area, it just *might* occur to you that you could do well in another area, or still another area, or you might perhaps some day come up with the belief that you were all right after all!

"Week after week I speak to you of the vitality of your being. Week after week you look at your beliefs, and say, 'There, I have no vitality! This belief overwhelms me. What a mountain it is!'

"Now, when you list what appears to be groups of negative beliefs, opposite that list, on each occasion, write your positive beliefs. There are none of you who do not have positive beliefs, and each of those beliefs are working for you now.

"Do not let them become invisible, for when they do, you deny the integrity of your own being, and deny the dimension of your being and your experience. Do not structure your present lives to the lists of your negative experience. Do not structure your lives to lists of your negative beliefs, but through lists of your positive accomplishments and beliefs. If you do this, the so-called negative ones *will* fall apart. But do not hold those in your attention. Do not play negative movies upon your inner eyelids."

"A belief, once dropped, seems quite silly," George Rhoads observes. "All the agony, the wondering, waiting, hopeless flailing, that the belief induced is something I do not care to dwell upon.

"My example: for more years than I care to recall, I broke my head trying to sell paintings," George says. "I saw artists doing inferior work, selling it at ridiculous undeserved prices, while my good work was ignored. As an artist, I was acceptable to myself, if not to the world. The rest of my life, outside art, seemed a hopeless morass . . . I could not ally myself or commit myself to anything but my work. For this I felt often that there was something wrong with me. How could I find impossible what others entered into with such ease and abandon?

"Despite my abhorrence of the cutthroat (as I saw it) business world and the politics of the art world, I managed to produce paintings and have successful shows at a top New York gallery. But . . . I began to feel that I was dirtying myself by accepting money for my work. I did not face this belief at the time. I felt that the people who bought my paintings did not deserve them or understand them. I preferred to give my work away to those who really appreciated it. To make money for it seemed wrong—a sort of prostitution.

"I was nominated for a Prix de Rome,"[5] George says. "The final decision was between me and another artist. He got the prize. I was indifferent. [My sales] fell off, my gallery dropped me. I had a show at another gallery—a disaster. I felt an odd sort of rightness and inevitability about these events.

"I turned to hackwork. Bad painting was what the world deserved, so they would get it. Yet I could not produce bad work. I turned to super-realistic painting: *trompe l'oeil.* I did it well. Here, by contrast to my more exuberant work, I did not expose myself—so I believed. I hid behind technique. Here I could do a good job and get paid for it, avoiding the effects of my belief in an undeserving world."

Although George would later find some solace in meditation, his basic beliefs about wealth and art would plague him for years. He lived in small, cramped houses with unreliable plumbing, ancient heating systems, and endless unaffordable upkeep. He constantly found himself at the edge of poverty, barely able to buy art materials or pay the rent. A sculpture commission or painting sale would always manage to come along in time to keep him going—but barely. In the midst of his worst moments, his father would call him on the phone to tell him to get a "regular" job.

By the time of Seth's belief assignments, George was often in despair, feeling that he was trapped by forces he couldn't understand or control. Yet he accepted the premise that beliefs form reality and began to work with his beliefs in earnest—determined to change them in the face of what looked like sheer practical idiocy. By the time he answered my questionnaire in the winter of 1979, George's world had started to change shape: he's had several large shows of audiokinetic sculpture at galleries in upstate New York, Chicago, and New York City; is regularly creating sculptures for shopping mall interiors; sells paintings on commission; and even has an art patron who deals with the business side of things and invests in furthering George's career. Recently, George bought a big old house in a village near Elmira. "I'm not rich, but things are much better," he says.[6]

"The beliefs that brought about this [former] situation are gone," he says. "Still, I thought one day that it was perhaps time that I sell some more paintings. Then a few days later a stranger knocked on my door. This did not happen often to me; I lived out of sight of human habitation, on a road hard to find. It was a cold day. The roads were slippery. The stranger turned out to be a local art collector, who wanted to buy a painting!

"I have gone to great pains to outline some old beliefs and the development of events that went with them," George says. "Maybe these revelations will be of value to somebody. Maybe writing these things down is a way of cleaning out little hidden pockets of belief that escaped the general housecleaning. This housecleaning has been heavy going for me. In retrospect I spent vast energy of thought and action on futility. But now it is done. On to new challenges!"

"George's example is one of the best of how you can really change your life if you're willing to work with your beliefs," observes Rob, who probably understands better than most the conflicts that surrounded George's efforts. "He really worked at it, and it was successful. It's a perfect illustration of what's possible."

"All of you, as I . . . say in my book [*The Nature of Personal Reality*]—commercial!—relate to ideas of good and evil, to the value judgment you place upon such things as guilt, wealth, color, and race," Seth said in explaining a belief assignment in 1973. "Some of you consider poverty a sign of virtue and good, so that you look at someone who has money and immediately you think that they are not spiritually attuned—that there is something wrong with them.[7] They must take advantage of someone. They must be nasty—they are Capitalists! You think of someone who is poor as being spiritual.

"I want you to examine your beliefs about several things—all involving good and evil, health, wealth, and color. For example, is white pure and black evil? Is health good and the sign of God's blessing, or is illness the sign of spiritual understanding and good for your soul?

"Is wealth good, and in your mind a sign of God's goodness, or is it instead a sign of spiritual lack? If you believe that the poor are virtuous, that poverty means spirituality, then you will be ashamed of money. If you believe, however, that wealth means goodness, you will be ashamed of poverty.

"If you are liberal, and yet believe that white means spiritual and black means evil, then you may find yourselves in some very embarrassing situations when you meet black people and try to relate to them.

"Each of you must examine those beliefs for yourselves. Does black mean the unconscious and white the 'life of reason'? Do you equate, you males, black also with homosexuality? Those of you who file psychological principles away, or have in the past . . . where do you place Jung's ideas of black and symbolism and your own sexuality?

"If you believe that beliefs cause reality (and they do) . . . then what is your attitude toward the poor? Do you say, 'They caused that reality, too bad! That is their hard luck!'?

"These are the kinds of questions that I want you to consider."

Another time Seth told us, "There have been great poems written about the great search of the soul for God, and how the soul runs and flees from God, but many people run far faster from an encounter with their own soul than they would from any God. God is, after all, supposed to be outside—some spiritual being that you can blame or praise.

"I challenge you to encounter yourself playfully and joyfully; to look at your beliefs as objectively as you would a flower or a rock or a skunk, or a chunk of coal. Simply be aware of the content of your own conscious mind. Learn to use your intellect and your intuitions together, and you will discover that there is no competition. You do not need to fear that you will be devoured by your emotions. You do not need to fear that your intellect will lead you astray. You do not need to fear anything.

"The freedom has always been yours. And each of you is here because you know it! And even when you playfully taunt me, or ask me for answers—then you are testing me and testing yourself. You have been given pat answers and accepted these answers for too long! Therefore have I always challenged you toward new questions and your own answers. And Ruburt has always stayed away from any such aura in which he was therefore accepted as an authority as far as others were concerned. You are your own authorities. You are your own authorities!

"No matter how tempted you are to look to others, *you are your own authority.* And the answers literally—literally—come from within yourself, and I mean now through your private experience, [and] cannot be given to you by another—they must *be* experienced.

"I can only lead you toward a recognition of those truths and help open your own inner doorways and help you use your own minds and intellect, until in one miraculous moment, your intellect and your intuitions click together and work like magic; and *then* you will know what I have been saying all this time, and the words will open, and so will you each open . . .

"No one can take those journeys but you. Whatever you do, wherever you go, or whatever you think, no one can go where you go or think what you think, in the same way. In certain terms, the truth is not the same for each of you.

"Is it true that the sunlight falls on one certain corner of the yard, and then false to say that it falls in another corner of the yard? But when you insist that truth is one thing, and must be said or experienced in one way, then you are saying that one patch of sunlight is true and the other must hence be false.

"So each of you are true, and in the authority and validity of your trueness you have at least an inclination of what truth is. And you can follow that inclination—that hint. You must follow it inward into yourselves, for no other person has your consciousness. No one else can do with it what you can do, or experience what you can experience. And in being true to your private experience, you enrich the experience of the universe, for you are a part of All That Is, materialized as you are.

"Now, I do not intend to give this speech at the street corners. It is *your* speech, given by you, in certain terms, to yourself. And so, again, I return you joyfully to those selves."

"The exercises in beliefs were profound," Warren Atkinson concludes. "They caused me to realize that we are masters of our destiny and so is everyone. This led to a great respect by me of the Godliness of everyone."

CHAPTER 6

ESP Revisited: Life and Death and Similar Weird Events

Grandma Mullin's Portraiture
(1887-1972)

How did that lovely oval lady
on the wall end up
the cheap square color photo
in my book, wrinkled,
shapeless as a sack,
content with cigarettes and cards,
and at the end, lost
inside her own reflection?

Occult men take journeys
out of the body, and thus
know themselves
eternal—
What are the journeys of the flesh?
What trick escapes our spirit
that we never know
Who that lovely oval lady was?

Photographs—
you gaze and gaze
A hint, like ghost aromas—
a voice, like déjà vu—
rustlings in an empty room.

—SMW

THE OLD HOTEL LOBBY WAS CROWDED and blaring with the noise of a rock band. Once considered posh accommodations for incoming railway passengers, the place was now just another bar near Elmira's deserted train station. Jane and Rob and I sat at a table by the dance floor, sipping drinks and watching people step and gyrate in the swirling lights. Now and then Jane and Rob would get up and join them, laughing about being (in their early forties and fifties, respectively) the oldest couple on the floor. The evening was fun and companionable; the racket a pleasant break from solitary work.

Rob gathered up our glasses and went to get more drinks. Ten minutes went by, then twenty. Was the bar *that* crowded? "He's probably in animated conversation with somebody," Jane sighed, affectionately. Finally, Rob came with our drinks, wending his way back through the crowd. And sure enough, right behind him was a glum-looking man in his mid-twenties, carrying a beer and pushing nervously past the knots of people.

Rob distributed our glasses and sat down on the other side of the table, gesturing for the fellow to sit between Jane and me. "He's read *The Seth Material*," Rob said, innocently enough.

Brad—as I'll call him—slumped into the chair and introduced himself with a mixture of friendliness and wary desolation. Physically, he was a real bruiser—his muscles bulged inside the sleeves of his black T-shirt. But he was on edge, and troubled. The band took a break, and in the lesser din, Brad told us that he'd just returned from duty in Vietnam, where it seemed that all his ideals had been shattered forever. He wasn't working. He didn't know what to do with himself. Like many servicemen in that situation, he was just drifting, lost, aching inside; months had passed and he couldn't snap out of it.

He gulped his beer. Jane was smoking a cigarette, listening to Brad and watching the crowd. Suddenly, she looked up at me. In that second, I felt that curious mental tingling, and an onslaught of images rushed into my mind. They connected, I knew, with Brad's childhood and with his recent military experience.

"Well, Brad," Jane said at that point. "I'm getting some impressions, and . . . I don't know, I could be wrong, but what I'm getting is that . . . ," and she proceeded to describe in detail an incident that she thought had happened to Brad in Vietnam.

Incredibly, it was exactly the same incident that I'd picked up on.

"Yes, that's right," I said, interrupting Jane's last few words, "and besides that, there was . . . ," I filled in other details as they sped through me. "And wait, wait, I get it! That connects with a time in your childhood, when you were about three years old, and . . . ," I saw Brad with a tall, severe woman dressed in a fashionable white dress, toddler Brad sitting on the ground at her feet, crying. The scene filled in, its meaning shouting in my skull; the words tumbled out, one after another, almost faster than I could shape them.

Jane's eyes were bright, alert. "Yes, and that also has to do with a thing involving a woman you went with, before 'Nam . . . , " Jane broke in, going on to describe the details of that relationship—which both of us kept adding to at intervals.

Brad was staring from one of us to the other, his mouth open. "That's right!" he kept exclaiming. "How did you—where are you *getting* all this stuff!" Jane and I were barely aware of his reaction. However we were doing it, there was a sense of precision, of correctness about those impressions that couldn't be denied. We were really caught up in it. The information was specific: dates, names, scenes—some, especially the Vietnam scenes, not very pleasant. We zeroed in on the background of his troubles, but also on some of his happiest moments, and advised him to concentrate on those "better" memories. Rob just sat there, listening.

"Wait, I'm getting something else," I said breathlessly. "It's a scene—I'm getting this thing about you [Brad] in the time of the early settlers in this country; I mean the *earliest* ones—something about a freeman, a man who'd been in prison, a man named John something—John Redfield, Wrenfield, something like that . . . "

"Right!" Jane broke in. "I see him too—and something about an island, or an island-like place—like, you were one of a company under this militaristic leader type; you'd been sort of rounded up to get up this company of settlers, because there'd been failed attempts there before—"

"Yeah, and something about your being part of those early settlers in Virginia or someplace that disappeared, you know, the Roanoke colony,[1] and about your—god, disappearing with them . . . "

"Right," Jane said, "and you still have this thing now about the dilemma of abjectly following, ah, patterns of order, like your military service now, but not knowing what to do about it and hating yourself for it." Speaking quickly, Jane added several more minutes of detail about Brad's connections with that colonist self, again including names, dates, and locations that she thought could be checked through historical records.

By then, poor Brad was popeyed. Back and forth we went, like a couple of crazed ping-pong players. Finally, Brad told us that everything we'd said about his background was accurate; it all made complete sense to him. The historical stuff, he added, "sounded right," but he really *did* have to be going. As he grabbed his beer glass and stood up, we noticed for the first time how upset he was. "Thanks, really, thanks a lot, you've been a great help," he mumbled. "I gotta go now, but thanks . . . " He hurried away and disappeared through the barroom.

Rob shook his head at us. "You two scared that poor kid to death!" he said with exaggerated severity. "What were you *doing* to him?" And really, in looking back on that incident, I have to admit that we weren't being very kind, keeping at it like that in the face of Brad's obvious horror. Simultaneously correct personal impressions from two complete strangers? It was weird, even to us—because, as excited as we were about the correlations, it gave us, as usual, more questions than answers. Since our impressions of his remembered this-life past, about which we knew nothing, were correct, was there any reason to suppose that the "historical stuff" was any less correct? But where had the information come from? Was Brad, in his dark mood, broadcasting like a desperate SOS beacon? Was our recitation of his own past going to answer his needs? Or had Jane and I simply reacted to Brad's rock-bottom despair by demonstrating some of the possibilities inherent in the psyche?

* * *

Daily events—ordinary ones and odd ones—were the real cornerstones of Jane's ESP class. A typical Tuesday night's conversation sprang from members' personal lives, and from what we'd been doing during the week. Seth's own comments rarely dominated the entire evening, and were instead part of the fabric of class. The weeks we spent reading aloud the yet-unpublished manuscript of *The Nature of Personal Reality* were the only time we read directly from any of Seth's works as a class project. This was not a group dedicated to page 275 in our hymnals, in other words. It was a group that learned to look upon daily life as a "medium" in itself. Our concepts of what constituted the paranormal and the supernatural (along with what constituted the so-called mundane) were undergoing radical changes. Our everyday lives were becoming more miraculous; our perceptions sharpened with a certain new quality of alertness. How much more startling a correct prediction than the clairvoyance of springtime? How categorizable indeed was ESP?

As seen in chapter 2, many class members had backgrounds filled with "peculiar" experiences. Nadine Renard was one of those whose adult life contained a multitude of odd events, not the least of which involves the musical talents of her youngest son.

In 1967 Nadine and her husband purchased an elegant brick house in one of Elmira's nicest neighborhoods. Only fifteen years old, the dwelling had been designed by the original owners as a retirement home. However, "the first day we moved in," Nadine says, "I felt an evil smell and presence and I sat and cried—I wanted out! I always felt a presence in the house. My three-year-old son Steve saw a 'spirit' in his bedroom. The front bedroom was always freezing—heating contractors couldn't find anything wrong. Drafts occurred, objects moved.

"A forty-pound brass light fixture rotated on the table. Shades were ripped off rollers in the night in the den, the original owners' music room. One day a pipe wrench flew across the cellar and landed next to my feet. During this time, many persons appeared to me [including] my dead aunt . . . who had died the previous year of a brain tumor. I had many out-of-body journeys at that time . . . "

While the Renards were living in this house, Nadine's son Mark was born. "He was a very difficult and precocious baby," Nadine says. "He sang at two months and talked at six months. At age three, after he was taught the basic notes, he started playing the piano and he took off from there! He would go through books and books of music and lecture to me constantly on Bach and Beethoven, on why they had written certain kinds of music; or he'd stop in the middle of a piece and tell me what these passages were supposed to express—at age three! And he was right, and he had no way of knowing all this stuff—he got this material out of the air somewhere; he had no access to it. He'd do this at his music lessons, and his teachers would practically fall off their chairs! This was a definite case of a prodigy . . ." By the age of five, Mark was giving recitals in classical piano, demonstrating a highly advanced and sophisticated technique. ("The first time I was so embarrassed—he didn't know how to zipper his jacket afterwards!" Nadine told class!)[2] "In the meantime, my next oldest son was accurately predicting mail deliveries."

Nadine and her husband sold their strangely behaving house in 1969. Later, they learned that the original owners had both died in the place, along with an alcoholic relative "who died or lost his mind in the cellar." It was Nadine's feeling that the house and her family's peculiar "psychic" qualities were somehow intertwined, possibly feeding back and forth through some kind of unrecognized energy. Nothing was ever proven about Nadine's house, but since anyone could prove that her son was the piano prodigy Nadine said he was, nobody in class doubted her descriptions of other events.

Nadine's weird house was an exceptional experience, but throughout class years, other members did do some unusual things with their consciousnesses. Gert Barber started experimenting with "mirror trances"—staring into a mirror while slipping into alpha and deeper states—and soon reported that she'd developed the ability to see faces other than her own in the glass. One, she reported, was a scar-faced priest, and this image would leap into focus within seconds after she started her alpha trance. While the vision of a scar-faced priest sounded suspiciously like an ex-nun's perfect insult, Seth did tell Gert that she had been a priest once " . . . and that is one of your hang-ups, in Ruburt's terms!" he added. "You are [however] doing very well with this visualization of the various portions of the self." Seth then went on to give Gert some insights on her convent relationship with another nun. "You would have projected [feelings of affection] upon a priest [instead of the other nun], but this frightened you even more, because the male relationship held for you a feeling of terror," Seth told her.

"You did not, you see, project them upon a person who could immediately answer them in kind, with no strings attached . . . you did not want that kind of relationship. You were only hiding in the thoughts of such a relationship . . . with a male that you were afraid to take on. Male in general."

Gert's mirror images (however insightful) could certainly be classified as weird, but I'm convinced that this kind of image projection is common—except that most people either forget such incidents, rationalize away their significance, or never recognize them for what they are in the first place.

Consider, for example, someone that I used to see regularly—and in public.

I see him now, in my mind's eye, as plainly as I first saw him twenty years ago—in, of all places, the local bowling alley.

I am fourteen years old, a member of a high-school bowling league. About forty girls are bowling, squealing, screaming, leaping up and down—filling the place with the noise and effervescence of kids playing a Saturday morning's game. I roll my ball down the alley, where it arcs in the beautiful hook that I learned to throw only that morning. As fine and as sure as a hawk diving for its prey, the ball zooms in on the pins. Crash! Wiggling in perfect geometry, the pins scatter to the alley floor. A strike!

I turn, flushed with the excitement of the moment, and see him standing there, on the other side of the team benches, smiling at me. He is an old man wearing an ankle-length brown coat, holding his worn brown hat in his old oak-leaf hands. His cheekbones stand out inside dry, apple-smooth skin. A few whisps of gray hair are smoothed over his skull. I grin back. He nods, his mouth opening in the return smile; he makes a small wave with his right hand. People bustle back and forth past him.

I wait for my ball to come back; this is the tenth frame and I get to shoot again. I pick up my ball, throw it: this time, all pins but one disappear. I turn back to smile at the old man, and he is watching me with utter delight; and I know that he has a special affection for me, that he has stopped just to watch me.

Minutes later, he is gone. But for a year or so he will show up to watch nearly every bowling match I play in. I will never see him walk in or walk out. We will always wave and smile at one another. And I will never have the nerve to walk back and talk with him.

Years later, at my high school class reunion, I asked one of the women who bowled with me on that team if she remembered the day I pointed the old man out to her. "I don't remember what you said about the old guy, but I do remember asking you if you knew who he was," I told her.

"What old man?" my classmate said. "I don't remember seeing any old man."

Which really didn't surprise me by then.

The memory of that old fellow—his huge, totally inappropriate brown coat and his loving smile—haunted me for years. Who was he, that he appeared in bowling alleys all over the city of Elmira? Intuitively, I knew that he was connected with me in a way that defied explanation—until one Tuesday in 1970, I decided on impulse to ask Seth who the old man was.

Seth stared at me somberly as I asked the question. "He was a probable self of your grandfather's," Seth answered, interrupting my rambling explanation. "He kept in touch with you, and you were able to see him because of your own abilities. He noticed you, even as you noticed him, and in his probability he wondered who you were—but he liked you."

I blinked. The old man's form fell into place with a simple correctness: Yes, this was exactly who that old man was. He'd even looked like my grandfather as Grandpa had looked a year or two before his death. "He was a portion of your grandfather that your grandfather as you knew him could not be, and in many ways he was much freer than your grandfather.

"Now, he had a hobby and he made small dolls," Seth went on, sitting back in Jane's chair and tapping thumb and forefinger against her chin. "These were dolls made of wood, and into them he projected all of his creative energy; and he made a doll that looked like you and he called it Susan, without ever knowing where he got the name. He did not know it was your name or who you were. He lived in Germany in his reality. He was born in his reality in 1831 and died in 1897. But you were able to see him. In out-of-body states, he projected into your reality. We will give you more information on it as we are able to." (Seth never did so, however.)

Tears stung my eyes. How infinite were the biological connections of your heritage, that a grandfather and his granddaughter could communicate all across their chosen realities?

And Jee-zus H. Christ! I thought, as Seth withdrew, what would have happened back then if—if only I'd walked up to that old man and talked to him!?

Believe me, I've kicked myself many, many times for not doing so. In a later class, I asked Seth, hopefully, if I would have more to do in my lifetime with that probable person of my grandfather's self. "Indeed," Seth answered, "I am answering in the affirmative." Now I've made it a point to keep a corner of my inner radar "open" for any hint of this character's reappearance—although I somehow doubt that he'd still be dressed in that shabby old brown coat.

But again, I think that this kind of experience is more common than is supposed. One night in 1971, I received a phone call from Bernice Zale, who'd roomed with me in college. The night before, she said, an odd thing had happened to her husband, Donald. The Zales had gone out to dinner with friends and were sitting in the restaurant bar when Don, who for weeks had been struggling with some difficult career decisions, left the group and moved to an empty stool in one corner of the barroom.

Bernice said that she'd let him go so that he could be alone for a while with his problems, but that a few minutes later she'd looked up to see Don in animated conversation—with himself! Laughing affectionately, she'd pointed this out to their friends. However, when they drove home that evening, Bernice said that she'd started to tease Don for talking to himself in the middle of a restaurant, and Don had reacted with angry astonishment. "What do you mean, talking to myself?" he demanded. "For God's sake, I was talking to that old guy all night long!"

"What old guy?" Bernice asked, puzzled. "I didn't see any old guy—you were sitting by yourself."

Stunned, Don had yelled at her to "stop making stupid jokes!" Bernice said that it took some doing on her part to convince Don that she wasn't up to some elaborate put-on. Don had seen and talked with "a very nice old fellow" for a couple of hours, and as far as Don was concerned, the old guy was as real as Bernice and their friends. "Don said that for some reason, he just spilled all his problems out to this old man," Bernice told me. "He said that he didn't know why he thought a stranger would care, but the old man listened very carefully and asked him some smart, thought-provoking questions. The guy never said anything like 'Do this or do that'—just the kind of stuff that Don could intuitively pick up on, and think, 'Yes, of course, that's true.' Don said it was as though the old guy had known him all his life."

Soon thereafter, Don made the decisions that led him into a successful administrative career in social work. And I remembered Bernice's story about the "invisible" old man during a class discussion a few weeks later on root assumptions and the meanings behind physical objects.

"The creation of individual symbols of self," I mused aloud as Seth finished a short delivery on the subject. "It's what Donald Zale did in that incident in the bar, isn't it?"

"It was indeed," Seth said, smiling.

"Then—that old man was himself," I concluded.

"It was indeed," Seth repeated. "You are so close, some of you, to understanding what cannot be verbalized, and yet I cannot give you a boost because they must come from you." Seth then said that he'd been aware of Don's experience and had "helped him out," though he didn't elaborate—and I didn't ask.

I sent a copy of the class transcript with Seth's remarks to Donald and Bernice; and the idea that Don's mysteriously understanding old man might have been himself personified seemed quite acceptable and logical to them both.[3]

These perceptions—like the childhood experiences of many class members—remind me of another "sighting" I experienced in my teen years, and for which Seth had another kind of provocative explanation. I include it here because of the continuing interest in unidentified flying objects (UFOs)—and because of the implications in Seth's answer as to the source of at least some of these objects.

Again, I was fourteen or fifteen years old. My friend Evelyn and I were walking along the road toward my house one summer afternoon. It was a beautiful day; the sun was warm and the sky clear. We ambled along, talking about flying saucers—of all things!—and what they might be. All at once, I looked up at the pine trees that lined the road near my parents' yard—and saw it there: a huge oval-shaped object, blue on top and light yellow on the bottom, cruising slowly above the tops of the trees. It made no sound.

"Oh, my gawd!" I yelled, grabbing Evelyn's arm. "Look! Look! There's one now—a flying saucer!"

Evelyn looked up and then grabbed my arm. "Oh, no, you're right," she yelled, "It is, it *is*!" We ran up the road to get underneath the thing—it was no more than twenty feet above the trees, which were about that far from where we stood. As we ran, it kept on moving over the treetops, over my parents' house, and eventually to the hills ringing the nearby horizon—where it hovered for a few seconds and then dipped suddenly and sharply down behind the trees.

We'd been close enough to see it plainly—and it wasn't a weather balloon (which I'd seen before) or a dirigible. It had been smooth, silent, and steady as it moved through the summer air. My parents were inside the house and hadn't seen it—and we never found anybody else who'd seen it, either.

In 1974, a Sethian dissertation on the "shapes of letters" and the Sumari language reminded me again of that thing zooming through my teenaged skies. I waited for a chance to ask Seth about it and couldn't help laughing to myself as I recalled it; now it reminded me of the plastic container for Silly-Putty that my son played with: oval-shaped, blue on top, yellow on the bottom.

"Seth?" I interjected at last. "Uh—speaking of the shapes of things, could you give me some idea of what that thing was that my friend and I saw in the sky when I was about fourteen? I mean," I smirked, "it wasn't a Silly-Putty container, was it?"

Seth stared at me for a second and said gravely, "It was not. But its shape will change."

Its shape will . . . what? I thought. "Well, the reason I asked," I fumbled, confused, "I thought it might have some connection—"

"It has a connection—before you ask anything else—with an event in what you *think* of as the future, and some of your future comprehension had to do with the way you perceived that particular event in your past," he said.

"Oh," I responded, thinking of Evelyn's part in the incident. "Well, then it also concerned my friend?" I asked.

"Indeed," Seth said dryly. "That is all I will tell you for now, but you must realize that the event exists not only in the past, but in the future; and in a way, it was a sign sent from a future self into the past." With that, Seth withdrew: another kind of UFO, I thought, dipping down behind the horizon of Jane's psychic hills.

Seth had commented on UFOs once before in class, in 1971, during a discussion on the "pulsing" nature of atoms and its relationship to flying saucer reports and out-of-body experiences: "In some respects, this is what happens in some of your flying-saucer incidents, for you do not have a vehicle

In 1963, while writing poetry, Jane Roberts had what she calls her "psychic initiation": "Suddenly," she explains, "my consciousness left my body, and my mind was barraged by ideas that were astonishing and new to me at the time." Prompted by this experience, she set out to explore psychic activity and write a book about it. Her research and personal experiments led, eventually, to Seth's speaking through her as well as to her book *How to Develop Your ESP Power*, published in 1966. The photo above, taken in 1969, appeared in her next book, *The Seth Material*, published in 1970. Below, Jane speaks for Seth while her husband, Robert Butts, takes dictation, 1969. (Photos taken by Rich Conz. Courtesy of Robert Butts.)

The 458 West Water Street apartment house where from 1967–1975 Jane held her Tuesday night ESP class. (Photo courtesy of Rich Kendall.)

In this photo taken by Rob Butts in 1969, Sue Watkins appears with her eleven-day-old son Sean and Sean's father, "Ned" Watkins.* As recounted in *CWS*, book 2, appendix 3, Sue and Ned were given a private session by Seth in which he advised them on their troubled marriage. (Photo courtesy of Robert Butts.)

*All names appearing within quotation marks indicate pseudonyms used by the author in *Conversations with Seth*.

Class members "Warren Atkinson," "Darla Solomon," and "Florence MacIntyre" in Jane and Rob's living room, 1973. (Photo courtesy of "Geoffrey Beam.")

"Diane Best" and artist George Rhoads, whose in-class doodles became the illustrations for *Conversations with Seth*. (Photo courtesy of "Geoffrey Beam.")

Jane in her rocker, during class, around 1973. Her cigarette smoking was the subject of interesting debate at various times throughout class years. From left to right, front row: Sue Watkins, "Lauren Delmarie," "Will Petrosky." From left to right, back row: "Darla Solomon," "Diane Best," "Derek Bartholomew," and "Florence MacIntyre." (Photo courtesy of "Geoffrey Beam.")

The "New York Boys" stop at the Roscoe Diner, halfway to Elmira, on a Tuesday night in 1973. The Boys drove 500 miles round trip each week to attend Jane's class. From left to right: Dan Stimmerman, "Lauren DelMarie," "Will Petrosky," Richie Kendall (holding a doodle of a flower with eyes), "Bobby Agan" (a.k.a. Robert Axelrod), "Darlene" (a girlfriend of "Kurt's" who attended class on a few occasions), and "Kurt Johns." (Photo courtesy of Rick Stack, a.k.a. "Rudy Storch.")

"Rudy Storch," "Harold Wiles," and "Lauren DelMarie," 1974. Despite differences in age and life philosophies, class members shared a "family of consciousness" affection for one another that went beyond the heated disagreements. (Photo courtesy of Rich Kendall.)

"Renée Levine" and "Jean Strand," 1974.
(Photo courtesy of "Will Petrosky.")

"Aunt Hattie" makes her appearance at the 1973 Halloween cross-dress class (see chapter 9). (Photo courtesy of "Harold Wiles.")

"Tim DiAngelo" and Richie Kendall, around 1974. (Photo courtesy of Rich Kendall.)

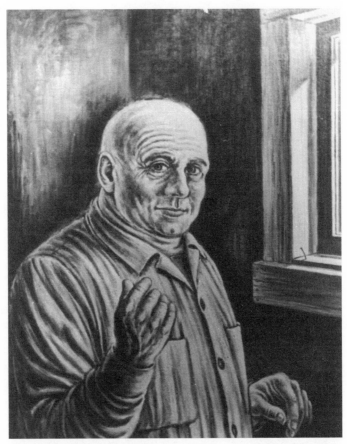

Rob Butts painted this image of Seth from a vision he had in 1968, five years after Jane began speaking for the "energy personality essence no longer focused in physical reality." Since this painting (along with many others) hung on the living room wall in Jane and Rob's apartment, it's not surprising that class members encountered this figure in dreams, sometimes with amusing embellishments—wearing a three-piece suit at a cocktail party, sitting in dream coffee shops, walking down dream streets in monk's garb, et cetera. (Photo courtesy of Robert Butts.)

such as the one you think you perceive. I am speaking of only certain cases, where you have visitors from other realities.

"What happens is that you have an attempt to exchange camouflage realities," Seth continued. "The beings entering your plane cannot appear within it as themselves. Since their atomic structure is not the same as yours, distortions must occur in order to make any contact possible. Thus you are greeted with a certain set of sense data. You then try to figure out what is happening—but the sense data, you see, means that the event is already distorted to some degree. The physical vehicles that are often perceived are your interpretation of the event that is actually occurring.

"Our friend back here," Seth added humorously, indicating Ned, "could well appear, you see, as a UFO in another aspect of reality, and frighten the inhabitants. You forget that consciousness is the only true vehicle. No part of your consciousness is imprisoned within you. It materializes in one aspect or another. I use the word 'materializes' because it makes sense to you, but it is distortive since it predisposes an appearance within matter. Yet all realities, as you know, are not physical.

"It is theoretically possible, for example, for any of you to disperse your consciousness and become a part of any object in [this] room—or fly apart, to disperse yourself out into space—without leaving your sense of identity. This is not practical in your terms, yet many of you do it to gain refreshment while you are sleeping. Consciousness by its very characteristics carries the burden of perception. This is the kind of consciousness you are used to thinking of. You cannot imagine it without perception in your terms; and yet consciousness can be vital and alive without your idea of perception. The last part of that sentence is important."[4]

ESP . . . weird events. But—why weird? Why segregated from a set of accepted events labeled as "normal?" Why wouldn't an anguished ex-soldier seek out an encounter that could lead him to ask new questions about the quality of reality? A young girl's developing abilities might naturally turn to a loving encounter with a grandfatherly figure and, in so doing, help shape her understanding of personality and perception itself. A young man, worried about his future, might easily turn to his own "future" self, personified by a "wise old man"; or a woman with ambiguous sexual yearnings might indeed objectify these dilemmas through a male mirror image—and then be compelled to seek an explanation for *that*. How can we then classify and shelve such inherent abilities so carelessly as to label them as "ESP," or as "UFOs," thus placing them outside the realm of what we think of as the practical senses? Yet it was through the perception of common daily events rather than through the paranormal that class really began to scratch the surface of what consciousness contains.

In June 1973, Rudy Storch described a series of accidents that had happened to him in the space of a week or two. First, Rudy said, every time he picked up a knife he'd inadvertently slice his fingers. Then he and fellow class member Lauren Delmarie were in a minor auto accident. But the spectacular high point of all of this had happened the previous week, right after Jane's class, when the New York group drove to a local fast-food restaurant to get some hamburgers for the five-hour drive home. Rudy, in complete obliviousness, had walked right through the restaurant's plate-glass window—shattering glass all over himself and the floor. Although Rudy hadn't been seriously hurt, the experience had obviously stunned him.

"A man who throws stones through plate glass is one thing, and a man who walks through them is another!" Seth put in, as Rudy started pouring wine for himself and some others.

"Ah, Seth—uh, did this happen because I'm completely delirious, or was it maybe because of certain beliefs that I've had?" Rudy asked from his wine-pouring position on the floor.

"You know the answer to the question—for beliefs are, of course, involved!" Seth answered, leaning over in Jane's chair.

"Well, I've been thinking of these, and I've come up with a few answers," Rudy said. "I wouldn't be asking you, except I've been getting hurt so often—"

"Problem solving also continues in your terms!" Seth roared, interrupting.

Rudy rolled his large, mournful eyes and perpetual grin around the room, mugging an expression of "Oh! Brother! Here we go again!" Then he turned back to Seth, who was waiting patiently. "Well, when I first started slicing my body, I came to the conclusion that this was caused by my fears," Rudy said. "I had beliefs that the universe was fraught with evil and danger, and that I was creating this reality. So then, I thought that literally if I took that belief out of it, that I would never get hurt, and that in one context my body was invulnerable to danger, because I create my own reality . . . although, there is, uh, the common-sense level . . ."

Seth suddenly leaned forward and tapped Rudy's forehead. "You want to prove your bravery and you are still setting up tests for yourself!" Seth said. "You are pleased that you came through the trial with as little difficulty as you did. It is in the manner of what you think of as initiation rites into manhood. And this is coupled with ideas that you had regarding psychic initiation. 'See, I walked through glass, and I live! I have only a few scrapes—Hail to Me!' Next you will want to walk on hot coals!"

Class screamed with laughter, but Rudy sat mouth agape, wine glass in hand. "Simply be aware of your own beliefs in that area, and you will have no more of these difficulties," Seth continued. "Remember, however, how your friends think of this, and how you talk about it, and what an event it was:

'and our friend Rudy walked through glass!' Think of the attention that you received!

"Now, I return you to your festivities, and I suggest that you have a good glass of wine! Do not worry. Simply be aware of your beliefs, and realize that beside the physical scrapes, in your terms you got a lot of goodies, and you wanted them.

"I am going to return you to the class for now," Seth said to the rest of us. "I want him [Rudy] to digest what I have said!"

Seth withdrew, and instantly a dozen voices jumped in to tell Jane what had been going on. Several people brought up "accidents" that had happened to them that week. Priscilla Lantini had gouged a chunk out of her ankle while mowing the lawn. I had stubbed my toe on a rock, and thought for a while that I'd broken it. Betty DiAngelo said she'd slashed her finger with a potato peeler while fixing dinner. But none of these, we all admitted, could compare with Rudy's glass-defying feat.

"I can't imagine what 'goodies' I got out of it, though," Rudy said. "Does Seth mean, you know, that five cuts and a bruise are goodies?" Rudy looked up at Jane in exaggerated innocence.

"Seth-baiting! Seth-baiting!" someone yelled.

"Let me clear this up," Seth responded, as Jane slipped obligingly into trance. "The attention was a goodie! And do not be ashamed of it—you all want attention! You also, however, did not trust yourself in physical reality. You did not trust that you would survive. You did not trust your body. You were 'spooking out the universe!' You wanted some kind of proof that you could be hurt and survive—some kind of deep confidence in the inner integrity of your physical being that could supply impetus—that the body could heal itself.

"There were other connecting beliefs—the danger, in your terms, was *invisible*. Therefore, through the experience, you gave yourself the confidence that you could travel through invisible dangers, and come out with but a few bruises—that even dangers that you could not see could be conquered; that you would indeed survive.

"On another level, this has to do with invisible beliefs, for you had been thinking of them. You can also travel through invisible beliefs."

"Without making them visible?" Rudy asked.

"The effect became quite visible!" Seth roared, to the accompanying roar of laughter from class. Seth smiled at all of us, and pointed his finger at Rudy.

"The experience had meaning on many levels . . . but any accident—and this applies to each of you—is no accident," Seth continued. "Your good health or your poor health is no accident. All of this has meaning to you. Our friend did not *happen* to walk through a plate-glass window. It was no cosmic or particular accident in which he was involved.

"If you cut your finger, it is no accident. If you stub your toe, it is no accident. If you come down with the flu, or with a virus, it is no accident. If you have a chronic physical difficulty, it is no accident. If you are creative, it is no accident. If you get good news, it is no accident. If lovely things happen to you, it is no accident.

"You form your reality. And this applies all the way down the scale—from your consciousness that you think of, to the tiniest molecule in Lauren's eye!"

Bob, another member of the New York bunch, spoke up. "I was thinking about my motorcycle accident," he said. "It was basically the same thing. It's true that I solved a lot of problems, but I can't help thinking that I could have solved the same problems without doing something so radical."

"Perhaps now you will work out problems at conscious levels," Seth told him. "It is only when you are not willing to face consciously your own beliefs, and face them through and make distinctions, that seemingly unconscious accidents occur: when all of a sudden you are not as quick as you should be; or, when all of a sudden, your reactions are not as good when a car comes that should not be there. Each of you has your own way, and an event that seems horrendous from the outside—from the inside, from your private viewpoints, may be something else entirely."

As Seth spoke about these symbolic yet "horrendous" events, I remembered a class in 1970 when poor tender-hearted Rachael Clayton had sobbed out the story of a household tragedy: the week before she'd let Tabby, her cat, outside, and he'd been killed by a car. "I loved that cat so," she whispered, her face soaked with tears. "He was the sweetest, dearest thing. I don't understand it. Why would he want to leave me? What did I do? Oh, I never should have let him go out that night!" We all felt terrible for Rachael—she'd talked many times about her funny, affectionate cat.

I remember Seth coming through that night with great precision of motion: for a change, he folded Jane's glasses carefully, placed them solidly upon the coffee table, positioned Jane's body within the chair with studied neatness. "Will you let me address a few words to you?" he asked Rachael, with elaborate old-fashioned courtesy.

Rachael blew her nose, saying nothing.

"I am awaiting for your answer," Seth said gently. "Far be it from me to speak to you if you would rather not hear what I have to say."

"I'll listen," Rachael said, in a resigned voice.

"We have had more enthusiastic responses," Seth responded with an impish hint of his usual self. "Now, this is a preliminary. The rest will follow as you are ready for it, and if you rush up in rage against me, then I will leave Ruburt to face it! So, listen!"

Rachael crossed her arms in front of her and waited.

"Now, consciousness is a beautiful personified precarious thing," Seth began. "You cannot really see it or feel it or touch it and yet you know its characteristics. The cat taught you to love again and to open up again. You were also close to hiding within your home with the cat and ignoring physical reality. The love which was awakened is to be directed in other areas—"

"But—" Rachael sputtered in protest.

"—and you may speak when I am finished, but for this one time, I will have my say," Seth went on. "The cat awakened your love. You knew this was to happen and you chose the means. Now, in so doing, you also gave affection to the animal and awakened within it characteristics it did not have earlier. In other words, you stretched the extensions of its own awareness and conscious-ness. You brought it up, to put it very simply. The consciousness of the cat grew and developed. You taught it communication.

"Now, I am not speaking of physical communication, but you opened up its awareness. Though it seems to you perhaps at this point tragic, the facts are that the real tragedy would have occurred had the cat lived, in your terms, and had you curled up in it, in your house on the corner, and turned your love inward to the animal, rather than outward, for there are people who need it.

"When you think in terms of remarriage, for example, or when your children urge it upon you, then you think in terms of yourself," Seth told Rachael. "You do not think in terms of those who need love and affection and who are more lonely than yourself, lacking children, and who are looking for not only affection but the simple courtesy that another individual can show by recognizing their existence. You were not able to translate or transform that love outward.

"At the same time, you extended the consciousness of the animal; it became more than it was. Its consciousness was ready to leave and adopt another form. Now, I will give you more information on this later and I will give you some advice that you may take or not, as you decide.

"There is nothing wrong and much good in loving animals," Seth added. "However, when you love any one thing so strongly that it begins to exclude others, then you need to think . . . Now, the animal went on as a youngster leaves the house and grows up. You aided in the evolution of its conscious-ness, then allowed it its freedom. You will meet its consciousness again in another form.

"You knew—and I am not implying guilt," Seth emphasized to Rachael again. "You knew what was going to happen when you let the animal out. The animal felt no pain; it left its body immediately. You aided in the devel-opment of its consciousness and it helped you by renewing your love, but as the animal changed its form, so also now this reawakened love must look outward. There are people who agonize for companionship and who have not known what love is. When you let it be known, telepathically, that your awareness of sensitivity and love has been reawakened, others can perceive it and come to it as a light. It will find its way and draw others who need it."

And in the week following his words on Tabby's death, Seth reiterated his words on "accidents" as class discussed a flood in East Pakistan, in which thousands had died. "In nature, there are no accidents," he began. "If you accept the possibility of the slightest, smallest, most insignificant accident, then indeed you open a Pandora's Box, for logically, there cannot be simply one small accident, but a universe in which accidents are not the exception but the rule. A universe in which, therefore, following logically, your consciousness is a combination of an accidental conglomeration of atoms and molecules without reason or cause that will vanish into nonexistence forever even as, indeed, they would have come from nonexistence.

"Once you accept, you see, that idea, then if you follow your thought completely enough, you must accept the idea of a random accidental universe, in which you are at the mercy of any accident, in which mind or purpose have little meaning, in which you are at the mercy of all random happenings, in which 300,000 human beings can be swept off the face of the planet without reason, without cause, simply at the whim of an accidental happening.

"And if that is the universe in which you believe that you live, then it is a dire and foreboding universe, indeed," Seth continued, his voice ponderously loud. "In that universe, the individual has little hope, for he will return to the nonexistence that his random physical creation came from. Following that line of thought, then, if you follow this through, a group of atoms and molecules were accidentally sparked into consciousness and song and then will return to the chaos from which they came; and the individual has no control over his destiny, for it can be swept aside at any point by random fate, over which he has no recourse.

"All of this can be related to ordinary life. Whenever you think that you have a headache, simply because you have a headache; or you bump into a door simply because you bump into a door; or you have an accident simply because you happen to be in a particular place at a particular time; whenever you feel yourself powerless, then you think that accidents happen and that you have no control over them. The only answer is to realize that you form physical events, individually and *en masse*. And as I have said time and time again, you form the physical reality that you know."

"You know," Rudy recalls of Seth's "accident" explanation "at first I wasn't satisfied with Seth's answer. I just couldn't understand what he meant by saying that I got 'goodies' from walking through a window! I mean, there I was, bleeding like a stuck pig from cuts on my hand and knee, and a guy at a booth is telling me, 'Don't worry, kid, when you get to the hospital, they'll just cut your leg off'—as it was, my knee needed nine stitches!

"I remember we'd just come from class and I was feeling really full of exuberance," Rudy recalls. "Really happy, you know, bounding around. Then—*wham!* Like, what a stunning blow, literally. I sat there in the restaurant, sort of swimming in and out of it, thinking, 'God, if this can happen to me if I create my own reality, *what next?* As though I were saying to myself, 'See what happens when you let go and you dare trust yourself? You get slapped down!" And the owner of the place was freaking out about her window . . .

"Then Seth really hit me with the core of it all—that I was dealing [in the incident] with invisible beliefs! That this was what I'd set myself up to do; that I didn't trust my own energy; that I felt afraid of it and felt that my own energy could destroy me. And it's true that right after it happened, I felt weirdly relieved and happy! As though I'd found out that I *could* survive; that I could trust my body not to get hurt in spite of such a terrible accident—and Seth came right down on that!"

"Do not overlay the personal daily aspects of your life with preconceived ideas about who you are, what you are, where you are, why you are," Seth says in volume 2 of *The "Unknown" Reality*. "Become aware of the original nature of any given moment as it exists for you. Forget what you have been told about time and space. Refuse to accept ideas that limit the dimensions of your own natural being. Again, the unknown reality is what you are."[5]

CHAPTER 7

The Sumari (and Others) Come Home

Follow Yourself

While the child weeps,
the old man speaks—
Oh hear
Oh hear—
While the child weeps,
the old man speaks:
Follow yourself
Follow yourself.
Follow the answers
that spring like flowers
that never grew;
like suns that never shone—
like a lover
who never lay in bed with you—
Oh hear
Oh hear—
Follow yourself
Follow yourself . . .

—lyrics from a Sumari trance by Jane Roberts;
simultaneously extemporized on the dulcimer
by class member Dan Stimmerman

I DON'T LIKE ORGANIZATIONS. I'm automatically suspicious of groups—any groups. Ritual, ceremony, and all forms of gesticulated chanting gobble-dygook turn me off fast. To imply that I'd ever sit still while somebody spoke to me in a language that doesn't exist—hardly! Or that I'd join in with a bunch of people singing spontaneously, in perfect synchronism, without missing a beat, in unrehearsed words that none of us understood—never! Or that I would ever find myself moved to tears as somebody wailed a chant that seemed to come from an invisible gang of observers standing around the edge of the room—

Drop dead!

And yet—

I'd been trying to figure out how to write this chapter; how to capture the Sumari development, the songs and "mini-dramas," the verbal and non-verbal meanings behind it. Jane had already explained Sumari in *Adventures in Consciousness;* Seth had also explored the phenomenon in his own books. What more could be said? Besides, aspects of Sumari (like reincarnation) could sound pretty silly, if you let them stand still. Yet, as always, it contained an undeniable emotional validity. How to express it?

I'd worked all day on it, thinking, writing, pacing, rejecting, and by 10 P.M., I'd had it. I went, bleary-eyed, to bed. But as I lay there, that familiar inner alertness at once possessed me, and that chant began, running again and again through my mind:

Sumari
Ispania
Wena nefarie
Dena dena nefarie
Lona
Lona
Lona
Sumari-i-i-i-i . . .

The last syllable wailed off the end of the scale, as Jane had wailed it that night in November of 1971, again and again, as I tossed and turned; again and again . . .

It's a call, I thought, that feeling of acceleration tugging at me—I'm calling on the Sumari for help. But as soon as I thought this, I shoved it away in disgust and finally fell asleep.

Zing! I was suddenly sitting bolt upright in bed. My clock radio's numbers were glowing the midnight hour. Yet it seemed that just seconds ago I'd heard that weird chant ringing through my skull; just seconds ago that I'd soared up out of my body, through the ceiling, flying out over a dark and liquid landscape; just an infinite second ago that I'd floated down on a beautiful spring meadow, where everybody who ever attended Jane's class was sitting among the flowers on picnic blankets, laughing and feasting, each blanket filled with ornate scrumptiousness that (my dream self mused) only the Victorian Age could have conjured up without guilt. Eddie Feinstein was even using a sterling silver salt shaker—complete with tiny claw-and-hammer sterling silver legs.

All at once, everyone—the whole field full of people—looked up and shouted, "Our hearts were young and gay!" (the title of a book I'd enjoyed as a teenager). Immediately I was propelled into my parents' large garage, where I saw, to my amazement, that a printing shop was growing—literally growing, like a time-lapse garden film—out of the garage walls and floors. All the means to express my ideas were springing up before me as I watched—lovely old Linotypes, drawers full of hand-carved wooden type fonts, a fantastic Mergenthaler printing press—and all without effort on my part. Once these machines appeared (all of them old printing methods, yet newly created), all I had to do was express myself through them, and their beauty would touch the world.

Which was, I realized in my midnight bed, the perfect Sumari answer to my Sumari chapter frustrations.

"Thanks, guys," I said to all those feasting class friends, and I jotted the dream down and went back to sleep.

Indeed, as Jane notes in chapter 7 of *Adventures in Consciousness,* upthrusts of energy and creativity are given to us from the psyche precisely when they are needed—and too often go unrecognized for what they are. Of all the things the Sumari development was, it was most of all a dramatic and obvious explosion of intuitive knowledge—shattering even our notions of symbolism. You simply couldn't mistake it for anything else. It was an incredible leap in Jane's already incredible abilities; and, I think, in the innate abilities of the class unit. Through Jane's artistry, it was also highly demonstrative, which sometimes made people extremely uncomfortable. And its appearance brought with it, once again, more questions than a lifetime could answer.

There were a multitude of needs beneath the surface of class that autumn of 1971—some of them only half-recognized by members themselves. As Jane relates in *Adventures,* Rob's father had died earlier in the year, and now his mother's health was failing. *Seth Speaks* had been typed and mailed off to its publisher, a project birthed and gone. Then on November 16, Jane's father died. At about the same time, November 11, Arnold Pearson's father also died.

My husband and I had divorced that July of 1971. My two-year-old son and I had been living with my parents, but after an unsuccessful attempt at a home typesetting business, I'd taken a job in Elmira and moved into my own apartment, just down the street from Jane and Rob. My job required that I leave Sean with a babysitter during the day, which filled me with guilt, anger, and loneliness—so much so that I'd sometimes go into the ladies' room at work and cry. Then on the night of November 16—the date of Jane's father's death—I dreamed of Arnold Pearson being in some kind of danger (I didn't know about either death yet). As I came half-awake from the dream, I saw the figure of a naked woman standing at the foot of my bed. Smoothly she bent, touched my toes, and vanished.

That same fall, George Rhoads and his wife bought a house near Elmira. Their marriage was not going well. (George was not yet a class member, although he'd read some of Jane's books by then.) Faith Briggs was having serious ear problems (see *CWS,* book 2, appendix 3) and was facing a delicate operation to relieve the trouble. In addition, she and her husband were having equally serious financial woes. Occasional class member Bernice Zale was struggling with a pervading miasma of depression that seemed to drain every speck of energy from her days. Bette Zahorian, Florence MacIntyre, and several others had sons who could be drafted and sent to Vietnam at any time.

(Some of those sons, for that matter, were in class.) Rachael Clayton was still mourning her husband's death of a few years before. Two of Arnold and Molly Pearson's sons had "dropped out" and were traveling around the country— aimlessly, their parents feared.

All in all, a dozen facts of daily life accumulated within class context that autumn—not unusually so, perhaps; but then, all of Jane's excursions into the psyche (including the Seth material itself), and by inference our own excursions, had been in answer to just these kinds of dear familiar needs.

The season had slipped into November's drear that Tuesday, the 23rd; about a dozen people had showed up, and we were laughing and talking as usual. The heat was banging up through the apartment's old steam radiators; a chill wet wind was rattling the windows. Jane talked about her father, Delmar, and his wild, brawling life. Arnold briefly mentioned his father's passing. Gert Barber told some more anecdotes about life in a convent. Vanessa, who attended class at that time with her sister Valerie, passed out copies of a local college newspaper, in which she'd published an article on Jane and ESP. Class seemed quiet enough—in fact, a couple of people said they were feeling down-right sleepy. I had the vague impression that Jane's attention was focused elsewhere, but attributed it to her father's death. Part of me wondered, in dismay, if we'd end up exploring the ramifications of grief that night—some-thing that in those days would have made me extremely embarrassed.

At 9:30, Jane called a break. Several of us got in line for the john or wandered into the little kitchen to yak. Bette Zahorian sat in her chair, look-ing glum. I smiled at her, but at that precise moment, my inner antennae perked up. Something was going on, something was whispering right beneath the familiar motions we were going through; right beneath the words and sentences and in the curve of our elbows and knees and lips. Objects in the room were suddenly bright and clear; as I looked, it seemed that each thing's color became more brilliant, more itself, more—real. Super-real. I watched Jane as she came back from the rooms across the hallway and sat down in her rocking chair. She was facing the bay windows from the other side of the big, barnlike room, made so cozy by the philodendron-tangled room divider that housed books, sculptures, pretty rocks, and a large black ashtray appropriately labeled, "BUTTS."

Jane adjusted her glasses and sat quietly, tapping the chair arm with her long fingernails (painted blue this evening)—a familiar gesture. "Break's over!" she called. Immediately, Gert and Sheila began to repeat for us their break conversation on "separate" or trance personalities. The conversation didn't get through to me somehow, but by then my own attention was elsewhere.

"I think there's a damn crowd of people in this room tonight," Bette stated; at nearly the same time, Jane said, "Wait a minute," in a soft voice. We waited. "I'm getting this hole-ripped-in-the-universe thing again," Jane said at last, referring to an expansion-of-consciousness experience she'd recently had during her Wednesday creative writing class.[1] "I'm getting . . . " she paused, lowered her eyes, lightly tapped her fingers against her lips. "Oh, it's . . . well, it's like, it's . . . there's this hole ripped in the universe outside those windows, and it's like . . . like this group of people seem to be . . . uh, well, coming in, around the room . . . "

Jane's voice was quick and light, almost apologetic. Her eyes were wide and dark, as they are during Seth trances—but this was no Seth trance, by any means. You could see that she was really getting something—it was as though her small corporeal self were traveling faster than light, whirling through the fabric of space and out the other side, right there before our eyes. I thought of my peculiar impression of the "speed" of the Seth sessions,[2] but something else was going on here; some event was really piling up. "I think—it's like their teacher, or whatever . . . is standing by the table in front of the windows . . ." Jane trailed off, caught up in it. We all sat still, waiting. I was on the floor in front of Jane's rocker. All the lights were on.

Abruptly, Jane said, "Sue, hand me a pencil and paper, please." I grabbed some notebook sheets and a pen from Gert and gave them to Jane, who immediately started writing. "Well," she said after a moment, "I got this— uh, these words, from this group or whatever, I'm hearing this babble of stuff, uh, not English, and I think I'm supposed to say them, or something, Sue, and what the hell, and so I wrote them down, and they're—" her voice was suddenly loud and full—"and they're like this: SUMARI—ISPANIA—WENA NEFARIE—" each word was louder than the last, and Jane threw the paper to the floor, arched back in her chair, filled her lungs with a huge, ecstatic gasp, and literally screamed "DENA, DENA NEFARIE, LONA LONA LONA, SU-U-U-U-U-MAR-R-R-R-I-I-I-I-I!"

The words wailed off the ceiling and echoed up and down the hallway outside. The hairs on my neck rose right up and tingled; tears stung my eyes, a sharp, white-hot thrill echoing through me just as that wail was ringing through the walls of the stately old three-story house. I was shocked and appalled and utterly transformed. And still today, writing this chapter or reading Jane's recollections, the memory of that chant brings an electric rush surging through me, tingling again in the roots of my scalp and the layers of my skin.

Jane was still arched in her chair, her eyes moving rapidly behind her closed lids. "Jane?" Sally Benson said, reaching over to touch her arm. "Jane, are you—"

At Sally's touch, Jane opened her eyes and sat forward, smiling around at each one of us. "It is with this always we begin, and we begin our classes," a soft, warm voice whispered. "It is with this chant always that we begin our endeavors in our space. It is not your own, and only a translation, for we do not use verbal communication. It is always with a facsimile of what we have heard that we begin our work, and in many guises and in many ways you are acquainted with our activities."

Jane's eyes were wide open, almost unblinking, the voice liquid and soft, like a spring night. I could sense, as Jane spoke these words, a great confusion of voices, or of people, buzzing somewhere just around the corner of my sight and hearing. To me, the room was packed, crowded beyond its physical capacity to hold us all—and indeed, reading this session over eight years later, I was surprised to recall that there were actually only thirteen of us there.

The warm voice went on: "We have always been here in your terms as you have always been in other places and other times, and there is a great familiarity and wonder on our part that you are still involved in these endeavors which were begun in your terms so many centuries ago, and in ways that you cannot now presently comprehend." Jane's later description for her feelings in trance was that "an astonishing graciousness" seemed to fill her. "Gracious" is certainly the attitude this voice fulfilled—as though we were all dear, precious, and living memories of a time and place nearly lost in the clouds of myth—almost as we might remember childhood stories about our ancestors.

"There are cities that we have built that you have helped build in other areas in your time," the voice said. "We have been here many times, and you have been where we are." Jane's eyes looked all around the room again, and suddenly she lifted up her head and wailed again, "Su-u-u-mar-r-r-i-i-i!"

With that, Jane began speaking in a deeper, ponderous voice. "And I am Sumari in another guise," it said. "And all of you have your guises and your masks that you wear and have worn. I am Sumari in another guise. And all of these guises are myself, and all of your guises are yourselves. And as I dwell in many realities, so dwell you in many realities."

My eyes were focused on Jane's face, but as this voice spoke of many realities, I became aware of two things simultaneously: a strong subjective feeling that I was vastly, incredibly ancient, and looking back fondly on a scene that centuries ago had turned to dust and bones; and secondly, that standing behind Jane's chair was a three-dimensional, quite solid golden figure, its head nearly reaching the ceiling. This figure stayed put even as I stared at it in mild surprise, though there were no details within its bulk. It was at this point, Jane later said, that she felt the personality characteristics of an old man and young boy at once—"an ancient boy," she says in *Adventures in Consciousness*[3]—the ancient and the new, combined.

Again, the room seemed full, spinning with motion and light and sound at the periphery of perception. The gold-yellow figure faded, but in its place

I kept getting strong mental images of tiers and tiers of dwellings, or of city-structures—waiting, it seemed to me, in a kind of "hold" position on the other side of space, building up enough energy to "burst" through.

Later, when class compared notes, we found that all of us had experienced some kind of altered focus of attention, including "visions" of groups of figures standing around the room. Rob, as it turned out (as Jane describes in *Adventures),* had also seen a vision—his of bright, jagged light, appearing as he sat typing in the apartment kitchen across the hallway, consciously unaware of what was going on in class.

"We are all Sumari . . . and you are all Sumari, and never forget that you are all Sumari, and have always been Sumari," the second, deeper voice was saying.

"Are there other family names?" Gert asked.

"It is the name of your family," the voice repeated. "It has always been the name of your family."

When the voice was finished speaking, it took Jane many long minutes to come out of trance—in itself unusual for her. By then it was past 11 o'clock, and time for class to end. We trailed out of the room, saying good night to Jane, who stayed seated, answering us only vaguely, her attention still drawn in other directions.

The night was fiercely cold and damp. As I started down the street, I seemed to be stepping out of a session of dream-talk. "What was that all about?" I said to Vanessa and Valerie, who were getting in their car. I felt uncomfortable—yet triumphant, in some mysterious way. But this had been Jane's doing, of course, a new turn in Jane's development. Still, the next night, when I volunteered to record and type up the regular Seth session so Rob would be free to ask questions, Seth went on at great length about Sumari—not only as an important turn in Jane's abilities, but as a psychic alliance, or "family of consciousness" that existed "in all levels of activity . . . who come together for certain reasons, varying reasons; whose individual inclinations are somewhat the same . . . you may think of the guilds in the Middle Ages, for example," Seth told Rob. "It is a membership of choice, in other words; of attraction and respect, and usually this is bound by like purposes and endeavor. These are true families . . .

"Their main activities take place in other levels of consciousness. You are on missions, in certain terms. You do attend meetings, when you are in the sleep state [and] between lives. You work through many layers of reality at the same time. Now, these are the people, for example . . . the strangers that you see in your dreams. You are affecting each other's realities."

Seth went on to describe the Sumari "family" and its "strong psychic alliance and . . . the agility with which they can manipulate between systems, consciously, with purpose, and with some exuberance. They are given much more, for example, to ideas than to the various camouflage realities within systems . . . Many groups, you see, deal exclusively with the camouflage reality between systems, with building it up, with its maintenance. [The Sumari] initiate the birth of systems. They constantly carry communications between systems, and they deal with the initiation and communication of ideas . . .

"The time, simply, was right for the [Sumari] information to come through," Seth said. "'Two [class] members had lost members of their own family. They were ready, therefore, to learn of their greater family . . . and you can be involved in this work only so long, you see, before you become acquainted with your true associates . . . You are being recognized, in your terms, as your present personalities, by your guild again. You are now ready to take up conscious membership. It is a way to acquaint your conscious self with your real and deep alliances." Seth added that while all those in class the night before were of this Sumari clan, as were others who came to Jane's class, there were other "families" of consciousness allied in their own particular endeavors.[4]

After this first appearance, Jane's Sumari trances changed rapidly from week to week. In the following class, Jane explained some of Seth's information on the Sumari "family." "Seth made some crack about my 'dislike of brotherhoods, alive or dead,'" Jane laughed. "He said the Sumari were temperamentally suited to creative work but 'didn't like to hang around to mow the grass,' which is, I guess, a pretty good description!"

Then, easily and smoothly, Jane slipped into trance, and the Sumari personality was there, wide-eyed and smiling, a certain softness about her face not lent to her by Seth's presence. This time, though, the words she used were not in English. At first, I thought she was speaking in French or Latin—or some version of the two mixed together. But it wasn't any language as we knew languages; it was language-like sound, rolling from Jane's lips with an odd eloquence, accompanied by lovely, graceful gestures.

"This soft, almost inaudible voice of last week's personality came through Jane, talking seriously, pleadingly, and lovingly with Sue, Sally, and Florence in an altogether strange tongue," Faith Briggs recalls of that night. "At one time Jane absolutely conked the back of her neck on the straight-backed chair she was in, so Gert put a soft pillow behind her head . . .

"Jane went through all kinds of impersonations," Faith says, "like matching up characteristics of the present group of Sally and Florence with their age-old counterparts, singing lullaby-type songs, changing expression and tone and manner of voice, and ending up with this *Su-u-u-mar-i-i-i!* in a long drawn-out call. At one point I had goose-bumps all over. Jane was trying so hard, in trance, to get the group [in front of her] to repeat and understand the words she was using. Like 'Old Home' week!"

The Sumari trance-person spoke to each one of us in this nonlanguage. I tried for a few minutes to translate it word for word (a technique that doesn't work no matter what the language is); then I just relaxed and listened to the sound as you might listen to music. Sumari-Jane then gestured to me, pointed up the street in the direction of my apartment, and pantomimed a mother rocking her baby to sleep, all the while speaking in those tender, velvety word-sounds. It was sweet and obviously appropriate, but I found that I was simply not very comfortable with what was going on—its emotional expression was just too overt for me. And then, quite without warning, Sumari-Jane broke into song!

I'd heard Jane sing in her "own" voice, and I can vouch for the fact that she can't carry a tune very well at all. Although she loves all forms of music from rock to classical, she has no musical training (except Catholic school choir). But the Sumari songs combined many incredible facets of ability, including a vocal sophistication and range normally beyond her. "Jane, who had no knowledge or training as a singer, did what trained vocalists do," acknowledge Warren and Camille Atkinson, who are both musicians and music teachers.

Flowing from Jane with ease and joy, the Sumari songs were often inter-spersed with spoken Sumari and displayed a psychological acuity as deft as Seth's—but without words. Her Sumari was like songs of the psyche; they captured an individual's inner "sound" and its relationship within the class. She might, for instance, sing in Sumari to two or three of us, using gestures, musical tones and rhythms, and a variety of voice ranges from a high soprano to a growling tenor, to express our own levels of interaction. Several times, the early Sumari songs were addressed to Rob and me and two of our so-called past selves, Nebene and Shirin.

As Jane describes it in chapter 5 of *Adventures in Consciousness,* Nebene and Shirin were personalities that Rob and I had supposedly been in the first century A.D.: he, a rigid, disciplined teacher and I, a bratty, defiant student. We'd come upon these other selves quite spontaneously one Friday night; simultaneously perceiving images of the school and the surrounding land-scape in identical detail. Jane and I also saw images of the Nebene character in the living room, and I'd had the weird experience of feeling Shirin coalesce within me and peek out through my eyes at the twentieth-century room: like having a set of your vaguely defined feelings suddenly acquire an identity of their own, complete with a "history" of another time and place.

Since that evening, though, Rob and I hadn't explored this mutual memory further for a number of reasons—a simple lack of time, to start with. But now and then we'd kid one another about the "perfectionist" and the "snot" and largely ignore the implications of how these personalities might represent portions of our psychological frameworks.

Sumari seemed determined to get us to relate as Nebene and Shirin, however. Rob sat in on several classes in early 1972, and each time, Sumari-Jane would turn to us and suggest in words and song a struggle of conflicting emotions that these other people within us had dealt with in their lifetimes—or who represented these emotions to us now. Then Sumari would point to Rob, to me, and then wait expectantly in trance. She seemed to want us to express all of this to each other in Sumari. We never did. I was far too inhibited: Was I just supposed to make words up as I went along? That seemed silly. Yet, when Sumari-Jane grabbed a pen and paper and drew a series of geometrical diagrams as explanation of her intent, Rob immediately scribbled some words down and handed the note to me:

> Kranjo:
> Saja bundila a gre op rendo qersa tuma
> lunera Mabajundo.
> Petiloj re per.
> KE

It made perfect sense to me as I read it, as did the answering note I handed back:

> Te jingjo le é bordujo—
> mayando.

"Yes," Rob said, looking up from my scrawl. "Yes, that's right." Affection welled up between us, and I kissed him on the cheek, with the whole class, and Jane in trance, watching. Then Jane came out of trance and said, "What's this?"

"Uh, well . . . ," I gulped. Rob shrugged and laughed. It was like waking up from a dream and feeling it disappear from your mind. I couldn't even remember what the damn notes had meant to me, let alone the crazy diagrams. Jane looked at Rob's words and gave what she felt was its translation. "Kranjo, meaning 'baby' or 'young thing'—Shirin, apparently," she said. "Severity of great purpose does not allow for easy tears or laughter. Intuition meets where rules cannot follow." Was this an acknowledgment of Shirin's boisterous lesson to disciplinarian Nebene?

Jane didn't translate my little reply, though; instead, Sumari came through again and acted the part of a little girl, swishing Jane's ankle-length skirt and tossing her hair and whining in a singsong voice. If that was supposed to have been me, I was thoroughly embarrassed for myself. But in a smooth transition, Sumari-Jane sang to me in a vibrant, powerful vibrato, in which I understood that Shirin's bold insolence could help me in thrusting my creativity out into the world; while I could give her—or that part of me—insight and creative focus.

"Jane [had said] something which sounded like the word 'invocation,'" remembers Faith Briggs. "Immediately, [Jane] went into a long diatribe of about twenty minutes, speaking Sumari, but completely different in character [from earlier Sumari]. It evidently was supposed to be a characterization of the willful Shirin.

"Sue sat enjoying it and grinning impishly," Faith says of that scene. "At one point [Sue] said, 'Christ! I haven't changed in 2,000 years!' The Sumari mocked sleeping motions between Shirin and Bette [who apparently had been a nursemaid to Shirin]. As Shirin, [Sumari-Jane] taunted Bette, hurled abuse at her, drank wine, traded [a] bead necklace with Sue, used wanton and flirting posture with Arnold Pearson . . . and in general, raised hell! Oboy!"

Finished with Shirin, Sumari-Jane then proceeded to characterize for Gert, Florence, and Bette, their multilayered roles in class. To Gert, Sumari indicated a nun's habit, prayers, and robotlike movements, which gradually softened to a portrayal of grief. To Florence, Sumari played a sexy young girl—and then yelled a song of challenge to the sky. After a long, staccatoed song to Bette, Jane came out of trance. Immediately, Bette blurted out, "I knew that I was supposed to go around to everybody, touch their temples, and say, 'Eko-Eko Sumari.' Well, I didn't!" She glared around the room, daring somebody to ask why not.

"When you sang to me," Florence told Jane, "for the first time, I wanted my husband here with me. That's a strange reaction, I guess—he's not that interested in all of this."

"It was a lament for myself," Gert said, puzzled. "I understood it then, while you were doing it. I felt like every cell of my body knew what you were saying."

I do think that the Sumari dramas were meant to lead us, through our emotions, into a knowing of our identities. The fact that Sumari-Jane spoke in music and nonlanguage meant that you, the listener, had to *feel* an interpretation ("I cried and cried when I first heard Sumari," says Camille Atkinson) or tune out the whole event—which some members did, not liking the Sumari phenomenon at all ("Sumari was just so much noise to me," Harold Wiles recalls). I was caught somewhere in the middle of these reactions. Yet beyond their psychological import, the Sumari songs and poetry were, simply, superb works of art. Warren transposed the Sumari "Song of Creation" and played it for us on his cello one week—surprising nobody more than Jane at the work's sophisticated beauty.[5]

In Jane and Rob's private sessions, Seth gave extensive information on the nature of language behind physical systems, and how the Sumari was supposed to be leading us, through the quality of sound, away from the accepted structure of words and into the basic, multidimensional expression of being. "As I have said often, language is used as often to distort as it is to clearly communicate," Seth told Rob soon after the Sumari had appeared. "There is a structure within the Sumari language, but it is not one based upon logic. Some of its effectiveness has to do with the synchronization of its rhythms with bodily rhythm. The sounds themselves activate portions of the brain not usually used in any conscious manner. It is a disciplined language in that spontaneity has a far greater order than any you recognize.

"The word 'Shambaline' [for example], connotes the changing faces that the inner self adopts through its various experiences," Seth told Rob. "Now, this is a word that hints of relationships for which you have no word. 'Shambalina Garapharti' [means] 'the changing faces of the soul smile and laugh at each other.' Now all of that is in one phrase.

"By saying the words and opening your perception, the meaning becomes clear in a way that cannot be stated in verbal terms, using your recognizable but rigid language pattern; so we will be dealing then with concepts as well as feelings, but seeking them through the use of a new method, and sometimes translating them back and forth for practice." And class being the testing ground that it was, Seth's explanations of Sumari were "tried out" in the strangest ways—beginning with the "Sumari circle."

Seth had been speaking at length to us that December Tuesday about the inner doors that Sumari could open. "Each of you receives revelations every moment of your lives," he was saying. "Your life is a revelation. We are trying to lead you gently so that you will accept the revelations of your peers. Within you are answers and questions. The questions are to lead you to your own answers, and the answers will not be the same.

"The revelations have come through the centuries; the revelations *are* the centuries. The centuries are transparent. You can look through this history that you know. The selves that sit there know other selves. There are revelations within you that do not need words; they need to rise up like new planets into your own consciousness, and you need to greet them gently and not give them labels or names.

"So we are leading you away from labels and names, and for a while you may feel confused or lonely, for you only feel safe when you can name an experience; and you want to know, What is it? What is its name? Is this [Sumari] language a truth? Did it exist in the past? What *is* it?

"We want you to do away with the normal punctuation of your experience, for you put periods and question marks and dashes where they do not belong . . . the words are steppingstones to lead you into other areas of experience. Within the word is a wordless knowledge. Now you need the sounds to remind you.

"In time—in your time—you will dispense even with the sounds. You will be walking backward, in your terms, into the heart of perception; therefore you will leave behind many of the truths that are now familiar to you, the words that you take for granted. For when you consider an experience, you apply words to it much more than feeling: Does this word apply, or does that word apply, or what is it? And without its label, dare I experience this unknown?"

Seth's words were slow and measured, unlike his usual jaunty self; it seemed that each syllable was being handed down through Jane's skull with peculiar emphasis. As Seth finished, Florence took a notepad out of her purse and drew a design on it (figure 10). "I've been doodling this for years," she said hesitantly, "but now it seems really important that I show it to you." She held the notepad up, displaying the doodle, and handed it to Jane, who went into Sumari trance. Holding out Florence's drawing, Sumari spoke to each one of us in turn in a quick, delighted tone of voice. That done, Sumari-Jane sat back in the rocker, closed her eyes, and began a low, rhythmic, singsong chant that went on and on, punctuated throughout by the pounding of her clenched fist on the chair arm. On and on, on and on, Sumari-Jane rocked gently, back and forth—*thump! thump!*— chanting and pounding, chanting and pounding. Gradually, this chant-song grew more and more powerful, until suddenly—with a perfect abruptness that surprised no one until the evening was over—every single one of us stood up and joined right in with this song, roaring it loud and clear and never missing a beat or fumbling a word. We walked in procession around Jane's chair, me included, singing in resounding, echoing voices, the "words" perfectly clear-cut and ungarbled, though not of any language any of us knew afterward. The power and ancient, symbolic clarity rang through the room, and we were totally within the experience, freely participating without reservation. In those moments, we understood the intent and source of this "circle" without doubt—and expressed it.

Figure 10. Florence MacIntyre's drawing

All at the same instant, everybody stopped. The song was finished. Sumari-Jane then directed several of us, in Sumari, to change places: Florence was supposed to stand in front of the bay windows and look out over the snowy night; I was supposed to face the closed apartment door. It all seemed completely appropriate and logical, symbolic and literal. We stood in our places for a moment, and then simultaneously, Florence and I turned toward one another and walked to the center of the room. Smoothly, Florence knelt in front of me and touched my toes—an action that stunned me in the first flash of confoundment I'd felt through this whole experience. I stepped away from her, embarrassed—and the group feeling evaporated. It wasn't until much later that I connected Florence's gesture with my dream-vision on November 16, which I hadn't described in class.

Jane was out of trance, staring: there we all were, standing around in a circle. "Ah, folks," she said, laughing, "what is going on this time?" Actually, Jane said that she'd been aware of the "circle" and its actions and meaning the whole time, and it had seemed a perfectly natural thing to do. Yet, what was it all about? Jane couldn't believe that we'd all stood up and shouted out that chant, right along with her, but several tape recorders had been left on throughout, and we played the tapes back to prove it. And it seemed that each one of us had understood the whole event—*while* it happened.

"I don't know," Bette mused darkly, "now I feel ridiculous."

I remembered a dream I'd had a few nights before, in which I'd been one of a group of robed people, swaying and dancing while the rising sun lit up a flat, black pyramid on the distant horizon. Had we been recalling some kind of ceremony from long ago?

"You were indeed involved in a variation of an ancient ceremony, in which you were all, in your terms, at one time involved," Seth told us the following week. "This was your translation of it in terms that you can understand, as what you are now is a translation of yourself in terms that you can understand.

"But remember, all of you, that your reality is structured not in logical terms as you think of logic. But that your most chaotic dream, that most important symbolic episode, and experiences that you have had that seem so unstructured to you, that these have their own inner structure that is intuitive. You understand that structure very well, whether or not you consciously admit that recognition."

Still, some members of class never did accept the Sumari phenomenon easily. After the "Sumari circle," Jane's Sumari trances would often include directions for specific members to stand in front of others, or walk around the room in a certain fashion, or perhaps exchange small items of clothing or jewelry. Some of us responded eagerly, and others didn't. In one of these mini-dramas, Bette Zahorian refused to participate until Sumari-Jane had nudged her, gently, for most of the evening: finally Bette got up, grumbling, and consented to move from person to person, touching their foreheads—the impulse she'd admitted to having in previous classes. "But I'll be damned if I'll learn another language!" Bette snorted later in protest. "How come we sit here and listen to this and do funny things, anyway? Just what are we doing?"

"Well, there are emotional realities involved, Bette," Jane said. "But I understand your predicament, because I ask myself those kinds of questions, too." Jane described an experiment that she and Rob had tried, in which they'd turned on the tape recorder and conversed in Sumari for several hours, just letting the words flow without plan. "The translation is emotional," Jane said. "You have, like new ideas of sound, like in pre-language . . ."

"I don't know, I just think that I sit here week after week not knowing what's going on," Bette answered. "I think some people here get more information than others do and I feel left out. Why was I supposed to go around to everybody and say that stuff in Sumari? I don't know why, but I felt like doing it. Why? What was I *doing?* Nobody tells me anything."

At once, Jane's glasses were whipped off, and Seth's voice bellowed across the room. "The Sumari always come home," he told Bette with great mock seriousness. "They have never left home and they know where home is, and none of you have left your home and the [Sumari] in you knows that very well. Now, I do not play favorites, and you know that very well and when you need help you get it, and when others need help, they get it."

"Yes, but I think I was set up for that," Bette retorted angrily. "I'm putting into words what others might be thinking."

"I did not say you were set up—I just said I do not play favorites," he replied. "Now, you knew what you were supposed to do [in touching foreheads], and it took you a good two hours to do it, and now you want a medal!"

"No, I don't want a medal," Bette said. "I would just like to know why I did it, because I don't *know* why I did it."

"Then you should ask *yourself* why you did it. And if you quit telling yourself that you do not know why you did it, then you would know that you already knew why you did it!"

Bette's eyes narrowed into little black beads. "And you aren't going to tell me why I did it, are you?"

"You tell *me* why you did it—I am not used to such goings-on," Seth answered humorously. "Why did you do it?"

"I don't know," Bette sighed, resigned.

"It was a lovely benediction. Why can't you leave it at that?"

Bette heaved another sigh. "All right. I won't argue with you, Seth. I'll drop it if you say so."

"You never drop anything," Seth grinned. "It would not be nearly as much fun if you did. I am not reprimanding you!

"Some Sumari come home quicker than others and some Sumari take their time," Seth said, after a pause. "Now, I do not want to tell you all the answers to the Sumari development, for some of the answers you are to find out for yourselves, and some of the answers cannot happen unless you discover them for yourselves . . . and the Sumari chants are to lead each of you further into your own realities."

"There are significances in the vowels and syllables and sounds that will be explained to you as you learn what they are through experience," Seth said in another class. "You are able to use your inner senses while you are in this room; therefore, you are to use your own inner perceptions. Be aware of your feelings and interpret them. The vowels and syllables do affect you differently, not only as a group, but individually, and they are meant to.

"To the extent that you understand this, you will be able to utilize much of this material to your own benefit, at home and in your dreams and in healing and in maintaining the effectiveness and integrity of your own physical image."

Seth also told us many times to be on the lookout for other Sumari: that there was a natural recognition among members of these consciousness "families."

"It's funny about recognition of Sumari people," Priscilla Lantini says. "I was working nights [as a waitress] in the restaurant and a couple sat down at one of my tables. Throughout their dinner we exchanged pleasantries, and I felt I knew them. Finally I asked if I had seen them before, if they were from Elmira or maybe they were friends of one of my children. They said they were from New Jersey and felt they knew me from somewhere, too. It was their first time in Elmira, and they were here to see Jane because they had read the Seth books and were very interested, but could not get ahold of her! Yes, I feel what Sumari is, and yes I do feel we know each other."

Indeed, most class members immediately understood what Seth meant and could describe many such encounters—as I'm sure readers can, too.

Another way in which Sumari was personalized for class members was when Seth (at Rob's request) gave many of us our entity names. Like Jane's "Ruburt" and Rob's "Joseph," these names are supposed to express a person's whole self, or "the image of the sum of your various personalities in the past and future," as Seth explains in *The Seth Material*. "The names are a sound that you make—that your mind makes, when it meets with the universe, as the leaves each have a sound that they make as they move against the sky," Seth added in an informal class gathering in 1979. "So, your mind sounds. And that sound has a certain identification. It is the sound of the movement of the leaves of your mind."

To give some examples, according to Seth, my entity name is "Oranda"; George Rhoads's is "Fromage";[6] Florence MacIntyre's, "Fentori"; Bette's, "Varneldi"; Gert Barber's, "Meor"; Harold's, "Larlee"; Priscilla Lantini's, "Sorta"; Richie Kendall's, "Ringdano"; Mary Strand's, "Peter"; Jed Martz's, "Torlara"; Lauren DelMarie's, "Pan"; Zelda Graydon's, "Fromadon"; Rudy Storch's, "Norvelinda." In a two-year span, one class member's entity name changed, according to Seth, from "Igor" to "Fornestor": "He is a new self," Seth explained, even while admonishing that names are basically meaningless. We stared at Phil appraisingly: Was this a probability emerged right before our eyes?

Sumari-Jane also gave little personalized songs to several class members; these, Seth told us, could be hummed or sung in private moments to regain feelings of affirmation, or for help in healing and "general maintenance of the physical image." These tiny songs were exquisitely lovely, and inexpressible in print, of course;[7] but like entity names, they expressed a person's inner "tone"; and each one was completely different, as each Sumari song was different from all the others.

"I don't know about this entity name stuff," Lauren DelMarie complained one evening after Seth had called him "Pan—who plays his pipes on the mountainsides." "I mean, like, what if I wake up some morning and find myself with goat's feet?"

Jane laughed, and pointed to Rob's portrait of Seth hanging on the wall by the TV set. "Look, when Robbie wakes up some morning and finds *that* sleeping next to him, we all worry," she said.

"*Seth Sleeps,*" Warren added.

"I remember the first time I heard Sumari," recalls Betty DiAngelo in a long and lyrical passage about the experience. "Although I didn't write down my impressions, it was an instant mind expansion. I could almost hear a popping sound as I switched channels . . . sometimes I had the feel of finally arriving home after a long journey; other times it was like the pleasant and peaceful feeling one gets walking after a new snowfall. Sometimes it had a beautiful sadness or longing to it. Too, it was a stabilizing and centering experience, like turning a dial to just the right spot, where reception is strongest and clearest.

"I remember once having the distinct impression that Sumari was coming from everywhere—the walls, the plants in the room, and even the ground underneath. Last but not least was the wonderment caused by such a feat on Jane's part. Surely we were witnessing, and part of, a miraculous or magical happening. It felt good and right to be a person, something we don't affirm often enough, as we spend so much time castigating ourselves and the human race as a whole.

"Jane's singing was the means by which we took Sumari journeys together; the vehicle was used as if we were on a bus and Jane was the bus driver," Betty says. "While we were all in the same vehicle, going to the same destination, we were each seeing the landscape uniquely through our individual selves.

"I dared not admit at first to myself how excited I was with the concept . . . of the Sumari family. How contradictory for me—I have been a zealous anti-groupie since I was a child. But at first it was as if I was peeking out through hands held over my face. I liked the esoteric aspects of the Sumari family idea . . . I couldn't ignore it . . . how else to explain the familial trust among class members and the feeling that we *were* some sort of family? There was so much openness and communication in class—much taken-for-granted trust; a natural aspect of class and not one we worked on . . .

"Sumari poetry addresses itself to the entity in time and is an experience on many levels, like all substantial literature is. And it doesn't just speak to the Sumari family . . . [Jane's] poems seem to me like precious and delightful gifts whose newness never wears off but is experienced anew each time one goes back to them."

George Rhoads remembers Sumari in a seasonal fashion.

"Sumari is the drama of the inner self, symbolized and condensed, like a waking dream in the form of music," he says. "Sumari does not judge or interpret or explain. It elucidates the totality of being as it becomes a creation in its own right.

"There are themes that recur from song to song, both in words and melody. One song grows and evolves into the next. The new song harks back to the old as it plunges into the new, and each combination is unique. In the songs that come through Jane, from the somewhat formal, structured patterns of the winter came heavily emotional and dramatic themes, concerned with problems and attitudes. Then with spring came the more fluid and primitive songs, evoking new psychic concerns. Even in these, different as they were from the early songs, there were traces and hints of themes that were stated far earlier.

"This evolution of the Sumari songs parallels the development of the class as a whole. We went from a baffled viewpoint limited by personal problems and an attitude of searching, to the area of the realization of beliefs, including and transcending theories and problems, to the realization of the power of the present, which is the controlling point of beliefs, and then on into creative play with the beliefs themselves. The final songs seemed to open the door to worlds of alternate reality.

"The Sumari song has a meaning on many levels," George concludes, "and is always saying that the joy and agony, the emptiness and fullness, the confusion and enlightenment, are simply song."

"There was a richness of symbols," Dan Stimmerman says. "The fall rolled around and the changes in the earth that mean so much to me were often the language of Seth and the poetry of Jane and the Sumari."

CHAPTER 8

Reincarnation: Survival of the Fitting?

Reincarnational
with Thanks to W.B. Yeats and A Vision

Born in the minutes
before the moon turns new,
I give my backward gaze
to probable pasts,
to real and unreal histories
I fashion into song . . .

With lace to dress my collar,
as I lean upon my cane—
with palsied limb I climb
those garden steps again;
and angry curse my sisters
for the weakness of our sex.
To be woman and be crippled
was to be doubly vexed . . .

Born in the minutes
before the moon turns new,
before my Queen I fall upon
my knees and plead the life of
that good Lord, my friend—
in whose public grace
I could bow but could not
kiss his face . . .

Before the moon turns new,
the swans sweep by and bridge
the centuries between my Lord's
estate and mine—
swans who hook on their feather down,
dreams and memories begot
before the old fictitious moon
turned face around, pretending
all that was, was not.

—Dan Stimmerman, 1973

"Now you can move freely through your consciousness, and experience other times, other places, other selves that you are," Jane was saying. "Those selves that you were in our terms live within the atoms and molecules of your being, and they can become as aware of you as you can become aware of them . . . "

I opened my eyes and looked up. Jane was leading us through a mobility-of-consciousness experiment in that November class of 1970, and even she was sitting with her eyes closed as she delivered the long, soothing monologue. I glanced idly around at the room full of people, everyone in various positions of repose, keeping mental pace with Jane's words. It was a pleasant, fulfilling scene. I gazed across the room at Laurie, a recent newcomer, who should have been sitting on the blue sofa.

She wasn't.

Sitting in Laurie's place, as plain and as three-dimensional as the rest of the room, a grotesquely emaciated and shabby-looking old man was staring vacantly back at me. His mouth hung slack; his face drooped in folds of weathered skin. Whispers of white hair stuck out at odd angles from his skull. The figure stayed for a few seconds and vanished, exchanging proper places with Laurie.

When Jane finished, I related what I'd seen, along with some other impressions: I "knew" that the old man had lived in the early 1900s and died of tuberculosis in a slum-section rooming house of an American city. Particularly, I kept seeing this old man on a rainy street, ambling listlessly, in a filthy sweater and pants—with no one, nothing, to call his own. The images were vivid, almost superimposed on Jane's living room.

Laurie listened, blushing. "I don't know why, but that makes some weird kind of total sense to me," she said.

At that, Jane removed her glasses. "The information was completely correct," Seth told Laurie, "and it has something to do with the problem upon which you are working, so that you can use this in asking questions of your own unconscious and of your own deeper self." Seth gestured to indicate Laurie's overweight condition. "The idea of being slim and slender reminds you of this earlier consumptive self."

Laurie nodded. "Is that why I can't get a clear picture of myself as I want to be?" she asked.

"It is indeed, and also you feel that the added weight is insurance against consumption," Seth said. "In the past, however, you had the disease for your own purposes. In the past life, you did not have an understanding nor appreciation of physical reality and you did not feel that you could manipulate within it easily, effectively, or well. You disliked physical life . . . yet in that life you learned a sense of compassion that you did not have earlier in the life previously, in which you were a soldier. In *that* life you were given to violence, and had no deep understanding of your fellow man . . . you were a very strong and large male.

"You had only contempt for those who were physically weak. Your activities in that life thoroughly disgusted you because of the wars in which you were involved. These wars were closely connected with the Crusades . . . Because of your contempt for yourself in that life, you chose a next life in which your physical image was very small and weakly, and in having that image, you learned the nature of compassion. Where once you had used force, you now felt the brunt of force. Where once you had no use for the weak, you found yourself indeed among their number . . .

"In your mind, the slim body means a predisposition to illness and a lack of strength," Seth continued. "Now, knowing this and working with your inner self will help you change your physical body. What you actually want, you see, is the body of the warrior to protect you, and you are not that warrior anymore."

After cautioning Laurie not to think that guilt for the warrior's actions was implied ("True compassion is strength, but you did not know that and so you had to teach it to yourself"), Seth then turned to another student and delivered a lengthy account of the man's inner reasons for having a birth defect in this life—reasons, Seth said, which had been expressed through some sort of physical defect in all of the man's lives. "In each of your lives, you have carried what to you is a badge," Seth told him. "In each life, you chose to affect one portion or another of your physical image so that it could not function correctly, as a reminder to yourself, and even to the present physical self, that you were not wholeheartedly embarking upon these lifetime adventures . . . To you, it is a constant reminder.

"These were all symbols, to some extent, of a refusal to completely enter into the experiences that you yourself had chosen. In this life, you are to understand that you have put this distance between yourself and others; between the inner self and others that you know in physical reality, and that to completely fulfill those purposes you have set yourself, you must now relate emotionally to others, despite the badge that you have adopted."

Seth supplied the man with more details, and Jane came out of trance. As Laurie was filling Jane in on Seth's description of the warrior, my husband, Ned, remarked that he also felt as though he'd been a warlike person many times. "Like, maybe my hassles with the draft right now are because I'm trying to be the opposite of that," Ned said, referring to his futile efforts to gain a conscientious objector status or at least be declared a noncombatant. "I'd serve as a medic, but wow, I'd never kill anybody," he stated.

With that, Seth returned to tell Ned that both he and I had lived in Europe and participated in the Second World War; he as an intern and I as a nurse. "And the dreams that you have had are quite legitimate," Seth said to me, in reference to my recurring war dreams that I'd had since childhood, some of which I'd related in class.[1] Seth gave us detailed information on these lives, including family names, dates, our birthplaces, and other checkable facts.

"You were both propelled into the war seemingly because of circumstances and you both died violently, separately, in the war—you [Ned] in the ruins of a cathedral in Germany and she [me] later in France," Seth said. "In this life, therefore, you are against war, extremely dissatisfied with the current establishment and resentful because you fought the war that was to end all wars and now realize that no war will end all wars and that only peace will end all wars. Hence, you [Ned] will not accept a status in which you carry a gun." Seth then predicted, "though this, now, understand, is in the realm of probabilities," that unforeseen circumstances would prevent Ned from being drafted into the armed services.[2]

Seth's information (much of it not included here) certainly provided a fascinating speculation on the possible origins of my vivid, terrifying childhood war dreams, and the cold-sweat fear that I would plunge into at the age of four or five, when I'd snap awake in the night each time an airplane flew over our house. Had newspapers or adult conversation scared me that much? (We didn't have a TV until I was eleven.) Or were my fears actually recalling the physical experience of a me that I had been? Could it really be that I'd once been my own parents' contemporary, dying in the war my father had survived? Or was Seth craftily picking up on our psychological symbolism and giving us a useful, dramatic arena where we could work on our problems?

Before withdrawing, Seth gave more details to Laurie, connecting other details of the old man's life with incidents in her own past. For all of us, Seth's information had direct, personal meaning, connecting with subjective and "factual" incidents in our lives, and imparting valuable insight into the webworks of our days.

I thought of class scenes like this just recently as I leafed through an issue of a popular "psychic" magazine. Its pages were filled with advertisements for past-life readings: two for $10, three for $12.50, or send a poem and get an analysis of your personal vibrations. And what do you get for your money? I grumbled—another set of "reasons" why your life is the way it is, with the power for its direction transferred this time to your actions in centuries past? A nice new mythology to replace all the old shopworn ones?

In a sense, though, I couldn't very well complain—like the incident with Laurie (or with Nebene and Shirin), I've picked up that kind of information myself and participated in it, as have Jane and class members, too. But I couldn't help feeling that Jane's class dealt with "past" lives in a different way—with, for one thing, a balance of integrity; with a lack of straining for a neatly pigeon-holed set of "power" definitions.

Seth, of course, discusses reincarnation in his books, as Jane does in hers; and throughout class years, both gave past-life information to many people. However, such information was always presented within the context of a person's daily life, and never as a list of people and places for its own sake.

In *The Seth Material*, Seth explains reincarnation in terms of simultaneous time:

> Because you are obsessed with the idea of past, present, and future, you are forced to think of reincarnations as strung out one before the other. Indeed we speak of past lives because you are used to the time sequence concept. What you have instead is something like the development narrated in *The Three Faces of Eve*. You have dominant egos, all part of an inner identity, dominant in various existences. But the separate existences exist simultaneously. Only the egos involved make the time division. 145 B.C., A.D. 145, a thousand years in your past, and a thousand years in your future—all exist now . . .
>
> Since all events occur at once in actuality, there is little to be gained by saying that a past event causes a present one. Past experience does *not* cause present experience. You are forming past, present, and future—simultaneously. Since events appear to you in sequence, this is difficult to explain.
>
> When it is said that certain characteristics from a past life influence or cause present patterns of behavior, such statements—and I have made some of them—are highly simplified to make certain points clear.
>
> The whole self is aware of *all* of the experiences of *all* of its egos, and since one identity forms them, there are bound to be similarities between them and shared characteristics. The material I have given you on reincarnation is quite valid, particularly for working purposes, but it is a simplified version of what actually occurs (*The Seth Material* [Englewood Cliffs, NJ: Prentice-Hall, 1970], pp. 148–49).

Class did share its own kind of psychological gestalt, in which reincarnation was at least an acceptable reference point. Jane or Seth might pick up and relate past-life images; sometimes class members "tuned in" on each other. Eventually, this evolved into reincarnational dramas in which several people would reenact whole scenes from "past" times and places—or at least from portions of themselves not usually expressed. And while using the reincarnational framework for emotional and psychic catharsis was not original with us, the beauty of Jane's class was that we could play with this information without making it the final catch basin for every human reaction in every daily encounter—Jane saw quite firmly to that.

Jane's attitude toward reincarnation (like mine) was strongly ambivalent. The idea of physical life being expressed in many historical situations made emotional and intuitive sense to her. Intellectually, however, she was highly suspicious of the standard notion of reincarnation, particularly as any kind of pat answer to present problems. Thus, when class started to experience the theory of reincarnation in emotionally-charged drama form, Jane would often find herself in a most uncomfortable one-foot-on-the-dock, one-foot-in-the-boat position, at once intellectually scandalized and intuitively involved.

Even on those occasions when the inner logic of reincarnational events would "click," or when Seth gave past-life information that made complete sense to people, Jane worried about it for days afterwards. What was the meaning of such memories? Where did they come from? Were we creating the events through suggestion, combined with a need for emotional outlet? Or did we actually remember people who lived—in our terms—long before any of us were born? Or was the truth some combination of these? These questions demanded that class maintain a balance, from which Jane never let things stray too far.

"One thing I found impressive [about Jane]," Matt recalls, "was the way she would lean back and give class its own reins, without trying too hard to interject her own interpretations or beliefs. But I do remember one time when we were talking on the phone, and she commented that she'd terminated the reincarnational dramas. 'Why?' I asked, 'were the students getting too uptight?' 'No,' Jane said with a troubled laugh, 'they were getting too loose.'" Eventually, however, Jane's questioning would lead to her books on aspect psychology (including *Psychic Politics* and *Adventures in Consciousness*), and a new perspective of identity.

Jane and Rob started their fortuitous Ouija board experiment in 1963 with the conviction that nobody survived death once, let alone many times. They'd never had a psychic experience in their lives; they didn't remember their dreams. In contrast, I had a childhood stuffed full of vivid dreams and visions; I'd also stood fully conscious by the side of my bed many times, looking down upon my sleeping body. From the dreaming me's viewpoint, my waking life was a jumbled jigsaw puzzle, held together by a specialized logic that only my physical self fully understood. So whatever I accepted or rejected intellectually, by the time I started coming to Jane's class, I'd experienced an intense and undeniable knowledge from an early age that my Self was independent from the body of my daytime hours. However, I'd never explored the meaning of my experiences with the restless probing that Jane demonstrated in her work, and in class.

So, while I believe that communication between portions of the psyche goes on all the time, few events in class surprised me as much as an apparent connection between one of my most graphic childhood dreams and a recurring "reincarnational" episode in class.

In the dream, my Sue-ness would simply disappear, and "I" was running barefoot through the night, a fine film of sweat tingling my skin in the cool air; running powerfully in great long strides, wearing nothing but light, soft breeches to protect my loins and thighs; running for hours, carrying something in my hand, one thought running through my brain as I was running through the night: *You must get to the village in time! You must get to the village in time!* . . . and coming over the top of a moonlit rise, stopping too quickly, my breath falling ragged and my legs cramping, at the edge of a dry field of whispering grain; and the village below, in danger; burning, fire leaping up from the village and lapping up into the fields, flames dancing now all around me like bright flowers in the ripe grain . . .

WHAM! I'd wake up, terrified, slammed down onto the bed, that male dream self's knowledge of flight and fire searing through me; and I'd lie awake for a long time, seeing that fire spit up through the dry field (Of what? Wheat? Corn? Rye? Where?), my heart pounding like a galloping horse. Sometimes two or three of these other-me dreams would go on at the same time—"double dreaming," Rob would call it in *The "Unknown" Reality*.[3] I knew, somehow, that dreams were more than "just" dreams, no matter what daily surface event they might spring from; and that these dream experiences in particular were of a sort that I was supposed to remember and understand.

I also knew—with a simple interior knowing—that the runner in the night and the others were not "imaginary" in usual terms. They were alive, and my knowledge of them touched them, as their activities in my dreams touched me. This sense of subjective communication was absolutely clear. Yet at the time, there was nothing, anywhere, that even began to lend a framework to explain or contain what I was doing or how I was doing it. Any psychological studies on dreams that I read classified subjectivity as suspect: as the poor cousin of scientific logic. For some reason, I stubbornly refused to accept that premise. On the other hand, the theories of karma and nirvana were just as repellent; reincarnation in that context struck me as plain outrageous idiocy. In comparison, science seemed at least rational—except that its rationale then proceeded to deny subjectivity as being valid "experience" in the first place. In short, none of the accepted explanations for what I was doing lived up to the experiences themselves.[4]

And then there was the campfire.

One cold January Tuesday in 1969, class decided to meet at Rachael Clayton's house for a change. Her comfortable old Colonial was just around the corner from Jane and Rob's apartment building, in that section of Elmira inhabited by the elegance of an age gone by. Rachael's large, open living room was furnished with chairs and sofas of mixed antique vintage; a thick oriental rug warmed the floor. Rachael brought out coffee, tea, and soft drinks; Florence, Sally, and Theodore had brought some wine. I'd been coming to the Thursday beginner's class for a couple of months; this was one of my first times with the half-dozen or so Tuesday regulars.

Jane sat in a fat wing chair, sipping wine. We talked for a while about our backgrounds and the ideas we'd grown up with about death. I wasn't aware of anything unusual in the air, but gradually it seemed that our conversation was drifting; people's attentions were no longer focused on the words we were exchanging. Even Florence spoke dreamily, not really getting to the point, which was unusual for her. Then it came to me that everyone was talking about something that I'd missed completely. In addition, Jane was now sitting on the edge of the wing chair, her forgotten wine glass on the little round end table, and she was talking to Rachael in a heavy, round voice unlike her own—or Seth's. Her eyes were bright and alert, but these were not her characteristic speech mannerisms and gestures—or, again, Seth's.

"Rachael, if you stay in that circle, it is false security," Jane was saying in that strange voice.

"I can't leave until I can see where I'm going," Rachael answered. She wasn't looking at Jane, but staring off to Jane's right, toward the center of the room. She appeared to be in a light trance.

"There will be light, and somebody else," Jane said, "I think me. I just know it's false security to stay in the group—because you have to go beyond that group at that time."

I scowled mentally—because you have to go beyond that group at that time? The tenses were crazy, yet they made weird sense, too. At that moment, an odd twinge like the heightened awareness of impending inspiration tickled the fringes of my mental vision, and the image of low, dark, distant hills caught in the silhouette of a rising moon flooded my mind.

Jane and Rachael were still conversing in their peculiar dialogue. "You have the opportunity to make adjustments and to leave the group when the night comes," Jane was saying. "You have the same sort of thing that Jane had, but Jane is getting over it in this life . . . *In that time*, you did not leave the group and you should have. Now you have the opportunity to go back and leave the group.

"It's as if in our terms, you see, you could go back to a period of this life where you should have acted in a different way and you didn't," Jane said to Rachael. "Well, you have the opportunity now to go back into that existence and make it different in the present . . . because you can change . . . you can change what we would think of as the past through actions in our present. Do you follow me?"

Rachael nodded, slowly. The moonlit hills loomed clearly in my mind. Were they visual or not? Sometimes I've snapped out of daydreams and realized that I hadn't been seeing anything that was "really" in front of my eyes. Now I saw, or somehow perceived, those dark and ominous hills with a powerful sense of urgency that was in itself familiar. Really weird. And why was Jane referring to herself in the third person?

"The past in our terms doesn't cause present behavior," Jane continued, still speaking to Rachael. "You can go back now into that past and change it, in our present. You will have the opportunity to do it because of your intuitive understanding, and this is something that most people haven't developed enough to do."

Jane's gaze turned to me. "Ruburt," Florence said softly in explanation, referring to the entity name Seth had pinned on Jane. Oh, yeah? What did *that* mean? Was Jane speaking with a larger awareness, embodied by her whole self? "Actually, that circle and those people are as real as this room seems to the rest of you," Jane said. "Right now, this room doesn't seem very real to me."

Vaguely, I realized then that this was the scene of the "campfire," which had first appeared a couple of months before during a mobility-of-consciousness exercise. All Jane had told me about it was that several class members had simultaneously reported seeing ghostly, half-formed images of figures seated around a fire, a primitive village in the background. Aware that suggestion could be operating (including the fact that class was itself a group sitting in a circle around the living room), Jane encouraged everyone to focus on the images to see what they could get. To one extent or another—either through visual or mental images or feelings of "something going on"—all of the class members tuned in on this scene. Rachael was especially drawn by the feeling that she was one of those faceless people huddled by the firelight; that some ritual affecting her position within the circle was what drew her back there.

Jane was still addressing Rachael in that odd voice. "Now, you can, if you want to, and without any kind of coercion, look up and see Seth's face," she said. "And in the face you'll find confidence to leave the group at that time. The confidence you find then will serve you now, and help you in the daily life that you think you are leading now."

"Who are the unfriendly ones?" Rachael asked.

Once again, that terrific agony of urgency surged through me. "Starting with yourself, counting yourself, the third person down to your left at that time was in conflict with you . . ." Jane was saying, but at that instant, a lunge of acceleration seemed to shove me, too, within this daydream scene: Jane's voice was coming from far away, and the moon was up above the hills, casting a pale silver glow across the land; and I saw the figures huddled there, faces cowled in skins, the firelight red and orange against them; saw them, at first close up and then as though through a telescope, waiting there, as they had waited many times—waiting for . . .

"Wait a minute," Jane said sharply. "Answer me, will you? Over a knoll—I feel a rise there."

"Yes," Rachael concurred. "A grain or wheat field."

My stomach thudded in surprise, half pulling me out of the immediacy of the scene. "Okay . . . do you sense anybody beyond that?" Jane asked. Rachael nodded. "I sense somebody beyond that field," Jane went on, "coming from the [other] village that we talked about earlier. I sense you [Rachael] do not want to know that they are there . . . there's a figure out there in the wheat field that she [Rachael] doesn't want to face."

"Good gawd," I interjected for the first time. "I'm the one out in the field! That's me, that's my dream!" But the others were too wrapped up in it to pay much attention. Seth eventually came through with some information for Rachael about this "group," telling her that "there will be other times in class when we will be there [at the "campfire"] and you will decide to leave the group and take the journey that will take you there . . . and then, you will feel triumph."

It wasn't until the following week that I had the chance to describe my old recurring dream, which I hadn't even thought about in years. Jane and I shook our heads. I'd never mentioned this dream in class and until that January night, had been aware of only scanty details of the campfire. Dramatic coincidence? A creative equation of scenes on my part? A marvelous bit of group telepathy, combined with suggestion? Or a piece of a puzzle depicting my part in an event from long ago? Or all of the above?

And what did any of this prove? Or was trying to compile "proof" of past lives an end in itself? We didn't know what to think. That the campfire existed on some level of activity couldn't be denied—even if it were just serving as a common gathering place for us to flex our psychic muscles. Had I picked up on that, symbolically, in my dream of more than a decade before? Did this connect with the vision of flames that Dan MacIntyre and I saw leaping up around Jane's chair that night (as described in chapter 3)?

"The 'campfire'—strange," Rachael recalled of the scene in a recent letter to me, "the instant I began [to think about it], all the old feelings and images were back, along with goose bumps and chills. I never felt I was a true part of the campfire's circle, although I was there. It still seemed as if I was on the outside perimeter. Jane even said to me at one time I was more or less a transient figure.

"No faces were ever apparent [visually], although I felt many people I knew were present. Jane was there, but not as Seth. Seth *was* the one face I could distinguish, and he was centered, standing, near the fire . . . I still feel a cold strong wind blowing, and there were reeds or thick grasses covering the plain beyond, swaying in the wind . . . the runner was approaching through this. I had a feeling of foreboding and I was reluctant to see him [the runner], although I felt a deep love for this entity. I never felt I was wholly accepted as part of the circle. I felt on the outskirts of the gestalt.

"I still retain permanent feelings of the campfire," Rachael wrote. "In fact, I was at the campfire other times, but [not always] physical. Isn't it strange—from the time I met you [me, Sue], I was aware of a deep attaching feeling for you with the love you have for a comrade . . . at times it's a paternal feeling. There must be something in the past, or I never would have started this letter the way I did."

"In one way, there's the idea that what we are has these realities on other levels that we're just not able to use physically right now," Jane suggested once in class. "So, they're being expressed somewhere else, and by the time we get to them physically [as in reincarnational dramas], they're only approximations."

It was the personal experience of reincarnation, then, that class used, and sometimes without warning—like the case of "Matt's snit with Natalie," in the fall of 1972.

"I can't recall having any class that involved me so directly, or instigated such a smorgasbord of emotional reaction," Matt says. An occasional visitor to class, Matt had asked Seth during the early evening about an editing project he was working on. In answering his question, Seth said that Matt would eventually "have more authority and power" in his field, and referred to some past-life material he'd given to Matt a few years before.[5] This information involved Matt as a thirteenth-century French monk who had worked against the dogma of the Church. In a similar respect, Seth said that Matt was in a position to work against the kinds of modern dogma he encountered in the publishing world.

"Maybe you'd better explain your job a little," Jane suggested to Matt after Seth's remarks had been related to her.

"Usually in class, I made a point of keeping my mouth shut," Matt says. "On this occasion, though, when Jane specifically asked me to explain [my job], I talked for a bit . . . but, just as I was curbing my own penchant for running on and starting to wrap it all up, Natalie interjected, 'You have a big mouth!'"

The hushed shock that Natalie's completely uncharacteristic outburst produced nearly ground the whole class to a halt. "Uh—well, Natalie, maybe we ought to let Matt finish," Jane suggested hopefully, in the unusual silence.

"Oddly, I took this with great good nature, though I was mildly surprised," Matt says. "I figured that Natalie had been working through some belief system that called for her voicing whatever came into her head, and so did not take it 'personally.'"

But Natalie persisted.

"Har, dee, har, har, har," she snorted derisively at Matt's attempts to continue his explanation. "Aren't we the big serious know-it-all tonight?" Natalie, a normally gracious and friendly woman, was practically dripping with disdain. In her chair by the philodendron-covered bookcase, she squared her shoulders and drew herself up, apparently set for battle. A scornful sneer curled her lips as she glared at Matt.

"She was very arch, as if keeping back enormous and superior laughter," Matt says, "and as this kind of odd exchange continued, I had an odd reaction. Usually, when attacked personally by strangers, my response is to become airy and gracious. But in this case . . . I realized that the only way to stop Natalie's game was to remain mentally and emotionally inert."

Again, rather than confronting Natalie, Matt attempted another description of his job; while Jane, aware of the sudden undercurrents, watched alertly. Five words into his first sentence, Matt was cut off by another snort of contempt. "Ah, c'mon, Matty, why don't you tell 'em what's *really* going on?" Natalie taunted.

"No—I defer to my elder brother!" Matt snapped back, waving with sarcastic courtesy in Natalie's direction. Several people gasped in surprise. "I was rather pleased [at that reaction]—the Matt part of me," he says. "The substratum was increasingly pissed off."

"Okay, you two, hold it," Jane said, quietly interrupting Natalie's comeback. "What's going on?"

"*He* was a monk, all right!" Natalie cried, pointing at Matt, sitting barely more than arm's length from her. "And he was so goddamned-death on it all! He thought he was so goddamned superior! And he still does! Ha! They should only know!" Natalie, who rarely used strong language, was piling surprise upon surprise tonight.

"Natalie," Jane said cautiously, "are you sure? I mean, maybe you're projecting resentment onto Matt because of his age and education and position or something—"

"Ha!" Natalie cut Jane off like a thundercrash. "Just ask *him!* See what *he* says! *He's* the know-it-all!"

"Well," Jane said, "I *am* getting something on this, but I'd rather you two worked it out . . ." Quickly, with Natalie adding but a few disdainful agreements now and then, Matt described what *he* saw as the situation in question.

"As a monk in the thirteenth century, I had been very earnest," Matt says. "I had taken religion quite seriously . . . [now, in class,] I recalled Natalie as an elder monk by about twenty years, angular, tall, worldly and polished, and infuriatingly coy over issues that to me were of the deepest seriousness and concern. The bone of contention was not the question of faith, but [attitudes] toward it . . . Naturally, if you take this rather straitlaced monk that I was, you can see why Natalie's 'now' reaction was such a snickering assessment, seeing my whole 'serious' trip somewhat re-created in my sermonette on publishing."

In the middle of it all, Jane slipped into a Sumari trance, and delivered a loving song to both Matt and Natalie. "The message seemed to [suggest] a way in which Natalie and I could find a common meeting ground, or perhaps see ourselves in different perspective," Matt says. "I recall a mothering gesture that Jane made with her hands; quite moving. But Natalie reacted to the song with peals of laughter, and I realized that this monk part of me was probably *still* taking it too seriously. Or was Natalie taking it too frivolously? No matter; the implication that *she* understood the Sumari better than I did only irritated me the more.

"Later the class switched to some other topic, but I recall that as everyone was leaving, Natalie practically cornered me, with a big smile on her face, shaking my hand, and insisted that I look her in the eye in man-to-man fashion. The aftershock came when Jane explained to me that the reason for the class's amazement was that up to that evening, Natalie had sat on the sidelines, never opening her mouth! In short, I had produced some major catalytic change in her personality. And the kicker was that Natalie [a regular member from the beginning] never came back to class again!

"This is a yarn I relate to people who are skeptical of reincarnation," Matt adds, a bit tongue-in-cheek. "I say, 'Let's see you come up with a rational explanation for *this!*' And then I dump into their laps the Tale of Natalie and Me."

Jane's books contain several examples of class reincarnational experiences. (See, for example, *Adventures in Consciousness*: chapter 2, "A Reincarnational Drama and Other 'Unofficial' Events"; and chapter 5, "Reincarnation Hits Too Close to Home.") Some of these, like Matt and Natalie's "tiff," were dramatic and volatile; most involved dialogues of coinciding impressions. It would be impossible, and in some ways, pointless, to list them all here. In the end, these dramas represented a stage that class passed through in developing a more flexible awareness of the psyche.

For example, Elmira businessman Fred Lorton started coming to class in its last few years, and never witnessed one of these dramas or got a speck of reincarnational hints from Seth. Instead, Fred tackled the whole issue on his own.

"I have thought about past lives, wondered, wishing that Seth would simply trot out the last six or so and then I could dwell on them," Fred notes. "Using self-hypnosis, encouraged by Rob and Jane, this happened: One life, two sequences. First: finding myself at about 40,000 feet above Egypt, just as one would if you were in an airplane, I looked down at an area west of Alexandria and I shouted mentally, 'I lived there! I lived there!' End of session.

"One week later, under hypnosis, with self-suggestion of continuing the above, I saw a black woman, about thirty, in a small village of less than fifty people, living in a mud adobe hut, like a beehive with a tall pole next to it. [The pole] was the only wood in this desert area, and it looked strange. This girl was me . . . I ate fish and snails. I carried water from a stream in two jugs on a stick across my neck. The hot sand hurt my feet. I was terrified of darkness and thunderstorms. I made pottery but was not good at it.

"The wooden pole by my mud hut was from a small fishing boat that came there and was damaged. I found out that by entertaining these men who came by the sea, sleeping with them, feeding them, they gave me gifts, and I was quite happy.

"No memory of dying or suffering or any great happening," Fred records. "I did get the feeling that I was brought from far inland of Africa. This was as clear or clearer than my memory of yesterday. It was like watching wide-screen movies and lasted about twenty minutes.

"In another self-hypnosis 'short' of five minutes, I saw myself as twelve to fourteen years old, in India: poor eyesight, later became blind. [After waking] I wondered why I didn't feel any great pity for myself. Again, no memory of suffering or death."

In Fred's experiences, the concept of multidimensional existence literally came alive and brought about a revolution in his creative self-confidence besides. Similarly, an emotional understanding of the facets of identity was brought home to Lauren DelMarie, one of the New York group, in a most unusual vision he'd seen—while shaving.

"I was looking into the mirror and noticed that the lighting behind my image was different," Lauren told class. "I felt a little uptight but decided to go with it. The image in the mirror changed completely, and I saw the walls fade away and [become] replaced with a scene in the woods.

"There were a few Southern [Civil War] soldiers, who were standing around a Union soldier who had been captured. One of the men, an officer, I recognized as a different part of myself. That man was telling the captured man that if he did not tell him the information that he/I wanted, that he/I would cut his fingers off one at a time until he did talk. I felt really freaked out by this guy's behavior and wanted the experience to end, and so it did."

Later on, Lauren told class that he'd had several dreams with this Confederate soldier, one in which Lauren found himself "sitting inside his head, looking out of his eyes, feeling his thoughts—And, man, I'm telling you, some of his ideas about war and stuff really made me sick!"[6]

At this point, Seth entered the conversation. "Good evening," he said to Lauren. "And, if you sit inside his head, did it not occur to you that he also sits inside *your* head, and that your ideas change his ideas? For again, you live simultaneous lives. Your thoughts and attitudes now affect, in your terms, your future and your past; and so, through your current experience, that other self becomes aware of ideas that would not otherwise, in those terms, have occurred to him.

"And," Seth continued, grinning gleefully down at Lauren, "he is initially—initially—as appalled by your ideas as you are by his. And yet they do enter into his consciousness, so he wonders where these ideas of cowardice come from! That is *his* interpretation!

"But the knowledge that you have, in his terms, becomes available to him so that he can use it and interpret it in his terms, and therefore, if he chooses, change his behavior. There is always a give-and-take. You are therefore affecting his reality as he is yours, and both of you are learning. For he is sure of his own energy, and from him, you can learn to be certain and proud of your own—though I hope that you decide to use it in a different manner!

"He wakens, you see, from his own dream of you. Now, you will add other interpretations to your dream of him, and your own private dream symbols. And when he dreams of you, he has *his* own private dream symbols. But both of you, in your own way, will both retain the pertinent information."

Seth then turned to the rest of the class. "Now, because we will be dealing with reincarnational material, you can then expect information in your dreams, and also what may seem to you to be some surprising daytime encounters. The very fact of your intent acts as an impetus that will draw to you some of the information that you want. But you will have also to learn to decipher it. The past is now. The future is now. You are not suffering because of any crimes that you have committed in a past [life], and we want that clearly understood!"

In class a few weeks later, George Rhoads reported a dream in which he saw himself as a Scandinavian doctor living in an earlier century. In the dream, the doctor was being terrorized by a gang of men who invaded his house by the sea. George said that from his dreamer's perspective, he recognized that he and the doctor shared similar beliefs about the masses of people being destructive, threatening, and revengeful toward artists, educators, and others who didn't "conform." George said that he thought he might have helped the doctor realize that the invasion situation was brought about through an insistence on these beliefs. "The dream was also, of course, an exaggerated picture of some of my worst fears," George acknowledged.

"You did help him with that," Seth confirmed, whisking away Jane's glasses. "We will indeed become involved in reincarnational activity, and more in depth than you now suppose, when most of you get to that point of realization that the point of power is *now*—that you are not at the mercy of a reincarnational past.

"Why is it, do you suppose, that we have not discussed probabilities in the past?" Seth continued after a long pause. "Because some of you—" Seth leaned back in the chair and shut Jane's eyes "—and I will keep my eyes closed and not embarrass you, but you know who you are—some of you would be so taken by those dogmas that still cling to you, so that as soon as you thought in terms of probable realities and probable events, you would be bound to question, 'Where does karma fit in?' and 'What guilt have I about a probable existence?'

"You are, whether you know it or not, and you *know* it, training yourself. I am not training you; you are training yourself. So that when we deal with reincarnation—and we are dealing with reincarnation now, whether you know it or not, and you know it—then you will use some common sense! Common sense is esoteric!

"But when we deal with reincarnation, you will not automatically throw upon it old dogmas and old beliefs, and find excuses for the guilt that you have been taught to feel. It does you little good if you throw the concept of Original Sin out the window; if you recognize that much of Freud's theories were nonsense; if you recognize that you are not at the mercy of the past in this life; and consider yourself emancipated and free and hip and in—and instead throw upon yourselves the idea of karma, as it is interpreted, and believe instead that you are at the mercy of thirty centuries of a past, instead of thirty years! Where are you ahead? You have dug a grave of theories!

"Therefore, in the framework with which we will study reincarnation, *you* will be at the center. And from that center, you will then look at your future and your past, realizing however that the future is not predetermined—but that the past is not predetermined either!"

In a later class, Seth continued: "The miracle is within each of you now. The reincarnational material that you hoped for, you will find for yourselves . . . but you will also learn that those existences are now. They are simply different focuses taken by your consciousness and awareness."

"Seth?" Warren Atkinson raised his hand. "A question? Is it possible to, at this point, create an incarnation which is in the past, in our terms?"

Seth grinned from one of Jane's ears to the other. "It is indeed!" he roared at Warren. "You do it all the time."[7] Surprised laughter and applause rippled around the room. Seth waited a minute and continued: "When you understand that time does not exist as you think it does, when you put that together with the idea that the point of power is in the present, then you will not feel at the mercy of reincarnational selves, or see probable selves as a bugaboo, chasing your own consciousness through the night! You will see that your reality is now, and that from that reality, probabilities are cast outward as flowers cast outward their seeds.

"Do you therefore deny yourselves the seeds of yourselves? In the time that you know, you willingly and joyfully send out children into the generations of time as you understand it. So do you also send your children, if you want to look at it that way, into probable realities. You give birth to them, again as flowers send out their seeds."

"Well, Seth," Harold Wiles said, "is there anything that would prevent one of those probable selves from deciding to come into *this* physical existence as we know it, through the process of conception and birth?"

"There is not," Seth answered, his voice low and gravelly.

"Now, reality has no beginning and no end. Hopefully—hopefully, hopefully!—in your terms of time, you may get a glimmer of what I mean. There is indeed an expanding universe, and it is formed in the eternal present. You create your own reality. That works, and is true, whether or not you follow, or care to follow, into these other realms; whether or not you care that the universe has no beginning or end; whether or not you have an iota of interest in probable selves. You still form your own reality.

"So it is not necessary that all of you follow [into other realms]. For those of you who [do], however, I promise you an adventure, and a creative alteration of consciousness, and experiences beyond those in your terms that you have known. You look at the world around you and are amazed at its richness and variety—at its physical aspects. Do you think that the inner world is not that rich, and more rich and more valid? Do you think that there is but one kind of consciousness?

"Your world is constantly formed out of the vast unpredictability of consciousness. You form your own ideas of significance, and from it you form your idea of yourself and your world. You must stop thinking in terms of ordinary progression. It is bad enough when you start worrying about keeping up with the Joneses. It is something else, however, when you start worrying about which kind of self is superior to another kind!"

With these evocative hints, the meaning of reincarnation moved through class members' dreams and encounters, reappearing in the fall of 1974 in Seth's idea of counterparts (see *CWS*, book 2, chapter 6); but before we really got into reincarnation again, class ended—leaving us to explore it on our own. But in the final analysis, I keep returning to some remarks that Seth made in July, 1971, during a discussion of the reincarnational drama between Bette Zahorian and Joel Hess.[8]

"I have told you, the regular students, that you are finished with kindergarten," Seth said that night. "You have been telling secrets on another level, in reincarnational terms. It is an extension [of the secrets], an acceleration. I want you to look through the gods and the devils to see beyond these. I want you to look through the victim and the slayer. I want you to look through stereotyped images of good and evil until you understand what your own creativity is. I want you to understand that in this moment in your time, your very cells respond to what I say; not because I say it, but because your cells also speak through my voice and the forgotten portions of you to which you do not listen.

"The voice that cries in the wilderness is your own and the voice that answers from eons of time that you do not understand is your own! You have counterparts—you are not alone.[9] You have brothers and sisters that you do not recognize.

"Stratums that fly through the night, in your terms now, have known consciousness and song. The air that brushes past your cheek is alive. It too has known love and exhilaration, and will again.

"In what I am saying, there are answers for you, if you have the wits to catch on. In the power that you sense [in Seth's voice], there are answers if you have the wits to sense within yourself that same power. To feel within the timbres of the voice the ecstasy that sings through your own being. To listen to all the tales that your selves tell you, to the secrets that fly through the air. And that is what I have been telling you all this time."

CHAPTER 9

The Naked and the Dread: Or How We Took Off Our Clothes and Put On the Opposite Sex

Ode on Sex and Religion

I think religions of the West
misunderstand the naked breast.

I think religions of the East
love the soul but hate the beast.

Worldly gains and subjective slants
have plagued the body of romance.

Hundreds of years of fear and guilt
have come from what the mind has built

and then passed off as Godly laws.
I curse the nuns and bless the whores!
—from a poem by Barrie Gellis, 1976

I am trying to tell you that if you look inward, and study your own
sacredness and creativity and blessedness, and joy and power, as
closely as you study the sacred books of the gods, then you would
realize that all those books of the gods were based upon the greater
reality of the individual—the individual soul, and therefore based
upon your own reality. Do yourselves just honor . . .
—Seth in class, November 6, 1973

FOR YEARS, SETH HAD BEEN PROMISING us a class on sex. We'd badgered him about it on numerous occasions, wanting the nitty-gritty and yet afraid of it. I'm not sure now what it was that we expected. Did we think that Seth would turn into a super Dr. Reuben (a well-known sex therapist at the time) and speak for three hours on the true meaning of the penis and vagina? Did we think that each of us would be given the key to our particular sexual hassles, thereby embarrassing us beyond endurance but creating the love life of our dreams?

I don't think it was ever clear in members' minds. Discussions of the possibilities of Seth On Sex were filled with giddy, wicked glee—like kids wanting to play doctor but afraid they'll get caught. And then when our sexual nitty-gritty class did happen, none of us fully recognized it at the time for what it was.

Actually, the promised sex lesson came in two parts: the "Halloween Transvestite class" of October 30, 1973; and the "Spontaneously Naked class" of May 21, 1974. Both illustrated to perfection the personal incorporation of mass beliefs and how each of us as private people identify as sexual beings upon the earth.

In the fall of 1973, class belief assignments had dared us to reveal things about ourselves—and to ourselves—that in another age might have been considered unthinkable. Nationally, the feminist movement was building up steam. Gay Rights and the gay world itself were emerging as an openly available, if not yet completely acceptable, sexual alternative. Traditional concepts of male and female were exploding into whole new solar systems; beliefs groping, as it were, for new suns to revolve around. And it was class member Dan Stimmerman, who had known since childhood that he was homosexual, who opened the door on the first of our promised sex sessions.

"The problem for me was not that I was one sort of thing and other people were another," Dan says of his position in class. "In the midst of a mostly heterosexual class, I was one of two—most often one—gay members. There was a lot to be worked on, and in fact, my only talk with Seth involved sexual role identities. It wasn't a problem of being different. Being gay had ceased by then to be a problem of acceptance for myself. There was something more."

That October Tuesday, Dan, a talented musician who had played his music and read his poetry many times in class, had been expressing his sharply conflicting attitudes toward sex roles and creativity. Dan was a man and a lover of men; yet he saw men as the aggressors, the destroyers, the unfeeling. He was an artist and poet; and yet he saw creativity as feminine. On the other hand, Dan believed that to be a woman was to be biologically cursed. He admitted to frequent feelings of not existing, of having no identity at all. It was on the heels of Dan's remarks that Seth came through with some pointed comments about this endlessly-wrangled subject of aggression and passivity, male and female, strong and weak.

"Now . . . you do not understand the great aggressive thrust of creativity—the action it demands," Seth said. "It is because you do not understand the nature of passivity—which is aggression, action, that allows itself to follow an inner course of events. You think of creativity as weak, and violence as strong, and do not understand that birth, in those terms, is a violence—for it is an aggressive thrust into a new dimension; and in what you think of as passivity, there is also a joyful aggression.

"When you use the word 'aggression,' you automatically think it is a no-no! You think it means violence against another, or war, or disaster. You do not understand that your least thought, as an action, is an aggression against that which was not before the thought was. And, that the petals of a flower so passively do an aggression against the air as they open.

"You make distinctions and separations where there are none, because you attach such significance and distortion to a word that you use!" Seth concluded. "And now, give us a moment and listen to a song, a Sumari song, 'Aggression and Passivity.'"

Seth retreated, and Jane slid into the Sumari personality, who sang a strange and lovely song to Dan. It seemed that the "female" Sumari used deep, powerful tones and the "male" Sumari sang softly, almost timidly. It was enchanting and amusing. Dan looked stricken with huge, colliding emotions.

Jane came out of trance and lit a Pall Mall, barely listening to the recitation of Seth and explanation of Sumari.

"Listen, people," she said, sudden inspiration lighting up her entire body, "I've got the perfect assignment. It goes right along with all of this. Next week is Halloween, right? Well, listen, we're going to have a *real* trick or treat party. What I want you all to do is this: Each one of you come dressed up like the opposite sex, right?"

Pandemonium broke loose. Screams of laughter and exaggerated limp-wrist gestures flew through the autumn night. "What do you mean, dress up?" Warren Atkinson asked nervously.

"Just that," Jane said. "Dress up in any way you want to, like you think you'd dress if you were the opposite sex."

Pandemonium faded out. We stared at each other. Was this going to be fun, or wasn't it?

During the week, I for one definitely decided that it wasn't. How in God's name was I going to fit my large breasts and cherub face into a man's demeanor? It wasn't possible. Of course, I could stay home the next Tuesday but that seemed like the ultimate cowardly cop-out. "If you don't feel like doing anything, then don't—*I'm* not," another class member advised me, with some disgust.

Tuesday night rolled around, and I still hadn't figured out how to dress up like a man. Actually, at that time my clothes *were* men's clothes. I wore men's jeans and sweatshirts most of the time in an attempt to cover up the pounds that I could never seem to lose. I hadn't put on a dress in years. But I knew that it wasn't an issue of blue jeans and men's shirts. There was a risk involved here that I wasn't quite willing to take—some exposure of my womanhood that I didn't understand and didn't want to understand, either. In the end, I simply went to class dressed sloppier than usual.

I was among the first to arrive. Mary Strand was already there, dressed in boy's clothing, her light complexion darkened with heavy makeup and eye pencil. Priscilla Lantini had darkened her large almond eyes and high cheekbones with garish liner, and looked like a miniature Rhett Butler wearing a three-piece vested suit. She gave me a direct, sexually commanding stare, as a man attracted to a woman might do. It was unnerving—I found myself unable to respond to the make-believe of her act. It didn't feel made up at all. Jesus! What was going on?

"What's the matter, Sue—did you chicken out?" Mary yelled derisively. "I don't know," I shrugged, "I couldn't think of anything to do." This time, I was glad to be preoccupied by the usual bickering that went on between Mary and me—it was rescuing me from other kinds of interaction. Then I heard the door across the hall open and shut, and in walked Jane. She was dressed in green pants and a paisley shirt with a denim vest. A black beret tilted jauntily on her dark hair, and all was topped off by a heavily drawn-on Vandyke beard that gave her the all-around appearance of a rakish Frenchman—a more angular version of the little French character on the old *Hogan's Heroes* sitcom. The women laughed and applauded. Warren and Camille Atkinson sat quietly. Like George Rhoads and me, they hadn't dressed up either. When teased by Jean Strand, Warren announced loudly that there was "no way" that he would be caught "dressing up like a *woman*." His voice was filled with contempt and anger that was really uncharacteristic of Warren, an otherwise tender and empathic man. His attitude now was insulting. What did he fear? What, for that matter, did I?

George was puffing one of his smelly Turkish cigarettes and eying Mary speculatively. "Very good," he said finally.

"Yeah?" Mary countered. "In what way?"

"It's a marked improvement," George said, indicating her boyish costume. "It gets you away from the disguise of a matronly blonde that you usually wear."

Mary gaped at George in astonishment. I thought that she must be hurt and embarrassed—what the hell, George hadn't even participated—but before the conversation could go on, we heard the racket in the downstairs hallway that heralded the arrival of the Boys from New York. They were laughing and carrying on as usual all the way up the stairs—although you could hear, "Darling, please don't treat me this way!" and, "God, I love your eyes! Your lips! Your cleavage!" and you knew what was coming.

In they poured—the guys playing it to the hilt. Will Petrosky had on an ankle-length skirt, but with his usual socks and sandals and old black T-shirt. His long dark hair was frizzed and combed a little fancier tonight, and he had on lots of glossy lipstick, eye shadow, and blusher. He struck a Marilyn Monroe pose in the doorway and mugged some kisses, everyone hooting and catcalling in appreciation. Then he minced in and started playing up to me as though he were a woman seducing a man. He swiveled his hips and let his mouth fall full and slack and wet. I was utterly revolted. Was *that* how I'd looked when I thought *I* was being sexy?

Then Lauren DelMarie waltzed in, swaying sexily in a long thigh-slit skirt and new-stuffed breasts. His shoulder-length hair curled softly against gold gypsy earrings. He giggled and cooed over Jane and kissed her seductively, bending low so his Kleenex bosom brushed against Jane's arm. The rest

of us howled with laughter. Lauren batted his eyes and simpered with maniacal accuracy. We burst into encore applause.

The others began filling up the room. Dan, who often wore makeup in
his private life, came in behind the rest of the New York crowd, a little defiantly. His slender, delicate features had been carefully painted in blues and
golds and he was really beautiful, dressed in a silk pants suit with a long silk
scarf at his waist. Was he cross-dressing or not? The other men might have
been caricatures of what *his* sexuality naturally expressed. Kurt Johns had put
on some makeup but wore his same old clothes. Several others had also made
small gestures toward the Halloween idea, but one thing was obvious: more
of the men were willing to take this a lot farther than the women. The girls
who drove up with the New York bunch had generally done the same as I
had: just put on larger, sloppier clothes. Some wore fake mustaches. Diane
Best had frizzed up her hair and worn men's work clothes, somehow managing to look like Beethoven. One woman smoked a Tiparillo. That was it.

Roaring with laughter, the New York crew described how they'd brought
all their "transvestite" clothes with them in Jed's van to change after they got
to Elmira. "We could just see driving up here all dressed up and the whole
vanful of us getting stopped by the Troopers," Lauren whooped. "Can you
hear the explanation? 'Oh, yeah, officer, well, we're just a-goin' up to the Seth
class where this lady who speaks for a ghost said we should all dress a little,
you know, *funny* for Halloween—yeah, Halloween . . . ' Riiiiight! So we all
changed our clothes in the rest rooms at McDonald's!" What all those people
must have thought as they sat there eating Big Macs while this bunch of
hippies disappeared into the men's room and emerged fifteen minutes later as
hippies of the opposite sex is probably best left unknown.

Gert Barber arrived, puffing on a huge cigar. Like Lauren, she'd stuffed
her shirt—only Gert had stuffed it with brute's muscles instead of breasts.
She looked like a cartoonist's lumberjack. A dark wig and mustache completed her manly picture. "Hiya, chickie," she bellowed at Lauren, obviously
loving every minute of the masquerade. She strode over to her usual chair,
yanked it away from the wall as though she were going to mangle it, crashed
down into a sitting position, and let forth a positively stereotyped beer belch.
Lauren pulled his skirt up to his jockey shorts and daintily adjusted an imaginary stocking, even managing a blush when several of the "men" whistled.
Clearly, the evening was a smash hit in the annals of class. Who would walk
in next?

Downstairs, the ancient, ornate front door banged open again, the noise
echoing up the hallway. (I wondered how the other tenants in this building
stood it sometimes.) Now, from all the way up here on the second floor, you
could hear the *thump! thump! thump!* of uneven, heavy footsteps on the stairs,

a cane thudding on each one like an ax on a tree. "I never saw such a broken-down, moth-eaten, disgusting old house in my life!" the high, nasal voice of an old woman complained from the first landing. I glanced at Jane; she was scowling. How was she going to handle an unexpected visitor on this of all nights?

Jane squirmed impatiently in her rocker. "Will you look at those filthy pictures!" the voice whined from the upstairs hallway's gallery of posters and drawings. "What kind of place *is* this? I was told this was a spiritual meeting and *look* at that trash! My land, I never . . ."

Jane grimaced in dismay and turned toward the door just as a large, rather bulky old woman thumped into the room, thrashing her foxtail jacket around on her shoulders so the animals' glass eyes peered down the immense bosom of her tacky-gaudy matron's dress. Her face was immaculately powdered, her white-blue hair reeked with perfume, and she wore five or six rings on each hand. Utter silence greeted her: Who the hell was this?

"Well, just what kind of jackanape goings-on *is* this?" she yelled, banging her cane on the floor. A few people giggled. She glared out through her granny glasses.

"You know, it isn't nice to laugh at an old lady!" she cackled, suddenly cracking a familiar smile.

"HAROLD!" Jane screamed, and the recognition exploded on us all. For this was not somebody's disagreeable grandmother—it was Harold Wiles himself, class transvestite trump card and Halloween surprise supreme. He fooled everybody, and nobody could believe it. We looked and laughed all night, and dear old Aunt Hattie Harold would grin back and flutter a hankie, taking notes as usual with those horrible ringed fingers.

"I had a ball at that class!" Harold reports. "I understand that they were practically to the point of making book as to whether or not I would come dressed as a woman. Little did those class members know about the 'real me'! I had assistance from a cousin, who loaned me her wig. My wife helped me a great deal with my makeup. I thought I made a damn realistic eccentric old dowager! As I recall, Lauren DelMarie was a gorgeous female! I guess my only disappointment was that so few of the others had the guts to go whole hog into the experiment!"

Harold told class that he'd driven in full costume from his house to Jane's apartment, right through two police roadblocks: one diverting traffic around an accident and one diverting traffic around a fire. "All I could think of was, oh God, what if they stop me?" Harold said. "I finally decided that I'd just keep on playing an eccentric old lady who had her nephew's driver's license by mistake . . . The only thing that worried me about that was, what I would do if they put me in the ladies' jail all night long? How would I go to the bathroom? Can you see the manager of a local business in a mess like that?!"

We started dissecting our costumes and degree of participation. What did our outfits show us about our beliefs concerning male and female roles?

Obviously, both Priscilla and Gert saw the male as powerful and blatant. Camille Atkinson said that Priscilla was transformed from a "downtrodden" female into an image of power—in the form of maleness. Priscilla herself recalls that the Halloween class "let me know what kind of a male I am. Being brought up in a society that pits male against female, it's nice to be your opposite . . . I think it gave me an insight that very few people have."

On the other side of the fence, Lauren and Will had played up the coy, come-on sexuality they saw in femaleness, and they played it with much more power than they allowed themselves as men. You couldn't mistake it—Lauren and Will could get anything they wanted with their wiggles, their simpers, their learned gestures. As men, they normally saw themselves as Woody Allen schmucks. And they felt much more affection for these female selves than for the manhood of Lauren and Will.

Dan had also put on the makeup of an attractive woman, but without taking on "female" sexual attributes in the same way. If anything, he had simply adorned himself with the bright plumage of a sexuality not allowed men in our society—seductive in the way of the cherished, and not of the hunter. It was Dan's portrayal of womanhood that I liked the best, at any rate—Lauren's and Will's were funny, but Dan's just seemed to understand. Was this a nuance of homosexuality?

Yet Gert, who in later years would openly declare herself a lesbian and join a local Gay Rights group (surprising nobody from ESP days), was not portraying a male who was pleasant in the same respect: a physically powerful one, yes, but not a fellow you'd want to take home to mother. But in her way, like Dan, Gert was being defiant and defensive—and crudely vulnerable. Lauren and Will were making fun of themselves as well as encultured female games—and doing a great job of it; but their envy of what they saw as female power was hidden in a mawkish glamour. Nothing about Gert's man was glamorous. He had a sad desperation about him that couldn't laugh about it. It was Gert's idea of true sexual safety, personified. Lauren and Will saw no safety in sexuality whatsoever—it was *all* dangerous. Some was just more effective; and when it came right down to it, women at least could use sex to tap other kinds of power: male power they themselves lacked without having to compromise themselves in the marketplace.

And why hadn't I participated? For that matter, why hadn't most of the women there participated? Was it really our female characteristics that we feared, as the woman's movement told us we did? When I tried to imagine dressing up as convincingly as Harold had, I discovered that the prospect revolted me—so how could I therefore censure Warren for his corresponding sentiments? Did I fear maleness, see it as hiding some unimaginable depth of aggression and violence, as symbolizing in my mind all of the worst our civilization had come to? Did I hold my womanhood up as biologically troublesome, but spiritually superior? Was there a part of me that I protected from the aggression and power I saw as a male society; a part that was relieved to be discriminated against, to be left alone and squirreled safely away, untouched?

I recalled Seth's remarks the week before about our misinterpretation of aggression and passivity. Was Dan expressing his fears tonight of the extremes of both? Was Warren?

Jane's costume was raked over the coals last. We decided that she was definitely a disreputable Left Bank character, probably writing poetry in an attic room overlooking the Seine. Jane loved it. "That's the nicest thing you've said about me in years!" she said with a terrible imitation-French accent. And that, of course, was the perfect line for Seth's appearance.

"You are *all* the black sheep of the universe, and I have told you that before!" Seth began, to a chorus of cheers. "You are all the black sheep of the universe, and I will give you some hints tonight, because tonight—" here, Seth doffed Jane's beret, "I am such a young man!"

We all prepared ourselves for a blistering commentary on our chosen costumes for the evening, with personal analysis of what we had or hadn't done. Instead, Seth's voice went low and intimate. "There was once a god who was not a god—who was not a god, for you are dealing with legends," he said, nearly whispering. "There was a god in ancient Egypt, and his name was Seth, and he was disreputable. And he threw aside establishments, and whenever other gods rose up and said, 'We are the truth, we are pure and we are holy,' this disreputable god stood up, and with a voice like thunder, said: 'You are nincompoops!'"

"Right on, yeah," Lauren chimed in.

"And the other gods did not like him," Seth continued in his story-telling whisper, "and whenever they set up their altars, he came like thunder, but playfully, and tossed the altars asunder, and he said 'Storms are natural, and good, and a part of the earth, even as placid skies are. Winds are good. Questions are good. Males and females are good. Even gods and demons are good, if you must believe in demons. But, structures are limited!'

"And so this god, who was not a god, called Seth, went about kicking apart the structures, and he gathered about him others who kicked apart the structures. And they were themselves, whether they were male or female. Whether they thought of themselves as good or bad, or summer or winter, or as old or as young, they were creators. They were questioners.

"And whenever another personality set itself up and said, 'I am the god before you, and my word is law,' then Seth went about saying, 'You are a nincompoop,' and began again to kick apart the structures. And so you are yourselves, in your way, all Seths, for you kick apart the structures, and you are the black sheep of the religions, and the black sheep of the scientists, and the black sheep of the physicians, and the black sheep of your mothers and your fathers, and your sisters and your brothers.

"And yet, the mothers and the fathers and the sisters and the brothers listen," Seth went on in that quiet voice in that quiet room, "for they do not have the courage to be the black sheep, and they quail in the voice of the thunder that is so playful, though they do not understand it because they equate loudness with violence, and they think that the female is passive, and the male is aggressive, and that war and violence must then erupt from the reality of mankind."

With that, Seth threw back his head and shouted in a voice that rattled the windows: "*And so you are, indeed, all black sheep of the universe, and Sethites have always been the black sheep of the universe!*

"Now, to be a Sethite, you do not have to follow this Seth," Seth said in a lower key. "You simply follow the Seth in yourself, and that Seth in yourself is a questioner, and an explorer, and a creator. And the Seth in yourself knows when to passively flow with the wind that blows through the window above a summer town, and when to go against the force of your environment. You were Sethites before you met me, and there was a Seth before I was Seth, and the spirit follows through the ages as you know them.

"You are being given—and you are giving yourselves—your own lesson this evening about your own beliefs. See that each of you follow through with your own private questions! And I return you to your own disreputable class!"

Black sheep, eh? We laughed and hollered and congratulated ourselves. You could say this was a disreputable class, all right—certainly disreputable enough anyway to do what we had done in this outlandish experiment. (However, Seth would later deflate any budding black sheep cult with the observation that "my analogy should serve you well . . . but a sheep is a sheep! I am not saying that there is anything wrong with a good sheep, black, white, orange, or purple . . . a sheep who follows is an excellent sheep. He is a perfect sheep—becoming what only a sheep can be. He knows what to follow. He has a sense of his own integrity. He does not follow asses, for example. [But] realize that I am speaking on many levels. For no ass tries to follow sheep, either!")

But as often happened to even the most intriguing subjects, we somehow moved away from the implications of the Halloween class. The belief exercises continued; Jane and Rob finally birthed *The Nature of Personal Reality* after months of preparation; Dan left that winter for California; new people came to class; dream events absorbed our interest. Then in May of 1974, on the heels of a debate on the virtues of responsibility versus fun, Seth asked us to write out our beliefs on what we felt responsible for, but did not enjoy; how well such tasks were done and how effective they were; and what we did because it was fun and how effective *those* activities were; and how these ideas of fun and responsibility applied to our children or our parents (depending on the situation).

"I use the word 'fun' purposely," Seth pointed out with great fervor, "because when I use the word 'joy', you can hide behind it, and think, in what you think of as high spiritual terms, for 'joy' sounds spiritual, and 'fun' does not!"

And it became quite clear in class the next week, as we started reading these beliefs, that most of us placed no equation at all between things that were fun and things that were "responsibilities." Fun things were suspect: okay only if all your "real" work were done first. Some members judged fun as lacking responsibility; others appeared to cling to it to save them from responsibility. The gap seemed abysmal. Discussion had been going on for an hour or so, when someone made the lofty remark that our only fundamental duty was to take care of our bodies; it was the "spiritual" responsibility for being alive.

"You knew," Jane said later, "that it was one of those so-called spiritual statements that covered a multitude of stuff." And, reacting to it as only Jane could, she straightened up in her chair and grabbed the zipper that ran down the front of her ankle-length dress.

"Well, if we're gonna talk about bodies, we might as well look at them," she stated, and unzipped to her waist, pulled her arms free, and let the dress top fall into her lap. Underneath the dress, she was naked.

Pandemonium, as it so often did, ensued. Screams of hilarity and surprise rang out. I was sitting on the floor at the opposite end of the long coffee table from Jane; my cousin Mark Disbrow was perched on the sofa arm next to her. Jane shrugged a so-what gesture. "What the hell?" she said. "What could be more innocent than this?" She suggested a break. Nobody moved. Everybody was talking at once.

I didn't dare look at Jane, and I didn't dare not look at Jane. Philosophically, I held social nakedness as inconsequential; gasped over only by Victorian grandparents. In practice, I was embarrassed and uncomfortable to the point of feeling sick. What was behind that kind of reaction? Surely not the sight of another woman's body?

"Okay, if you think it's so great, why don't *you* do it next?" said an angry female voice.

It was Jean Strand, nagging at George, of all people. The two of them were sitting next to each other on the floor at Jane's right. "Well?" Jean demanded, punching George's lotus-crossed leg. "Well? If you're so free and all you do is have so much goddamned fun all the time, then why don't you just toss your clothes off too? Huh? Why not? How come you're keeping *your* clothes on, huh?"

"What if I don't feel like taking them off?" George asked, reasonably enough.

"Oh, the big cop-out!" Jean sneered. "Poor Georgie doesn't feel like it—aw-w-w-w!"

"Well, okay, piss on you! If that's what you want, that's what you'll get!" George shouted wickedly, and he leaped to his feet, untied the drawstring on his old pink and blue tie-dyed cut-off sweat pants, and dropped them and his undershorts to the floor. "There!" he yelled glee-fully at Jean, holding his T-shirt up above his belly button for full effect. "Is that what you wanted?"

Jean Strand

Jean wouldn't look. She hid her face in her hands and screamed.

Immediately, five or six other class members stood up and stripped off their clothes, John Dennison vehemently flinging his trousers across the room. Mary pulled off her T-top but left on her bra. Ira stood up and gulped, "Well, if that's all it is!" and dropped his pants around his ankles, sat down in his chair, stood back up, and pulled his pants back on—a flasher effect. Tim DiAngelo slipped out of his jeans without standing. Derek stripped to his underwear. And finally, Jean uncovered her eyes and removed her blouse— also leaving her bra on. Most of the others just sat, frozen, watching.

I wanted to disappear. I looked longingly at Jane: she was so tiny and lithe, not an ounce of fat. At that moment, I felt like a huge blob of Jell-O, burdened with watermelon breasts, and I was ashamed. There was no reason to feel that way, I told myself—after all, there sat Diane Best, much heavier than I was, with her enormous breasts bared like a magnificent Rubens. But in that moment, I hated myself for not being perfect; worse, I hated myself for hating myself. And then, my cousin topped it all off by saying, "You know, Jane, I gotta say this—you've got terrific tits!"

"Gee, thanks, Mark," Jane said easily. "But you know, *this is what you really are!*" She looked down the length of the table at me. "It is, Sue," she said. "You know that it is."

"Sure," I gulped, wanting to cry. George was replacing his shorts. Most of the others were putting their clothes back on, but Jane stayed bare, smoking a cigarette; and when Seth appeared a few minutes later, her exposed breasts underscoring Seth's voice sparked a fresh round of uncomfortable giggles.

"I simply want you to know that I approve, and I would approve more, and I will approve more, when you avail yourselves of the same freedom," he said, indicating Jane's bare bosom. "Do you realize what it would mean to you if you could? You are all looking for esoteric spirituality. Know thy bodies! Honor thy flesh! Feel the joy of thy corporeal being! Know that thou came naked into the world! The clothes are added. The stances are added. Love thy corporeal being, and deny not the integrity of the flesh. Then you will know what spirituality is. Then will you find the miracle of the marriage of flesh and soul in one, and you will not be ashamed of your bodies, nor afraid to show yourselves.

"If you are afraid to show yourselves in this room, then what façade do you erect for the benefit of others outside of this room? What façades do you erect to hide your own reality from yourselves, simply because you do not understand your own beauty, your own validity; because you are not sympathetic with yourselves; because you do not think of yourselves as lovely women or lovely men, but as errant children to be hidden away from yourselves and from others?

"I challenge you, then, and so does Ruburt, to face and meet the spirituality of your corporeal being! Then you will not need . . . to look to others for truth, but, looking at yourselves in the mirror, you will find the validity of your being and see the expression of All That Is as it is expressed through your individuality. What joy there is within you that you hide from yourselves and others, and what comradeship that you deny!

"Now, these classes are built around the nature of beliefs," Seth reminded us. "And this innocent and innocuous demonstration is meant precisely to make you question your own beliefs about your personal body, and its relationship with others. And that is your assignment for next week: Why did you remain clothed?"

At that, Renée Levine, who had been next in line to read her belief paper on fun and responsibility, uninhibitedly removed her shirt and bra. She held her belief paper in one hand and shook her head at Seth, who had not retreated. The two of them faced one another unashamed. "I feel free to do this," Renée said, gesturing at her body, "and yet I don't feel that that's any great freedom, you know, as far as that goes. I feel it's a very easy thing to do, and I don't think that it proves all of this stuff that you're saying it does."

"The others in the room, who do not find it easy, however, rationalize that it is easy," Seth replied.

"Yes," Renée whispered, "but things they find easy, I might not find easy."

"It is good that you understand that," Seth said, and withdrew, leaving Renée to read her beliefs about fun and responsibility—while topless.

And then things really hit the fan.

Renée's great uninhibited spirit of fun, it seemed, centered on a sexual freedom that the rest of us hardly dared imagine, let alone do. Renée, at age twenty-three, was sleeping with several different men without shame; and moreover read a rather fascinating account of how she'd been managing to usher a string of neighborhood boys into the family basement rec room since the age of thirteen, all without the boys knowing about each other or her parents knowing about any of it. She stated emphatically that while more conventional ideas of sexual behavior pressed in around her, she simply refused to comply against her desires. She would do what she wanted to do until she didn't feel like doing it any more, and that was that. She just loved to do it—and always had. So what? she asked. She felt responsible only to herself, and abided by her own rules. Sex was innocent, and life was fun—period.

Renée put down her belief paper.

To say that the room was thunderstruck would be inadequate beyond measure. Even by 1974, this example of aggressive, casual female sexuality was staggering for most of the people there. Groping for words, Fred Lorton said that he could relate to what Renée had written only as the father of a daughter. "Renée's probably doing okay," he said, "but I just don't relate with real understanding. I try, but . . ."

"Well I'm sorry, but I can't relate to it at all!" broke in Florence MacIntyre, who was sitting behind Renée. "I can't help but think that it's just a gross irresponsibility to act like that—to do that to your parents! How do you think they felt about it, Renée?"

Renée half-turned, her lovely breasts bobbing gracefully. Her calm was incredible—people were attacking her beliefs and she dared stay naked! Jane, also still naked, listened, smoking. "They didn't know," Renée said easily.

"Oh, phooey!" Florence sputtered. "You're acting like a child! A spoiled brat! Throwing yourself around like that. What does it accomplish? What are you contributing to the world, doing that? Nothing!" Florence's face was angry-red, words were tumbling out. "All you care about is yourself! That's not fun, that's just dumb! You're ducking responsibility for yourself, no matter what you think you believe!"

Tears filled Renée's eyes. "I am not!" she replied. "That's what I was trying to say—people press in with their judgments. I mean, what's bad about it? It's just sex, that's all. It doesn't hurt anybody else! I make sure nothing unwanted happens! I love it! It's fun! What difference does it make to—"

"I just don't understand how—" Florence interrupted, but Seth's voice cut in.

"Now, when our Lady of Florence realizes that her joyful self is a most responsible self, then she will realize that when she is being joyous, she is helping others; and when she is not being joyous, she is not helping others," Seth said. "I make, indeed, this statement of great heresy, my delightful Lady. When you are having fun, you are helping others. When you are not having fun, and telling yourself that you are helping others, you are not helping them or yourself!

"So when you think in terms of responsibility, and when you make a division in your mind between responsibility and joyful fulfillment, then you are denying yourself and the world much pleasure, and hiding, my dear Lady of Florence, from yourself and the world the great, joyful symphony that is yourself!

"When you are fulfilling the joyful nature of your being, you are helping yourself, and you are helping others. When you help others because you think you must, but it goes against the grain, then they know it, and you inflict upon them the obligation that you have no right to inflict; and then you say, 'Be nice to me because I am helping you—you have a responsibility' . . . "

"Seth!" Florence interrupted furiously. "Are you accusing me of doing my responsibilities without wanting to, without love for them? I love my work and my responsibility toward my children!" (Florence was a kindergarten teacher.)

"My dear Lady," Seth answered gently, "I am only trying to open you up to the love of your being, and to knock down the barriers in your own mind between what this girl [Renée] has said, and your interpretation of her experience and her remarks. I am only trying to acquaint you with the lovely joy of *your* own being, and help you melt those barriers that you still hold on to; that divide you from the joyous experience of your own nature."

Seth sat forward in the rocker, jutting Jane's chest out, eyes sparkling with glee. "Now, to show you how responsible *I* am, and how *nasty* the word 'fun' is, I have this to say [to all] of you!" he roared, flipping Jane's right nipple with his thumb in an outrageous burlesque-dancer move. "Oh, my God!" someone squealed. Seth waited for us to stop laughing and blushing, and then turned, with great tenderness, to Florence again.

"When you follow your own nature, you automatically and naturally feel for the needs of others," he said to her. "When you are joyful and free, and when you are having fun, you automatically feel . . . your oneness with all other creatures of the universe, and you know your place in All That Is. And when you are yourself, others look upon you with awe and joy and understanding, and you look the same upon them. And you help every other creature that shares with you the framework of this earth . . .

"When you recognize the joy of your own being, you give joy to others. All I ask from you—and no one has asked more, or less—is that you acknowledge the joyful right of your being to existence, and follow its great joyous nature, and *that* is fulfilling any responsibility that any god or self could put upon you!" Seth then added, "[Florence] knows that I love her, and she is simply not willing to acknowledge the fact that she can love herself. And that applies to each of you!"

Florence—as usual in these situations—was not convinced. Renée was slipping back into her clothes, much to the disappointment of Harold Wiles, who later remarked that he was thoroughly annoyed with Renée for sitting with her back to him the whole time she was topless.

"So I return you to yourselves," Seth observed. "Do you want to be returned to your conventional clothed selves? Then at least in your minds, divorce yourselves from those limitations, and even you [here he nodded at Mark] who think you are so free, I have only one thing, again, to say to you as long as you do your assignment for next week, and feel, of course, responsible enough to do it: again, it is this!" And Seth flipped Jane's nipple in Mark's direction. Mark laughed loudly, but most everyone else either forced a few giggles or sat in silence.

"If you find that sacrilegious, then examine the nature of your beliefs," Seth admonished, as it was clear that all of us were horrified to some degree. "It is too bad—you have lovely bodies—that you decided to hide them and what they represent."

During the week, I wrote a tortured essay on why fat was embarrassing. Camille refused to go farther than declaring herself "a very private person." Harold pondered the whole mess for days and wrote exactly nothing. In class the following Tuesday, however, Geoffrey Beam read a wonderful, funny, honest paper suggesting that clothing might be a fortress, built to represent specified characteristics that we want others to see and react to, "but at the same time carefully concealing that which we wish were not a part of us, and which we do not want others to know about . . . within which we hide ourselves from the world." Florence read her essay on not undressing, describing the creativity that could be expressed with clothes, and nicely skirting the battle of Renée's sexual beliefs from the week before—which was, of course, the perfect entrance for Seth, who assured Florence, "You cannot plead innocence, because you know me, and I know you, too well!"

Seth appraised each member of the class, one at a time, his eyes bright and knowing, before he went on. "You think of your bodies as you think of responsibilities!" he finally stated. "You think that vulnerability is wrong. Your freedom lies in your vulnerability to life, sensation, experience, song and being—being is vulnerable. It reacts. It lives. It feels. You cannot deny feelings without denying portions of your soul. Your attitudes toward your bodies are like your attitudes toward responsibility! Think of the correlation!

"When responsibility means doing what you do not want to do because you think that you should do it, then responsibility is not fun. Neither is it true responsibility, because you are not responding as an alive individual being. You are, instead, blindly following. You are not giving when you think that you are giving because you must be responsible, when you do not want to be.

"You do not help anyone when you help them but do not want to, in your terms . . . When you say, 'I love you' because you think you have a responsibility to say, 'I love you,' when you do not feel the emotion behind the words, then you are a liar, and the other person knows it.

"Naked! Think of it in a different way! Think of it as being joyfully free of those fortresses that you have that you do not recognize—that you are not as honest about having as our friend over here [Geoffrey]. At least, he is aware of his fortress, and to some extent he can and does make a palace of it.

"In the most vernacular of terms, you are beautiful people. There is nothing about yourselves that you must fear or be ashamed of. Your bodies on this earth serve as a representative of your soul . . . When you realize that there is nothing you need to hide, you are free to hide anything you want, out of your own desire or your own intent, but not because you are forced by your own fears to stand clearly before yourself or others.

"Now, you may look at pictures of animals—old animals, skinny animals, fat animals, wounded animals, beautiful animals, ugly animals. You may look at them . . . and think, 'What uniqueness!' And you see the integrity and uniqueness of the animals as you perceive them. Yet, you look at your own body images blindly, and if they do not live up to some ideal that you have set for yourselves, then you refuse . . . them what you would gladly give to any animal. You do not admit your own beauty—any of you—in flesh.

"If you see a wounded animal, you may still enjoy its beauty, or see it in its environment. You do not judge a twig as to which direction it grows in—up or down or straight or crooked. You can meditate over a twig, and yet you look at your own bodies and will not admit their validity, and when you do not admit their validity, you are putting your inner self down in a most vernacular of terms.

"If you are forty, you want your body to be twenty; if you are fat you want it to be skinny; if you are skinny you want it to be fat. You want a body that is not individualistic, a body that is not you. But your body *is* you and speaks your being and no one else's.

"The soul in flesh shows its individuality through its bone structure, the expression in its eyes, the tip of its ear, the tiniest joint in the smallest toe, the crook of its elbow, in the vagina and in the penis, and the hair and the fingernails, and all portions of the physical image."

When Seth withdrew for the last time that evening, and Jane rolled out of the long, deep trance, Mary Strand said, "Well, Seth just gave us our sex class, I suppose."

"You gave it to yourselves," Jane murmured. And although there had been other classes in which Seth had discoursed about sex roles,[1] you certainly couldn't deny that actions—our own actions—had literally fleshed out his words and shown us our creaturehood as we chose to live it. And while other encounter-type groups have indulged in disrobing to discover hang-ups and freedoms, I'd bet that very few of them were willing to hang their spirituality on the flip of a barenaked nipple.

"Looking back on the naked class, it seems carefree now," Mary Strand says. "There was very little nudity—some tops were bared; George and my sister did a quick pull-down that seems childishly hilarious in retrospect. Sue W. didn't choose to participate, and I removed my halter, which was daringly wicked by past and present standards, but it was spontaneous fun and sensual without losing innocence and deteriorating into the lurid."

"The 'naked class,'" Geoffrey Beam muses, five years later. "Certainly an unusual class, though not entirely unpredictable. I was mildly surprised by it, somewhat amused, somewhat offended; but at least it provided an outlet for some diverting commentary, along with an opportunity to suggest the idea that the clothing we select may serve as literally a costume . . . "

"It was really strange about that class," Jane recalls. "I was forty-five years old and I guess I figured that if a forty-five-year-old could take off her clothes, the others couldn't help but come out ahead! I thought the younger ones would have fewer inhibitions because they had great bodies, but it didn't work that way!

"Tim DiAngelo, for instance—he was in his early twenties and a physical-fitness bug—he had a great body! Yet he was embarrassed and actually apologized, saying that he'd had a better body when he was younger! Actually, the ones between twenty-five and thirty were more spontaneous . . .

"And spontaneous it was!" Jane laughed. "If I'd planned ahead of time to do that, I would have been too inhibited—I think . . . "

CHAPTER **10**

The Experiment Continues: Seth II, Mental Events, and the Birth of the City

Notes To a Young Man
To Dan

I

It has come to my inattention
That you neither attend nor inattend,
But see through the gods' illusions
And prayerfully refuse
To play a game.

Be careful in nothing.
Sidewalks are for a reason.
The half-wise can slip
Through his own footsteps
And find no hold.

II

The housewife polishes the drinking glass,
Cherishes the wood-dreaming table,
Shapes teacups and saucers from chunks of space,
Places them upon waxed squares of nothing
With a smile.

Help sculpt this dear nothingness
Into form so impermanent and lovely.
Hold up the universe. Attend
With love and sly wonder. The gods turn
Illusion inside out to truth.

III

Be careful of nothing.
The gods poke playful fingers through your cheeks
And roam like cosmic worms
Through the multi-dimensional apples
Of your smiles.

IV

The stupid say, 'The trees are real.'
They are wrong, but safe for now.
Their shade will disappear when the trees vanish.
Without bodies they will stagger
Like headless chickens.

The half-wise say, 'What illusion!
The shifting forms are shadows. I dismiss them.'

And precisely here the shapes are real
And trees weigh tons.
Beware a wind storm.

V

The wisemen say, 'The trees are real illusion.'
They are right and their shade
Will outlast trees.
They look out smiling
Through the faces of the molecules.

They spin astoundingly
Through the china cups and saucers.
Laughing, they pluck cherries out of thin air.
Be careful in nothing. Attend without attention.
How astonishing the game.

—Jane Roberts

Be alert for what seems to be coincidence. The things you
tell yourselves cannot be—those things are.

—Seth in class, July 16, 1974

It is not that your being exists in a lesser reality. It is that
you have not learned to recognize the extent of the reality
in which you do exist.

—Seth II

THE SEASONS ROLLED THEIR WARES through Jane and Rob's apartments; winter bringing its icy, rattling winds against the house, summer its faithful flock of hungry pigeons to the rooftops. The publication of Jane's books was bringing more and more people to class, too: visitors packed the living room, side by side with regular members, until some nights you were literally squeezed shoulder to shoulder. (One night, Mark Disbrow avoided the sardine situation in the apartment doorway by going back outside, climbing up the drainpipe, and crawling in through the kitchen window.) There was an acceleration permeating those Tuesday nights, and you could feel purpose and intent there even when it seemed that the same questions were being answered for the fiftieth time. Like the thread of the seasons, a constant multitude of events wound their ways through the fabric of Jane's class, just beneath the surface of the experiments, discussions and developments.

Sometimes we'd drop a subject, and months or years later it would reemerge within the context of other things that, superficially, seemed unrelated: the secrets sessions acting as a kind of training ground for the belief exercises; the door experiment serving to wake up our perceptions in dreams, leading us into "class" dreaming. Sometimes in our excitement, skepticism, or cursory treatment of a class event or Seth session, we'd completely overlook how we'd gotten to that point; or how our previous experiences had been lying dormant like seeds, ready to burst new growth upon us when we were properly warmed to the occasion.

"People didn't understand that at the time," Jane says. "They'd want so many classes on reincarnation, or so many on Sumari—but it just didn't *work* that way."

Actually, the psychological restructuring process that class provided as we learned a larger concept of identity wasn't apparent to me until recently, when I read through the 300 or so class Seth sessions in preparation for this book. It was then that I recognized some of those threads of events, and how their appearance led us into the literal wellspring of our daily lives.

In the summer of 1969, the personality of Seth II appeared in class for the first time. Jane had encountered this "larger" aspect of Seth during a session in April of 1968 (as described in *The Seth Material*), so we knew something about him (or her, or it—or whatever). But seeing this transformation was something else again.

Seth had been talking to us that night about psychological stability ("I wanted someone with a strong enough ego-structure to contain what will amount to forty years of mediumistic experience," Seth had been saying of Jane) and the many forms within personality. Speaking through Jane, Seth was as animated and jovial as usual, gesturing at Jane's overflowing ashtray and joking that "there are two simple requests that I have made—one, I have been asking Ruburt to stop smoking cigarettes, a dirty habit, and smoke cigars—and he will not do so!"

"What brand would you like?" offered Brad Lanton, who was taping and transcribing the sessions at that time.

"A fat one!" Seth answered, and paused, waiting for us to stop giggling about his beloved cigars and brandy that Jane soundly refused to consume on his behalf.[1] Then Seth turned gentle and soothing. "What I want you to know is this," he said, "I come here, I hope, as an endearing personality with characteristics that you can understand. Now these characteristics have been mine, and they *are* mine; and I am who I say I am. And yet, the Seth that you know, and that you find so endearing and understandable, is but a small portion of my reality—the portion that can relate with you most easily."

Seth looked at each one of us in turn, as though we were all cherished children. I remembered Rob's description of one of the first times Jane had actually spoken in Seth's voice. At the time, Jane had refused to sit down for the sessions, instead pacing the floor while in trance. Rob said that Jane, as Seth, walked to the big bay windows and stood there for a few moments, watching the falling snow glittering in the pale streetlights and hushed, winter cityscape. It was with that same nuance of long-ago that Seth spoke to us then: "It is a portion that has been physical . . . [to Theodore] that can understand your being overwhelmed with work; [to me] it is a portion that can understand your being full with child [I was six months pregnant]; [to Lydia] it is a portion that can understand the aspirations that you were unable to fulfill . . .

"And this part that you see and that appears in this room, and that can show joy, and show its existence and reality, that can call to you beyond space and time, that shows such energy, that shows you what energy can blow through such a small and slight frame [Jane's]—that self is a small part of my reality," Seth went on, leaning back in the chair and closing Jane's eyes. "For some time yet, you will need its familiarity. And you will need the human characteristics that you know—and that were mine—and they are still mine, for this self of mine that I show to you does still exist and grow.

"But beyond that self, there is another self, and still another self, of which I am fully aware. And that self can see through physical reality. And to that self, physical reality is like a breath of smoke in air—and that self does not need the characteristics that you know and find so endearing. And yet it is not an unemotional self; it is a self that has condensed emotions; and, it is not distant."

During this monologue Seth's voice boomed out louder and louder; but as it ended, Jane very abruptly came out of trance. However, instead of reaching for her glasses as usual, she stayed back in the chair, opening and closing her eyes. "It's like—I'm getting this pyramid effect," she said slowly, making a triangle shape with her hands over her head. "I'm getting that feeling like this pyramid coming down over my head and like I'm being pulled up through it—I mean, I know it's just an image, but . . ." her words trailed off; her eyes closed; her hands relaxed on the rocker's wide armrests. Indeed, it seemed that Jane's entire body shifted into a neutral gear, as though no personality were in it at all.

We watched, nonplussed. What the dickens was this?

Jane took several deep breaths, inhaling and exhaling in long, drawnout swoops of air, licking her lips repeatedly. And then she began to speak—

in a thin, high, completely unanimated voice that sounded like nothing human; like the voice that would speak for mathematics, if mathematics found its own voice. Brad had to turn up his recorder microphone as far as it would go to catch the high, flat words whining from Jane's lips: "And that self tells you that there is a reality beyond human reality, beyond human characteristics that you know . . . and within that reality, even I am dwarfed and there is knowledge that can never be verbal," the voice said. "And there is experience that can never be translated in human terms.

"Although this type of existence seems cold to you, it is a clear and crystal-like existence in which things are known that are beyond your comprehension—in which no time is needed in your terms for experience—in which the inner self condenses all human knowledge that has been received by you through your various existences and reincarnations, and it has been coded and exists indelibly."

Jane paused, licking her lips again. The words came slowly but steadily, without inflection, never varying from that high, computerlike whine. "Know," it said, "that within your physical atoms now the origins of all consciousness still sings and that all the human characteristics by which you know yourselves still exist within the eye of all our consciousness, never diminished but always present.

"So I am the Seth that is beyond the Seth that you know. And in me, the knowledge and vitality of that Seth still rings. In your terms, I am a future Seth. But the terms are meaningless to me, for he is what I was in your terms.

"We form the reality that you know," the voice continued. "We have spoken to you since the beginning of your time. We have inspired and helped those of your prophets who have looked to us . . . We want you to realize that there is consciousness without form; that there is consciousness with will and vitality that comes to you from beyond even those places that your Seth knows. We want you to realize that though it is hard for us to communicate, we spoke with your race before your race learned language. We gave you mental images, and upon these images you learned to form the world that you know.

"We gave you the pattern by which your physical selves are formed. We gave you the patterns, intricate, involved, and blessed, from which you form the reality of each physical thing you know. The most minute cell within your brain has been made from the patterns of consciousness which we have given you. We gave you the pattern upon which you formed your entire physical universe . . . and the comprehension that exists within each cell, the knowledge that each cell has, the desire for organization, was given by us. The entire webwork was initiated by us. We taught you to form the reality that you know."

The voice stopped. Jane sat still for several minutes, only her eyes moving back and forth beneath her closed lids.

Finally, Sally Benson reached out and touched her arm. "Jane?" she called. "Jane? Jane, are you here?"

"Yeah, I'm here," Jane said, her eyes still shut. At last, she opened her eyes, sat forward, and put on her glasses. "Whoosh!" she said. "I've still got that pyramid thing. I guess that was Seth II, right?"

In *The Seth Material* Jane described the Seth II phenomenon as "a future development" of Seth, containing the "present" Seth (and by implication, the "present" Jane) and yet as being more than that, with its own gestalt enriched at least to some degree by Jane's ability to contact it.[2] "Living past, present, and future," Jane said to us. All very fascinating— and unsettling. "Where is our old Seth?" Rachael Clayton demanded. "Is he going to come back, or is he gone for good?"

Rachael shouldn't have worried. By the next class, the "old" Seth was indeed back, joking and bantering with us as usual. But Seth II wasn't gone either; this personality appeared throughout class years, typically two or three weeks in a row at a time—and each time with the similar message: about a level of consciousness from which the physical universe as we know it had been birthed.

In a class that fall, Seth had been talking about reincarnation when he began to speak again of how the characteristics we knew him by were "only a *small* portion of [his] reality." "I use them often," he said, "as teaching tools. I appear to you . . . in familiar ways, so that you can sense the bonds between us that *do* exist. And yet there are freedoms that have nothing to do with human consciousness as you understand it. There are roads you will follow, and you will look back on the selves that you know as the first bare glimmerings of your birth.

"And so when I speak to you, I speak to you often in sympathy and compassion that you know so little and have so far to go—and yet you travel a road that I have also traveled, and so I can, to some extent, enter into your existence and understand reality as it appears to you . . ."

This time, aware of certain cues in Seth's words and of a feeling of acceleration in his speech, we suspected what was happening. And sure enough, Seth's voice trailed off, and Jane slipped into that strange Seth II trance, her body completely motionless except for her lips—in direct contrast to Seth's energetic self.

"Let the human characteristics by which you know me fade into their proper perspective," the thin, flat voice began. "Seth as you know him is in my own past, a reality that I scarcely remember. He is a portion of my reality and as such he continually exists. He does now exist in his own reality. Yet to me, all that is past.

"I am not only what he will one day become, in your terms, I am far more. And in me your Seth, while remaining a developing identity on his own, is a distant memory in my consciousness. We sent him to you, in your terms, in some indescribably distant past. He entered your universe in a reality I find difficult to remember. He gave guidance to your kind for eons of your time . . .

"I do not sufficiently understand the experience in which you are presently involved in your terms," the voice continued, and it was clear from the expression of that voice that the senses, as we knew them, were outside this being's experience. "We are involved in forming creations, realities, consciousness—worlds that are beyond your comprehension. Within these, Seth as you know him is a shadow within my awareness. Yet he is part of what I was. There seems to be a dim connection between him and the Ruburt that you know . . .

"We form the realities, we give birth to universes; but within you now I can tell you is the breath of creativity, the source of All That Is, of which you are a part . . ."

Jane stopped. Smoothly, she opened her eyes and the "regular" Seth spoke. "Now," he said, grinning, "we will come to get our good friend [Ruburt] back. He is lost in the Netherlands. Give us a moment."

Eventually, Jane came "back down through that damn pyramid thing," as she put it, and called a break; but almost immediately afterward, Seth II returned: "Do not imagine that we are not individuals or that because we seem alien to you that we do not know joy or creativity," it said. "Our joy forms universes . . . we possess the energy that gives your sun light . . . You each exist in my 'now' though you would not recognize the selves that you are. You will help create these realities of which I speak."

"I don't like that person," Rachael stated with finality as we discussed Seth II in a later class. "I want *our* Seth back! That thing is like talking to a machine—except that you can't really talk *to* it. Ugh!"

"He is not as scintillating as I am—but he has his reasons!" Seth responded, entering the conversation. "Now, despite my good-humored remarks about the personality you call Seth II, let me tell you something: You cannot translate the dimensions of his personality. What he is cannot be translated in your terms. His thoughts are not translated in those terms because you cannot rightfully call them thoughts in the way you are accustomed to thinking of thoughts! To him, a thought is a creative experience. What he thinks immediately *is* . . .

"His energy is beyond my knowledge—and his creativity is beyond my knowledge. I will not grow into what he is—we have our own ways to follow. And yet we are connected. And some of my energy, you see, also comes from him. Now, I happen to like *my* worlds better. Otherwise, I would not come here so often. I have always dealt with emotion, but *he* deals with those realities that make emotion *possible*."

Even though Seth would tell us many times over the years that he did not speak symbolically to us—or that his symbols were filled with quite personal, literal meaning—most of the import of these class sessions flew over our heads, leaving it more or less up to Jane and Rob to examine what was going on beneath their surface. And I know that there were times when understanding eluded them, and Jane considered ending class altogether; for one thing, while these feats of personality emanated from her own psyche, she wasn't even "there," so to speak, for most of their manifestations. Yet all of us were there in the first place because we at least suspected that we were far more dimensional creatures that we'd been led to believe in the past. And so I wonder how we could have missed the implications of the Seth II personality. At the time, I think we saw it as a weird but impersonal "Seth extension" whose words were eerie rhetoric, meant to demonstrate another of Jane's multifaceted abilities. I think now (as with the "regular" Seth), this personality's words combined literal and symbolic intent in a way that simply confounds our usual one-line consideration of events.

In January of 1970, the familiar Seth gave a long, emphatic dissertation on "rules," as he put it: "You create your universe—you create, within the system that you know, the world that you know. The rules are that within you there is knowledge and that you must look inward, not outward, to find it. The rules are that this universe is created by the thoughts that exist within each of your minds . . . and there are no exceptions."

As Seth finished his assurance that we in the physical universe "are not left alone or abandoned," Jane paused in trance, stilled Seth's exuberant gestures, and began speaking in the high, distinct voice of Seth II: "You do not understand multidimensional personality structures," it said. "This does not mean that they do not exist. It is true that our reality cannot be translated in your emotional terms. Emotions, as you know them, represent but the smallest glimmerings of our reality." Jane paused again, as though waiting for some vast distance to be breached. "We have always watched," the voice said, more softly than ever. "We are the watchers and the protectors—and you have never been alone. We tend you carefully as a gardener tends his beloved plants. We are concerned with your growth and nourishment.

"There are developments within your own identities with which you are not presently aware . . . you are indeed learning to be creators, and you are already, in your terms, creators.

"And by the products of your creations shall you learn to see yourselves and know what you are. And through the mirror of physical reality do you see materialized the inner selves. And through your creations shall you realize your abilities and your responsibilities, even as we."

With that, Jane was speaking for the old familiar Seth: "You are, I hope, in the midst of a garden of consciousness. And as a flower blooms, so are you made to bloom. And as a flower is supposed to flower, so are you meant to flower. You cannot see the garden, although you are in it, but there are emanations that are invisible to you. And I would be very happy if I were you, that there was someone around to keep order and to keep an eye on things and to take care of your spiritual nourishment when you had forgotten what the spirit was."

Florence MacIntyre, who had been quietly sipping wine up to this point, wrinkled her nose in disgust. "I certainly don't see *myself* as any old flower," she said. "I'd hate to have to depend on somebody else watering me!"

Seth turned to Florence with mock severity. "You see yourselves in physical form, and the analogy of plants upsets you . . . because you consider yourselves above a plant, and do not realize what a fine consciousness they possess," he said. "And yet, as a gardener sometimes at night walks through his garden and observes his plants, and gives added fertilizer to some, and waters others, and arranges others so that they get more sun—so your own entity walks through your soul and whispers instructions. And it would do you all well to listen!"

So, it flew past. Gardeners walking among the flowers? Was Seth II as far above us as we were above the plants? Well, maybe—if you accepted the idea of anything being "above" anything else.

In any case, a year and a half passed by. We told our secrets. The reincarnational dramas were running their brief course. Class dreams were increasing in frequency and detail. We played with different stages of alpha consciousness and became pretty adept at changing focus. Seth and Jane led us through expansion-of-consciousness exercises, using alpha states to perceive probabilities, meet various portions of the self, or just to get the "feel" of our own minds. (See *CWS*, book 2, appendix 1, for example.)

One Tuesday in June of 1971, Seth came through and suggested that we close our eyes and try to imaginatively follow his voice.[3] "In alpha 1 you are used to one short adjacent step away from what you call your consciousness," he said during the long, soothing soliloquy. "Now I want you to take one step beyond this. I want you to realize that you are indeed highly perceptive, that around you and about you in all directions, the inner senses reach; that you are in the midst of other realities, you are in the habit of blocking them out, and you are now learning to accept them; to open doors that have been closed . . .

"Beyond that door are realities of which you have always known and people with whom you have always been acquainted. I want you to freely open the inner eyes and see their faces. Open the inner core and hear their voices.

"I want you to walk freely and with joy within these other realities that exist now as surely as this room exists . . . and so one by one, the inner senses can begin to operate so that what you see can become clear and what you hear can become vocal and clear and strong . . . I want you to realize that you are getting glimpses of a reality that exists now, in your terms; that existed in the past; and in your terms, will exist in the future . . . "

After about fifteen minutes of these smoothly delivered directions, Seth told us, "Return fondly to your image and the knowledge of it, to the intimate knowledge of flesh and bone and cell; to the intimate knowledge of the earth from which now at least you spring . . . trust it and open your eyes and return your attention to the room."

During this exercise, many of us had experienced vivid mental images. I'd found myself standing beside a man who was in the middle of describing points of interest in the surrounding environment—which consisted of a flat, vast geometric plain leading to a distant city.[4] I felt as though I'd been daydreaming about a group of people I'd known long ago, instead of paying attention to the conversation at hand. Just then the man asked me a question, and I was quite embarrassed, since I'd been thinking about these people I'd once known and hadn't been listening to my companion at all. I was totally within this scene; in other words, it was not "just" an imaginary fantasy.

My friend was watching me curiously, however, even knowingly. "Do you know my name?" he asked.

I did, of course. Yet when I tried to think of it, I couldn't place it— the name had slipped right out of my head. At this point, I realized that Seth's voice had been in the distance all the time, and that I'd been conscious of his directions. Then I also realized, with some disappointment, that I didn't really belong here with my friend—yet. It was this place, I then remembered, that was the "daydream," not the room full of people that I'd remembered so fondly. But since my body was definitely there on the plain with this man, and not in that living room, as far as I was concerned, I felt rather confused.

"My name is Jason," the man said. "We've been associates for a long time." With that remark, I heard Seth's voice tell us to imagine our altered perceptions as a doorway. At once, a door opened within a huge pyramid that appeared on the horizon behind us. I knew that Seth would be ending the exercise soon, and I would be leaving my friend and that distant city. "Come back there with me," I suggested, referring to Jane's living room. "Can you do that? Wouldn't it be fun if you could?" We walked through the doorway, but when I opened my eyes in class, he wasn't there— of course. And now it felt strange to be remembering him, and that strange, geometric plain, as if it had been a dream.

Members described what they'd seen; several had encountered scenes as vivid and as utterly "real" as I had. It was exciting and intriguing. And although I never thought about that Jason character again until I read Jane's account of this class in *Adventures in Consciousness,* I assure you that those moments on that flat plain were every bit as "real" as any collection of moments that I can recall from my life as I know it.

"I am not finished with [class]," Seth said, entering the discussion. "We are going to get into more of an emotional level [in class]. I will not let you forget that, you see, but for tonight the experiment is not over . . . I want to give you a brief moment in which you sense, to some extent, the vast distances in which your own reality has its meaning, and the other dimensions of existence in which you also have your part."

Then Jane sat back in the chair, and after a long wait—at least five minutes—she started speaking for Seth II, her body once again gone slack.

"Certain translations are being made for you so that these communications make sense to you," Seth II said. "We help you maintain your lives as you help maintain existences of which you have no knowledge. We watch you as you watch others, yet so vast is the distance, in your terms, that communication is difficult.

"We do not watch as human forms. You perceive us that way in a distorted view. In your terms, our forms would be geometrical. We do not understand too clearly the nature of the reality that you are creating, even though the seeds were given to you by us."

I think that all of us were somewhere in the stages of alpha, the effects of the consciousness exercise still whispering through us. But I for one certainly snapped-to when I began to feel, subjectively but powerfully, that the room was *crowded with observers*—that's the phrase that kept running through my head—and when I looked up toward the high, white ceiling, and saw, to my considerable surprise, dozens of giant-sized faces looking placidly back.

I glanced around at the others. People were staring off in all directions, including at the ceiling, but some, like Bette Zahorian, were hastily taking notes. Seth II was continuing in that distant voice. I hardly listened to the words. The faces had stayed there, all around the perimeters of the ceiling: large, oval-shaped, cartoonlike faces, somewhat bloated and completely unanimated just like Seth II's voice. I assumed at the time, of course (as class members in general would), that there weren't faces up there in the same way that, say, our faces were in the room; just as I knew that my friend of the pyramid door hadn't been here in the same way that this living room was. On the other hand, it was ridiculous to deny my experience of that reality. I knew I'd been in a place that existed, in some fashion or another, although not in the same order of events as my usual daily life.

It's the same kind of credence that we'd learned to give our dreams: realities of complete validity, with meaning not only *for* us but *from* us; and while dreams don't infringe on daily physical life (or shouldn't, in those terms), they certainly enrich it—and more, make it possible in fundamental ways.

The same was true of these faces, except that in this case there was a physically-expressed image perceived, as it turned out, by many of us. And it would be a long time before the meaning of this kind of experience, and its relationship with my perception of Jason's reality, dream realities, and the circumstances of the daily physical world, would start to connect.

The faces vanished; Jane came out of trance. The room exploded in an uproar of talking, shouting people. At least a half a dozen of us had seen the crowd of round, expressionless faces around the ceiling. Several others who hadn't seen these images had strongly sensed "the watchers." Bette was particularly emphatic about the feeling that masses of beings— not human beings—had filled the living room during Seth II's speech. (In fact, she seemed quite insulted by it!) Two others had seen a pyramid over Jane's head while she'd been in the Seth II trance. And all of these impressions had been noted without cross-comparison, in a fully lighted room, with varying degrees of involvement.

The following week, Seth II came through once again, telling us several times that "the experiment continues." Experiment? What experiment? Whose experiment? "Who's his control group?" Joel laughed. And now and then we'd bring up this "experiment" and joke about how we were doing—and never associate the appearance that fall of Sumari, for example, with its "crowd" of people felt in the room by many of us; with its perception-shattering nonlanguage; with the first few words spoken by Jane in Sumari trance: "It is with this chant always that we begin our endeavors in our space . . . there are cities that we have built that you have helped build in other areas in your time . . . we have been here many times, and you have been where we are." For that matter, we didn't connect Seth II and the "experiment" with the concurrent upsurge in class dreaming; or with the emotional meaning of the belief exercises; or with any of these activities that were at least attempting to visualize other portions of our identities.

The realm of imagination had simply not been granted its due, even by this class. Subjective reality was interesting, fascinating, filled with exciting possibility, charged up to the eyeballs with emotion and outlets of expression—but not really a force in the world as we thought of it. We weren't aware of our own changing conscious stance, and of the personal meaning for each of us in Jane's expression of Seth, Seth II, Sumari, and all the rest—of the personal, practical meaning of mental events.

It's my opinion that all of these connections—along with the applicable meaning of mental events—emerged as a new kind of conscious awareness in class with the birth of the "city."

The fall of 1974 was brilliant and warm. Correlating dream reports were multiplying every week. Was it the magic of autumn? Many of us, myself included, had series of dreams about swimming across powerful rivers, or backward against whirlpools, or of being otherwise at odds with any kind of direction. "Like being in the transitional stage of birth contractions," I wrote in my dream notebook in late September. Two nights in a row, I was awakened at 3:00 A.M. by strange noises on my front porch: once by the sound of a huge dog barking by the door; and next by the sound of someone knocking furtively and turning the knob. Both times, I'd opened the door, terrified and armed with a baseball bat, just as the noises quit—and found nothing there. My house was on a rural road, the closest neighbor two miles away. What was I hearing?

Nationally, politics seemed drearier than ever. President Nixon had resigned from office, but only after calling the U.S. military to an alert status in the Middle East that summer. Some called the alert a sham on Nixon's part to try to improve his national image. Whatever his reasons, it brought the specter of war and the Bomb to the surface once again. Class members grumbled dejectedly that first Tuesday in October: in spite of anything we did and said in that room, the human race must be collectively insane. Once again, we'd dangled ourselves over the brink of destruction—this time in the name of Public Relations. What kind of belief system had brought us to this?

"You know, it's funny," Derek said as the evening was drawing to its close, "I've been reading in some scientific journals lately that the rotation of the Earth has recently accelerated in some minute degree. They can measure that, you know." Derek shrugged. "I don't know why that seems related to what we're talking about, but for some reason, it does."

George exhaled a cloud of Turkish tobacco smoke, frowning. "Maybe it's that we've all just slipped out of a world that blew itself up and we're still feeling the repercussions of all that energy, translated into rotation acceleration," he offered. "In the probability system we were in, see, the Mideast confrontation set off nuclear war—but we all decided not to get involved." He smiled innocently.

"What a cop-out!" Mary Strand jeered. "Just like a Sumari—you think you can flit around into any reality you feel like!" Everybody laughed. Mary had reported some swimming-against-the-stream dreams too. "It's all part of the Sumari Syndrome," Lauren explained, "like falling in love six times a week—and writing about it!"

"But there *was* an acceleration of the Earth's rotation," Derek said, bringing us back to our earthier worries. "It was *measured.* And if we create anything that happens, then why did we create that?"

It was quarter after eleven. Since class normally ended at eleven o'clock, this had looked like one of those Tuesdays that would pass by without Seth commenting on things. Members didn't sit around all evening and wait for Jane to bug out and let Seth come through, however—outside of some rowdy Seth-baiting, class was just as excited about comparing notes on our own experiences, dreams, or whatever, as about hearing Seth's remarks. Indeed, in at least the later years, I think Seth was like another (albeit wiser) class member who traveled distances unheard of by even the New York Boys to be with us. But their 500-mile round trip was one of the reasons (besides Jane's own writing schedule) that class ended at a reasonable hour. It usually took Jane and Rob an hour or more to clean up the living room after everybody left; and even though Rob had quit his part-time job (and could therefore attend class), the two of them liked to get up early in the morning to start their day's work.

So that particular evening, just when we were getting ready to leave, we were really surprised when Jane allowed Seth to suddenly enter the conversation. "You needed the time to talk together," he began. "The class group has been changing. You needed your own conversation and your own give-and-take.

"The class is its own entity!" Seth roared. "You are part of that entity. People come into class and leave the class, for the class is always changing, as each of you change."

Seth turned to Derek. "You are correct. There is an acceleration, and you are ready for it. It is your own. There is also a connection with the seasons, and remember that you also form the weather; and the acceleration that comes to you from the wind is, again, your own, objectified."

To the class in general, Seth continued, "Now, at certain times, dream activity is also accelerated, and this is indeed such a time. You have an opportunity, now, to know yourselves, and as you also exist in inner reality."

Seth's eyes were wide, dark, and penetrating. The room was stuffed with the magic of the autumn night and a fragrant wind blowing in through the open windows. "You have an opportunity now to open new roads, if you will," Seth said, a smile creeping across Jane's features. "You will be the new inhabitants. It can be your own city. You will have to make your own politics! They will be any kind you desire.

"You have enough class members now to form such a city. It will be used symbolically as a meeting place. You will have your own inner home, then, that you form for yourself.

"You should go there as a founder, each of you. You can begin forming that city now. And when you form such a city, you form it for yourself, and yet you also form it for others. And, in greater terms, of course, you have already formed it; and when you no longer need it, it will be used by others, and it will be a kind of inner landmark where others may use what you have created."

Part of me was fascinated. Part of me was horrified. Red flags waved in my brain. An inner city? Uh-oh. It sounded a bit too much like some kind of occult-records-hidden-in-the-mountains thing. Besides, I didn't like cities on the level I was dealing with now, let alone a level somewhere in the sky. And yet . . . Seth's words fit somehow, and I felt the call of challenge and adventure. It was exciting to think about the kinds of lucid dream correlations class might have, using this "city" as a symbolic meeting place. But the thing was, I had the uneasy feeling that this was one of those times when Seth was not speaking "symbolically."

"Now, I have hinted at multidimensional art, and this is multidimensional art indeed," Seth was saying. "Each of you has abilities peculiarly suited to form such an inner environment—such a 'Sumari city'— and so shall you then be pioneers in your own way. There are inner lands still to be conquered, for there are inner lands still to be formed. For when you create this city, you create the landscape and the reality in which it exists. The planning of your city should begin about now. Keep track of your dream activity!

"Now, I return you to yourselves, and to this room, and to the founding of your first inner Sumari city. You cannot complain about that city, for you will have formed it! Make it pleasant and warm for other dream travelers"—here, Seth stared directly at me—"and always be courteous to those who knock at the new doors!"

Seth withdrew. Class burst into a flurry of conversation, hardly stopping to tell Jane what had been said. "A dream city?" she said quizzically, frowning. "Hmmmm." Getting a word in edgewise, I quickly described the weird noises and knockings on my front porch during the week—had that been part of this city thing? It was already midnight, but as we kept on talking all at once, Seth came through again.

"There are old tales telling you that 'the way' is prepared—that there are many mansions in God's house, but who made the mansions?" he boomed.

"Now I am beginning to hint in '*Unknown*' *Reality* at a different kind of culture and activity. And I would like to see, in this space and time, a beginning made again of that kind of activity.[5] I would like to see you, then—and you can—build up an entirely valid culture, beginning with a city in another level of reality; where, if you believe what I am telling you, you can deal with mathematics—mathematics that you have not dreamed of as yet, and realities of which you are not as yet aware.

"You can, therefore, build an inner level of freedom that gives you access to far more information than you usually have. You can colonize an entire inner level of reality. To do so, you must give your best with dedication and joyful creativity.

"This will not be an imaginary city! It will have a greater reality than any physical city you know . . . there, you will hopefully work on developing skills . . . you will learn what you have forgotten, and yet when you do so you will learn something new. For you have all changed, and there is no such thing as dead knowledge or a dead skill . . .

"The city will have more than seven hills [like ancient Rome], and not all roads will lead to it; nor should all roads lead to it. Try, then, before you sleep, to remind yourself of your own endless creativity. Remind yourselves that what I say can definitely be accomplished. Try, before you sleep, to remind yourselves of the city, and to plan what you would do there, for you will do it!"

George called out, "Seth? Is that the city that I dreamed about last week, and described a little bit in class?"

"It was a distorted version, but other class members have also had such dreams, but they do not remember them," Seth said. "In your own way, you have been working toward such a program."

"Two things!" Rudy Storch shouted, waving his hand in Seth's face. "First off, a number of years ago, I had some dreams about a city. Could that be some kind of foreshadow? Secondly, is this city the kind of thing that Atlantis was?"

"I will not answer the second question, and the answer to the first question is yes," Seth said, and then added, "Yes, and no, to the second." Rudy laughed loudly. "All right!" he shouted.

Derek spoke up next. "When I was a really young child, I looked out one day from a window, toward the east, and I saw a very bright city off in the clouds somewhere, I was really impressed, and I still remember it, because it was so shiny. There is probably a connection between what I saw in that reality and the city that you're talking about."

"That is true," Seth affirmed. "But also, all of you will have an inner city, at which you are always at home, and among friends, and with your own family. You will always be with people who admire your own integrity, and you need not fear," he added, speaking to Derek.

Class finally closed, though members were talking and laughing all the way down the apartment house stairs and into the October night. What fun! Everybody was in a state of happy exhilaration. The following week, there were even more dream correlations than usual. Both George and I had recorded double dreams. In one part of mine, I'd been on a beach with Joel Hess, who hadn't been to class in three years. Both of us were children in the dream. At the same time, I'd found myself talking to a woman who said that she was me, at age thirty-five—a significant "future" me, she said. The following day, Joel called me up from Elmira— the first time we'd communicated in a couple of years—and in the ensuing conversation, he mentioned that he'd had a dream about me the night before, in which we'd been children sitting in a bank; both of our dream scenes were situated on the edge of a city.[6] (And six years later, at age thirty-five, I published this book.)

George had dreamed about teaching multidimensional sculpture in a fantastic building, with the New York Boys as students; several of the New York Boys had dreamed about a probable self of George's who was a professor of art. Two members had dreamed of each other on the same night; in both dreams, they'd been piling lumber up in preparation for "city construction." Again, class time flew by, and it was nearly 11:30 when Seth came through with more words about this city.

"Now, each of you in your own way have been working with the nature of reality and of creativity," he said. "There is much I have not told you about your city, for you will have to discover it for yourselves. And yet, there is, indeed, this other reality in which your creativity blossoms; and when you make plans here, they do indeed come to fruition. I am merely encouraging you to focus your joint energies in that direction. And if you do, you will have, in whatever terms, a dimension in which you can meet . . .

"You will be dealing with symbols, yet you will learn that symbols are reality, for you are symbols of yourselves that live and speak, and you do not think of yourselves as symbols. You do not understand that symbols live—that there is no symbol that does not have its own individual life.

"I speak to you theoretically of other realities. I challenge you now to be creative in another reality, as you are in this one. And if it seems to you— if it *seems* to you—because of your beliefs, that you are limited here, though you are not limited here, then I challenge each of you, joyfully, as in a game, to create a city, an environment, and perhaps a world in which no such limitations occur. And if you had your choice, what kind of world would you create?

"And so you have begun the building. For each of you, in your own way, will contribute. There are birds to be created to fly through those skies—and those birds are your thoughts, freed to their own fruition; and again, in other worlds, what wrens and robins and cardinals fly invisibly out of your skull to materialize in your city, and light upon the trees that are also the fruition of your desire?

"Now, there are books written programming out-of-body activities, where millions are told when you leave your body you will meet this demon or that demon, or this angry god, or that angry god, who commands any particular realm or reality; and you must do this or that or you will be annihilated. So the esoteric literature goes!

"So, instead, we will form a free city, and a free environment to which those people can come—where there are no demons and no rash gods; and where those who enter can read books about Buddhism if they prefer, or play at being Catholic priests. We will say, 'That is your right—you form your reality.' And we will allow those travelers that freedom.

"Now, you take it for granted, most of you, the fact that you can, indeed, travel out of the body. For centuries, in your terms, there have been no pleasant, recognizable roads for out-of-body travelers to follow. So I am suggesting that you create such a road and such a destination.

"Now, listen—you think there is nothing impossible, intrinsically, about building a platform in [outer] space—a handy place where supplies may be gathered. I am suggesting, then, a platform in inner reality; a safe place for travelers, and you can build it. It is as valid, and far more valid, than an orbiting city in the sky in physical terms, and it challenges your creative abilities far more.

"You need a good challenge—it is fun! Not because you *should* do it, but because you *desire* it and because it is fun, and because there is no other such creative challenge that you can throw down to yourselves— and no one else has ever thought of a better one thrown down to your-selves from future selves that you shall indeed encounter,[7] and you know you can do this and you know that you have done it; and on the face of the Earth, as you know it, there is no greater challenge that you can give yourselves . . . "

Or—that we *give* ourselves, because if we can in fact create such a place in such a fashion in a collective inner reality—then what else is there but here?

Imaginatively, of course.

CHAPTER 11

Health, Healing, and How We Walked Through Each Others' Bones

The Green Man

When the Green Man
steps out of the woods,
and he beckons,
will you go?
All made of leaves,
his words are slow—
When he beckons,
will you go?

Whispering to branches
in the pale green Spring,
he makes the leaf buds grow
worshipping the sun
in the tall oak trees,
he watches the heron come and go.

(Oh, go, go—
go with the Green man—go!)

While he is fast
on his dark green feet,
and the wind blows freely
in his hair—
lay aside for winter time,
your problems and your cares

(and go, go—
go with the Green Man—go!)

Quick! Before the leaves turn brown,
and the Green Man falls to sleeping
in the ground—
Ripe red wintergreen berries
to be gleaned,
when you go with the Green Man, go.

(place your hands in his hands of green—
place your hands in his hands of green.)

When the Green Man
steps out of the woods,
and he beckons,
Will you go?

—Dan Stimmerman, 1974

SHE WAS A PALE GHOST OF A GIRL, sitting passively on the floor, a bright green paisley scarf tied over her dark red hair; her face so flat, pasty white, that I had to force myself not to stare at her in disbelief. She was a visitor in class that October night in 1973, and even though it was nearly 10 P.M., she hadn't said a word, although I'd noticed her talking at length to Jane during break.

Not that anyone could get a word in edgewise anyway, I grumbled to myself. Tonight, the Boys from New York were really at their peak—everybody talking at once, and nobody getting more than a sentence or two in before being interrupted: a boisterous, lively, exasperating bunch, these guys. Usually, the great good fun of it all was worth the hassle—moreover, they'd given class a new kind of stimulus: an untamed, galumphing glee with a healthy dash of irreverence besides. But tonight, the noise and constant jostling to speak were just irritating. Wouldn't anybody shut up long enough to listen? Sitting there, my chair jammed among other chairs in the crowded room, I found myself boiling up into a lovely resentment of the whole crew. What had happened to the good old days when class sat quietly around the coffee table and discussed—sometimes with emotion—the possibilities behind Seth's theories?

The pall of cigarette smoke burned my eyes; my nose felt stuffed with wool. I thought of the forty-mile drive that awaited me after class. I thought of leaping out the window for some cool, fresh air, and for home. I thought of standing up in the middle of the room and screaming. At that moment, such thoughts were all quite delicious.

"Hold it!" Jane yelled, and a momentary quiet fell on the group for the first time that evening. Jane grinned at the tangled legs and arms and T-shirted bodies bunched around the floor of the living room. "Now that," she said, "is golden silence for you."

Immediately, thirty-five voices started talking at once, all of them vying for Jane's attention.

"HOLD IT!" Jane yelled again, good-naturedly. Sometimes, back then, I just couldn't understand that part of her. Here I sat, fuming at all this impertinence, while Jane seemed to bask in the racket and chaos. In her way, Jane has complete trust in sheer, untamed romp. But, for me, exuberance was turning into a real pain in the neck—if spontaneity knew its own discipline, then where the hell was it tonight?

"Listen," Jane said, looking around at us, "I think our visitor here has something she wants to say." Jane smiled down at the pale ghost-girl, who by this time had been jiggled and joggled over by the sofa at Will Petrosky's feet.

"Well," the girl said in a voice only shades less pale than her skin, "I've been sitting here listening to you all talk about your dreams and everything, and it's great . . . but, see, I have Hodgkin's disease."

Nobody said anything, for once, but I was too choked on frustrated resentments to register what the girl was talking about. I didn't even know what Hodgkin's disease was.[1] So what? I thought. She cast her eyes down in a strange, maidenly gesture, fumbling nervously with the scarf's knot under her chin.

"I read the books," she continued, "and I wanted to come to class, and I've been listening to you, but—"

"Cora," Jane said gently, interrupting the girl. My god, I thought, Jane's catching it too. "Cora," Jane repeated.

The girl looked up, confused. "What?" she said. The room waited expectantly.

"Cora," Jane said again. "Your name is Cora. Tell them."

"Tell them?" the girl answered back.

"Tell them that your name is Cora," Jane said, and then she leaned forward toward the girl and repeated, slowly and carefully, "Tell-them-what-your-name-is."

"Oh, sure," the girl said. "Well, yes, my name is Cora, and I've been trying to get it into my head about what you guys are saying about making your own reality and being spontan—"

Twenty voices lurched into gear. "Yep, the old joy-and-vitality bit!" several people yukked. "YOU! Be spontaneous—now!" Richie yelled at Lauren. Cora smiled at the people sitting on the floor with her. She didn't seem perturbed in the least by all the noise.

"Wait a minute," Jane said, removing her glasses. "I think we have a Sumari song for you, Cora—something about the cells and molecules of your body having names . . ." The room quieted down as Jane slipped into a delicate, lovely Sumari song that gradually built into a ringing crescendo of self-affirmation. The girl had never heard Sumari before, but her pale, angular face almost glowed with rapt attention. The song was punctuated throughout with pantomimed dancing motions as Jane swayed gracefully back and forth in her chair. At several points in the song, Sumari-Jane imitated Cora's own fumblings with her scarf, except that Sumari seemed to be encouraging her to remove it, or to at least be free of it in some way.

The song ended on a long, powerful note, and Jane came almost instantly out of trance. "Um . . ." she found her glasses and replaced them. "That was Sumari," she explained innocently.

"Oh, yes, it was beautiful," Cora said. "Was that Seth, or what was it? I really liked it."

Class immediately wound up again; several people jumped in with explanations tumbling all over. "Sumari's a family of consciousness," someone said; two or three others yelled a simultaneous explanation of "sounds that are about other levels of perception."

"I get the idea that it had something to do with telling you to acknowl-edge your own being in some way that you aren't doing," Jane said. "HOLD IT!" she shouted above the din of voices. "Let Cora tell her impression."

"I . . ." Cora hesitated, and incredibly, a chorus of voices interrupted her again. By this time, I was seething, ready to leave and slam the door behind me, when Will Petrosky suddenly caught the floor. "You don't have to cover up in here!" he shouted at the girl. "And so you don't need that scarf on either, like Sumari said!" And with that, he bounded forward, reached over, and in an exaggerated version of the Sumari gesture, yanked Cora's scarf from her head.

And with the scarf, horribly, came the red, red wig that Cora had been wearing to cover the poor, pale, utter baldness of her naked skull.

A silence more total than the tomb fell on the class, and Will cringed back on the sofa, his hand still locked in the grabbing gesture, a look of abso-

Will Petrosky

lute horror on his face; the horror that was envel-oping everyone, as it finally got through to us all what the girl had been talking about when she'd said "Hodgkin's disease."

I was scandalized: this was the ultimate inva-sion of privacy. But I must admit that I was also wickedly triumphant. There! I thought nastily, that's what you guys get! That'll teach you! Now maybe you'll learn something about manners!

Cora was calmly readjusting her wig and scarf. "Well now, that's one of the things that happens when you're on the drugs they put you on for this," she said easily, as though this violent revelation were nothing to her. "Lately, I've been able to do with-out some of them, and I've been in a period of remission . . . I read the books, and I think it's helped me some."

Complete silence reigned supreme. Petrosky looked as though he wanted to disappear into the Chemung River. Jane looked around, waiting.[2]

"What a lesson for those poor guys," Warren Atkinson recalls with affection. "Will's impulsive brashness brought feedback he did not expect! His face, his devastation, and the startled class are all etched in my memory. Suddenly we saw how near death she was and how she was hiding it while still trying to live."

"I think," Jane said quietly, "this is a good time to take a break."

Break, usually a circus of romping between the bathroom and the kitchen, was subdued, to say the least. Nobody had to yell that break was over, either. And after everyone slumped back in their places, Seth came through almost immediately.

"Now, I have a few words to say to some individuals, and first of all," he said, bending toward Cora, "I bid you my greetings, and I simply point out to you that you identified yourself here as a young lady with a disease. The first words you spoke identified yourself as a person with a disease. Your self-image is too involved in the disease that has a name that has been given it.

"Now hear me!" Seth boomed, his voice roaring out the autumn windows. "You have your own name—assert it in the joy of your being! And if you want to live in vitality and joy, then your name is more important than the name of any group of symptoms, for they have not the kind of reality that you have! And your glowing integrity identifies you here, so then accept the vitality of your being, and speak your own name over and over! For that name is the name given you in this space and in this time, and do not accept instead the name of a disease in which you lose, it seems, identity and strength. Do not quail before vocabulary! Your integrity and your beauty and your strength identify you here, and identify you for all time. Therefore, do not look wan. And forget thoughts of tragedy that are spelled out, and assert the vitality of your being!"

Cora was listening to Seth's words, huge as they were in that humbled room, with the same calm in which she had accepted everything else this evening. As for me, my heart was pounding hard with the strange shock of looking upon a person younger than I was, who was actually dying; someone who had been told that she had *this* much time left to be alive. How could she stand it? How could Seth's words make any difference now? It *was* humbling. And as I began to sort out my earlier feelings of rage, I realized that Will's impulsiveness had opened all our eyes—including Cora's—to an inescapable application of theory: her condition was either a result of her beliefs or else she was the victim of an indiscriminate insanity of impersonal cells. Facing her now, which could you accept?

"Now, if you decide to leave this world, that is your right, and go in joy and vitality," Seth was telling Cora. "But go because you know *you* decide to leave, and not as the victim of a disease that has been given a name. If you decide that you want to live, then live in your full glory and strength, *but make up your mind,* and do not allow yourself to be victimized.

"If you want to die, then *why* do you want to die? Know the reasons, and go because you have made up your mind, and go with strength and vitality, making your own decisions—but not as a victim, and not in tragedy, and not wan!

"If you decide to live, then tell yourself you want to live and know the reasons, and your body will repair itself in joy and glory," Seth added. "You are not a victim!"

With that, those dark, penetrating eyes turned to Petrosky. "The energy in this room is always apparent," Seth continued. "And it is one of the reasons why Ruburt does not tell you to shut up more frequently, even though some-times such thoughts abound!" I squirmed in my chair, blushing, but Seth went on with his usual dry composure.

"In this room, you have the energy that forms each of your worlds, and that reaches out with its great vitality to touch others. Therefore, as it surges through you, it is inexhaustible; and send it, therefore, to this girl, and let her use it as she wishes. Let her make her own decisions as each of you must make your own decisions. No god made victims—you make victims of yourselves by your beliefs.

"Now, let us see a smile and some apples in those cheeks," Seth said to Cora, reaching out to touch her under her chin. "I have died many times, but never as a victim, and each of you choose the time of your death and the time of your birth. As you trust in the ground of your being, then you will also share in the *joy* of your being and trust yourself—trust that what comes from you is good and adds to the universe. Trust in the integrity of your blood and the molecules. Trust that you are here for a reason."

When Jane came out of trance, she pointed out to Cora that she'd been identifying so strongly with her condition that she hadn't even given her name as an introduction, but had instead given the name of a disease. Cora admit-ted that she did this at other gatherings: at parties, in casual conversation, even in letters. She said she now realized how she'd actually been depending on the symptoms to give her a feeling of importance and strength: she, Cora, victimized by a disease, was bravely fighting it. Pending death, she acknowl-edged, had literally become her life's blood.

"I think our friend Will here did us a favor," Jane said, and perhaps that's what it was. We'd certainly never had a more direct confrontation with whether we really accepted that beliefs created our experience—or if we felt, underneath it all, that this was fascinating theory, but not "real."

For one thing, there is an abundance of "obvious" evidence that the physical body on its own is helpless; that good health is in fragile opposition to the powerful evil of disease; and that the body (like peace) requires con-stant vigilance against decay. And on the surface of historical evidence alone, it seems crazy not to accept the benefits of medical science—except that, looking at Cora, you had to wonder about the trade-offs of such benefits: diagnosis, treatment, and death, all medically tied up and labeled in a neat package, from which Cora was not likely to escape.

However, the traps inherent in placing all of your trust in an outside authority—medical, spiritual, or otherwise—are not so evident once you've accepted its terms. For Cora, only a newer drug would give her remission. For others, the method might be trickier. Recently I received a letter from a man in California who had attended class once in the early '70s. He'd "heard," he said, that Jane was dying of cancer and asked if I could verify this for him: "I have found it depressing, since if we make our own reality, and Jane has been learning this from the horse's mouth, so to speak, there doesn't seem to be much hope for the rest of us."

I assured him that Jane and Rob were both healthy and happily engrossed in their work,[3] but that relying on Jane's physical perfection as "proof" that you create your own reality was missing the point. "Jane isn't setting herself up as a new goddess on Earth," I wrote. "The point is that each of us makes his or her own experience, and if there's something there we don't like, we should examine that reality—not Jane's."

Well, I patted myself on the back for that one—yep, catch the guru weed early in the bud, I congratulated myself, forgetting for the moment how many times I'd terrified myself by reading cancer statistics and symptom lists. But not long afterward, I learned that a friend in Elmira had died at age thirty-five, after contending for several years with leukemia—and with a set of beliefs that at first glance might appear to be concentrating on health.

Bill had been a strict vegetarian and organic food advocate for nearly ten years. He balanced his diet carefully, never consumed sugar or alcohol, and maintained an active daily life. On second glance, however, you could see that food in Bill's world was dangerous business—one slip could cause havoc— and filled with potential spiritual disaster. (Eggs, for example, were "too high on the karmic scale" to eat—a status apparently not granted to the plant kingdom.) Bill and his wife were members of a meditative sect whose guru-type leader demanded denial of the flesh in all of its expressions for the sake of "purity"—they weren't supposed to have sex, for one thing ("We try very hard not to," Bill told me once, sighing for the weakness of his failures). At his request, Jane attempted on several occasions to give him some insight into the origins of his condition: for openers, it was obvious that in his eyes, the body was a literal cancer upon the spirit. And Bill died believing it—because this was what his "master" had decreed.

On the other hand, medical doctors are routinely granted the authority and power over our physical salvation: in Cora's case, she'd been pronounced dead several years before the fact—and she died in the spring of 1975, believing in the diagnosis. And in all of these systems, the self is granted very little authority or power of decision at all.

Certainly, little attention has been given to the ferreting out of beliefs behind medical conditions, or to why consciousness developed in the particular way it did, forgetting the inner origin of outer events. And so, in this regard, Seth didn't automatically "heal" anyone—nor did he, Jane, or class ever posture that they could. It was placed upon the individual to do this, as Seth's remarks to Cora implied. Health and the body's condition were treated as the result of beliefs: as a reflection of the inner order of logic, springing into physical expression. Help was offered through belief "therapy," alpha energy, or other methods; but with superb psychological respect, Seth (and Jane) gave people credit for being able to solve their own problems—for being themselves healers of physical difficulties, no matter what external system (including medical science) was used.

"What [do] you think about the odor of the Earth and of people—do they smell?" Seth once asked a visitor who'd wondered aloud why he had pains in his nose. "In derogatory terms . . . what portion of you believes that they smell, so that you want to close out half of the odor of that reality? That is all I will say, and it has a scented message!"

The literal and symbolic harmony of circumstance as expressed by Seth was hilariously evident in that kind of remark, as it was when I asked, for example, why a rash had covered my son's body in less than an hour one afternoon, turning him into a mottled, scarlet mess, and then disappeared as suddenly. "For a hint . . . while I will not give you an answer, consider your thoughts about invading armies," Seth replied. "Not of warring nations, now, but of invading armies; and the word 'armies' is important, in relationship to what you think of as reincarnational memories [as related in chapter 8]. And that is all I will say, and, as you know, it is far too much!"

Invading armies? Oh, hell, I thought, why isn't it ever anything simple like, "Your son is allergic to the dog," or, "Stop making him eat spinach?" No, it's something about figuring out what "invading armies" means! But once I'd deciphered this hint (insane mass forces attacking the innocent . . . hmmm . . . a process that actually took me several months), I achieved insight into my beliefs about children and disease that were far more "practical" than, say, a ghostly prescription for calamine lotion. The rash never did come back, and I also learned something about the power of suggestion and the interrelationship of beliefs within families.

"I feel that everyone causes their own illnesses for a subconscious purpose and can heal themselves if it 'suits' them at the time," says "Nurse Nadine" Renard. "However—my kids were sick all the time [at the time of class]! We ran to the doctor, but still they were sick, and consequently, I was preoccupied with them most of the time." Because her family considered her the one who supposedly understood both medical and psychic matters, Nadine felt responsible for keeping everyone healthy. One night in class, Nadine explained her family's struggles with a never-ending series of colds, sore throats, and flu. Despite her good intentions, she complained, this situation had left her with a terrible fear of germs—which seemed sensible in the face of things.

"You can get rid of all the illness," Seth advised her, "when you realize that you have the habit of creating and drawing it to you out of fear. What you fear most, you draw to yourself. Instead, you must concentrate upon what you *want*—and do not be so worried! You can learn to concentrate upon what you want and draw that to yourself, and to completely restructure the health habits of your family.

"Now, there are some past-life reasons for your attitudes and also for the profession in which you find yourself, but first of all, you must understand that you can draw health and vitality and strength to yourself and that you are not at the mercy of any poor crawling germ or little flying monsters that come to attack you or your family! I tell you this because there is a connection in your mind; illness becomes to you the symbol of something far different and far more profound. It becomes in your mind the symbol of evil, which attacks you—in your mind—in small ways as small illnesses.

"It often occurs that those who have strong healing abilities focus upon illness and sickness and are obsessed with it," Seth told Nadine. "It is in the same way that many ministers, given to thoughts of good and God, are obsessed with the idea of the devil and evil. You also have strong healing abilities, but these, so far in your personal life, have been latent because of your fear and your obsession in the other direction.

"If you will forgive me, it is somewhat like a woman with very earthy desires . . . who rigorously refuses to use them and dwells instead on thoughts of their evil, holding them back simply because she realizes they are so strong. In your own personal life, you are afraid to use your abilities of healing. You do not understand them, and yet in your profession you are free to use them and you have seen them work."

In a later class, Seth addressed himself again to Nadine, who had asked how she could change her thinking to keep her family well "instead of making them sick."

"Realize that you do not form events alone," Seth told her. "You are involved in a cooperative venture. You are not alone responsible for an event, therefore, in that usually others participate in its creation and for their own reasons.

"Now, the question cannot be answered simply in one evening," Seth continued, "but each living consciousness has its own defense system and its own vitality, and you should trust your own—[but] you do not trust your own. You do cooperate together to form the physical reality that you know, telepathically, through ways and means that are unknown to you. You weave these webs of psychic reality that then coalesce into physical reality. You do not weave them alone, necessarily—you weave them together. Your thoughts intertwine with the thoughts of others. You are responsible for your own thoughts.

"You need to learn the power of thought and emotion, but this should fill you with the joy of creativity. Once you realize that your thoughts form reality, then you are no longer slave to events . . . Why do you water your fears like weeds, and ensure that they do grow?

"Now, you are involved in healing—it is your interest. But you must also find the peace of your existence in the area where ill health does not exist, or you will indeed be dragged down into that aura. And therefore must you also begin to concentrate instead, and purposely, upon the healthy organisms and not imagine unhealthy ones. You would do better if you completely changed your focus away from health—because to you, health also means poor health!

"You are at a level where opposites seem to exist, though they do not exist," Seth added to the class in general. "Therefore, when you think of good, you think of evil, and when you think of health, you think of disease. It would be better if, when you find such thoughts occurring to you, you change your focus completely into another area. Find the area yourself, but have an area that engages your interest, a place of energy and peace—in which you realize that in your dealings with health and disease, you are dealing with shadows."

Nadine does say that her healing abilities, when freed from the anxieties of her immediate family, have apparently helped others. "I used suggestion on some neighbors with problems," she says. "I just tell 'em good stuff, and the doctors say they're amazed at how well they get over whatever it is."

One neighbor, Nadine says, had been through two cataract operations and was home only a few days when one eye swelled up, became inflamed, and began oozing. "It looked something awful, but I would say things like, 'You look great, Frances,' or something, or sometimes I would gently lay my hands across her face and tell her that her eye was well now," Nadine says. "Once in the middle of all this, Frances called me up and asked me if I could get her some strong pain pills. Well, I only had some Tylenol and that wouldn't give her much relief—I mean, her eye was swollen so you could see the stitches—so I told her the stuff was codeine and boy did she get relief! And her doctor later told me that her eyes healed much better than he'd thought they would.

"Another friend of mine died of cancer some time ago," Nadine says. "I used to go and just hold her hands and give her suggestions of peace, and then she would say she felt better and fall asleep, which was a lot to give her then, I guess."

Sending energy to friends, seeing the beliefs behind another's ills, or listening to Seth's astute psychological assessments were all easy enough to go along with when applied to someone else. But when the illness is your own (or a loved one's) and you're supposed to look around *your* discomfort or fear or immediate physical effects to grasp the root, then that little bit of necessary distance all too often evaporates.

One Monday afternoon in the summer of 1971, within the space of a few hours, a painful, throbbing abscess blossomed in my left ear. At the time, it just seemed like one more thing attached to a string of lousy days. George Rhoads and his wife, visiting my parents and me on their way out West, had delivered long and somewhat merciless health-food lectures on whatever I fed my son; during Sean's checkup that week, the pediatrician had stated flatly that because Sean ate several eggs a week, "He'll drop dead of a heart attack at age fifty and it'll be your fault." My divorce from Ned had been final for a month, and I was trying to force myself back into the job market. To complete the picture, the abscess had filled my skull with pain; moreover, I was filled with the fear that I'd end up as I had five years before, when a doctor had sloppily lanced an abscess in the same ear, landing me in the hospital with bacterial meningitis.

As I drove to class that Tuesday evening, determined to divert my attention from the earache, every detail of that hospital stay loomed up like nightmare lights: the shots of toothpaste-thick penicillin; the stiff, hot pain in my neck and head; the whirlpool smog of Demerol numbness.

In Jane's apartment, I slumped on the rug by the bathroom door and tried to concentrate on the people around me. Juanita, a recent newcomer, sat on the sofa, a wide, fixed grin on her somewhat care-worn face. Someone spoke to her and she didn't respond. The person sitting beside her on the sofa nudged her. "Hey, John said 'hello'!"

"What?" Juanita said loudly. "I'm sorry, I can't hear you." So—two of us here tonight have ear problems, I mused.

Class started with a discussion of our current experiments with alpha (see *CWS*, book 2, appendix 1). Juanita strained to hear, literally stretching herself half off the sofa. My ear pinged and stabbed; my neck ached. Visions of those hourly shots danced in my head. Given these kinds of troubles, the condition of the entire world looked pretty hopeless to me.

Jane was watching me with an expression of sympathy, combined with something like scientific alertness, a communication we often shared. I grinned at her and shook my head. On the phone that afternoon, I'd told her about the earache and about the earlier experience in 1966, when I'd lost a semester of college and ended a long-standing relationship with a man I'd known since high school. Now five years later, I was newly divorced and facing the need to stand on my own with a young child and no job. In both circumstances, I'd developed the same initial symptom. More than coincidence was involved, I knew, but somehow I just plain didn't want to think about it.

"It has something to do with the woman thing," Jane said, out of the blue, still watching me with that rapt alertness.

"It what?" I said. Class noise and chatter screened us into privacy. "The woman thing?"

"Right," Jane said. She waited. I didn't get it

"Hey, people," Jane called out to the class, "let's do some alpha on Sue and Juanita." She told them briefly what our troubles were; Juanita, it seemed, had a chronic blockage of the ear canal that was gradually destroying her hearing.

But before class could begin the alpha attempt, Jane's glasses were whipped off and Seth's old familiar "Now!" cut through all conversation.

"Both of you have this thing about noise!" Seth said—very noisily!—addressing Juanita and me. "I will speak to you both at once, therefore.

"The world is not as tumultuous as you imagine it to be, and you can hold your own within it," Seth told Juanita. "You can indeed! You can clear your own ears and your own vision [Juanita also wore very thick glasses]. All you have to do is realize that within yourself is the ability to face each day as you come to it. You are trying too hard now. You must relax and trust the inner self to see and to hear. The early troubles that helped trigger your difficulty you can now, as an adult, overcome by realizing that the inner self has its own knowledge and its own ways. You *can* hear me, and I will see to it that you do!

"Imagine yourself answering questions that have been put to you," Seth continued to Juanita. "You need not imagine that you are hearing clearly. If you imagine that you are answering the questions, then it will be taken for granted that you have heard them correctly. When you try too hard to hear or see, you hear and see less. Relax and let this be taken care of for you. Now, you do not trust the inner self to do these things, and you must learn to accept the inner ancient wisdom that is your own!"

I gulped. Me next! I flinched; my ear crackled jabs of pain. Seth turned to me, regarding me with what I hoped was only my interpretation of severity.

"And *you* must learn that love is noisy and can be a bother and can get in the way, and you must learn not to deny the validity of your own feelings in those directions where you are now tending to hide them from yourself," Seth said evenly. "Much later I will see that Ruburt tells you about it specifically. For now I will simply tell you that the earlier incident of which you spoke to Ruburt [the earache I'd had in 1966] *is* connected with this one. You know that it is, but you must think of what noise represents to you and what it is that you do not want to hear and why at this particular time you do not want to hear it."

Illogically, I remembered George Rhoads registering stern disapproval of Sean's Cheerios breakfast, while Sean had banged happily away on his highchair tray with a spoon—a noise unequaled for sheer nerve-destroying capability. "Then it's related to Sean?" I asked.

"It is connected with Sean, but it also has deeper roots," Seth answered. "I will see that Ruburt tells it to you. This also has to do, however, with the fear of exterior stimuli and the basic fear that it will sweep you away, destroy your person. You have, now, security, and these thoughts and feelings are highly erroneous. You have physical senses for a reason. They are to help you, not to hinder you. When you refuse to use them for whatever reason, you lessen your own abilities and your own effectiveness, as you know; but this is not ever thrust upon you. This is a method of learning and as you learn, you will solve the problem." Seth then addressed the group, pointing out that "each of you in your own way hides certain groupings of feelings from your-selves, so I am not necessarily directing this specifically at our friend here [me], except that she has the trouble with the ear this evening."

Finished, Seth disappeared through his dimensional doorway. I told Jane what he'd said.

"Sure," she replied, puffing on the Pall Mall that had been smoldering patiently in the ashtray, "it's a thing you have about noise, and . . ." Her eyes widened. "Food!"

Food?

"Sure, food—I get it," Jane continued, speaking rapidly. "Food repre-sents not only nourishment to you, but it's a symbol of your femaleness, see? The whole thing started this time when George and his wife and the doctor all got after you about how you're feeding Sean. You didn't want to hear it! Besides," she added, a bit conspiratorially, "*sex* and noise are connected in your mind—loud noise and violence and sex; you feel they could utterly shat-ter you, so you also eat too much to build up a protection against all of it, so you'll be left alone, from the whole works."

It made gorgeous sense, but . . . I jotted down some notes, and evaded it. Class did a Mu chant for Juanita and me,[4] and that night I went home feeling a little better. But the next morning, my ear was just as painful, and eventually, at my mother's insistence, I did end up in the hospital again, although this time no widespread infection ensued. I didn't face up to the beliefs Seth and Jane's remarks implied for many years, however—and in the meantime, I would deal with their manifestation in numerous forms, and not just as physical symptoms.

Class did try some healing experiments on itself, of course, as part of our exploration of the unplumbed properties of imagination and conscious-ness. In the early 1970s, alpha biofeedback was emerging as an accepted method of regulating some of the "involuntary" body functions. Alpha, one of the officially labeled brain waves, involves a relaxed awareness, and is not as intense a state as the "normal" beta level—or even a light trance. After a few inconclusive jousts with an alpha lamp (which was supposed to change colors to the individual eye as you switched brain wave levels), Jane suggested that we forget the lamp and try to see what subjective information might be avail-able in the alpha state.

To go into alpha, we'd usually imagine ourselves doing something inspiring, like painting or writing, or listening to music; then we'd "hold" that feeling. Some would instead imagine a tiny self standing off to one side of our heads (Jane's favorite method), or we'd concentrate on one of Rob's many paintings. At first, it was hard not to go deeper than alpha; but after a few weeks of practice, most of us were pretty adept at switching to that state whenever something unusual happened in class. It was like seeing an event from many sides at once, since you never lost track of "normal" perceptions—you added to them.

The experiment that class did most often in alpha—aside from altered-perception "journeys"—was to direct our collective awareness toward a volunteer and mentally rummage through his or her body, accepting any images we perceived in a lighthearted spirit of playful investigation. Anything that we "saw" that didn't "look right" was to be fixed up according to our own mental imagery. Class members would spend four or five minutes at this and then come out of alpha and write down what we'd perceived. The volunteer would then describe his reactions during the experiment, and we'd read our "findings." (To supplement it all, we'd send the person energy during the week.) It was great fun to see if members' alpha perceptions would coincide—and they often did.

After tripping imaginatively through Joel Hess, for instance, several of us made independent notes on seeing "inflamed muscles" around his spine and lower back. "I imagined that I had a miniature fire hose in my hands," Sally Benson said. "I made it spray some kind of soothing salve all over the place, and I made it work, too!"

Joel admitted that he'd strained his back that week, although for years it had ached chronically anyway. "I'd tell you all that it feels better tonight than it has in a long time," Joel said humorously, "but you'd probably all put it down as suggestion." Similarly, after trying out alpha on another student, several members reported that they'd seen Jeanette's stomach as "a forest of animals, prowling around and hunting one another." Some of us imagined tiny versions of ourselves chasing the predators out; others tried petting the animals and creating a miniature *Peaceable Kingdom* out of Jeanette's insides. Jeanette later said that for several weeks she'd been nervous and "tied up in knots," and that her stomach was often upset.

One class visitor swung into this alpha experiment with great revealing gusto. "I imagined myself going in your left lung," the woman told Jane enthusiastically, "and I found myself in a great big coal bin. It was really filthy dirty in there—yukk! So I started washing the walls with this giant squeegee and I opened the windows to let all the poison smoke out . . ."

"Uh, wait a minute," Jane said mildly. "Before you get too carried away with those suggestions, maybe you ought to examine your beliefs about my smoking."

"Beliefs?" the woman wailed. "What do beliefs have to do with it? I mean, everybody knows smoking is bad for you, and you of all people should know that it's bad, since you're . . . " the woman hesitated.

"Yes?" Jane baited. "I'm what?"

"Uh, well," the woman confessed, "you're speaking for Seth, after all, and involved in your spiritual work, and smoking is so unspiritual, and doesn't Seth tell you to stop it?"

Jane sighed. "Actually, he'd love it if I took up cigars," she said. "But to hell with that! Besides, I have great lungs!" And Jane bellowed a huge, drawn-out "Muuuuuu!" to prove it.

Class didn't interpret its alpha healing experiments in such a literal sense, but neither did we see them as being strictly symbolic or "imaginary," in usual terms. Also, alpha exercises were not used as a replacement, necessarily, for medical advice. They were used as a means to uncover the inner reasons for physical events (in this case, physical symptoms).

"I learned to believe in health," Arnold Pearson simply states, referring to his happy retirement years after class had ended. Mary Strand, a nurse, says that she taught her children to believe in health also, "and in their power to heal themselves. We've managed to avoid medication and doctors for several years, [although] old gods and beliefs still threaten me in times of trial." I'm sure the old gods threaten anyone who starts to bridge the gap between the selfhood that's been taught to us through centuries of human experience and the kind of selfhood as revealed, if only partly, in Jane's class. To understand private and mass reality as creations of the self is a radical departure, and few, if any, social frameworks exist that allow a balanced expedition into the worlds of circumstance.

CHAPTER 12

The War of the Idiot Flowers: In Which Dream Fish, Spontaneity, and the Draft Are Kicked Around

Consorting with the forms of the dead,
these spirits take you by the hand
and walk you from your bed.
—Where may we be headed?—
The world is a ghost to your dreaming,
Your dreams seem as ghosts to your world.
We take our worlds and we mix them;
into one another they spill.
We make a real hand ghostly—
We make a ghost's hands real.

—Dan Stimmerman, 1979

The pacifist sat upon the road
and gently stroked a quiet toad.
A stranger came intent to hit
but slipped upon a load of shit.

—Barrie Gellis, 1974

"The gods did not conceive the universe in
sorrow; this earth did not come from a tear.
You have formed your own tears."

—Seth in class, March 1972

OUTSIDE THOSE BAY WINDOWS, THE LATE '60s and early '70s marched on, the world boiling over, it seemed, in violence and social revolution. Riots ripped through the inner cities. Self-proclaimed prophets blew up buildings in the name of peace. The war in Vietnam raged on and on. Peaceful solutions were condemned by some as too slow a path to justice, scorned by others as naive. How could you put down your guns in a world full of weapons?

The Vietnam war and all its subsidiary questions of violence, aggression, patriotism, and dissent reached its tentacles down into Jane's class in those years as the men—and women—faced the very real possibility of personal involvement. Events around us often served to square us off on matters of philosophy: Was violence ever justified? If a ghetto riot drew attention to deplorable conditions and therefore initiated changes, then wasn't such an outbreak justified? What about the war—what about the ideal of peace? When did loyalty turn into fanaticism?

"The ends do not justify the means," Seth told us many times. "In fact in those terms, the ends *are* the means." No violence was ever justified, Seth said—not ever. "There is never any justification for violence . . . never any justification for threats. The means create the end. And if the means are violent, the ends are violent." Yet, what do you do if somebody shoots first?

During those years, while Ned and I were married, he struggled for months with the lengthy, complicated procedures required for the CO (Conscientious Objector) draft status—to no avail. Ned appealed his personal objections to military service before the district draft board in Buffalo. No dice: no CO. Now he would have to wait for the inevitable change in his college-student deferment. In the meantime, his moods leaped from deep despair to precarious exuberance as he dabbled intermittently with painting and tried to concentrate on his job in a local tree nursery.

The first class in December, 1970, fell on a cold, howling winter's night. Jane's living room was toasty warm, though; the radiators banged happily away in the big old-fashioned rooms, especially in the gargantuan tile bathroom. Class had standard jokes about that bathroom: the huge oval sink on its pedestal; the shower stall with its nine needle-nozzles; the toilet that would keep gurgling after a couple of flushes and often required the plumbing expertise of a class member to halt. But nothing seemed to reach Ned, not even this homey camaraderie. He sat on the floor, in a corner, smoking cigarettes, wrapped in a cocoon of misery and anger.

In class for the first time that night were Joel and Alison Hess. At the time, Joel was involved in antiwar organizations at Cornell and was also preaching in a small rural church near his home. He seemed to be a very serious man, and during break he volunteered some very serious statements about good and evil—particularly evil, and how its characteristics ruled the world.

"The only hope we have is for good people to discipline their innate tendency to do bad things," Joel stated in summary.

"Oh . . . bullshit," I answered, cautiously. Immediately, Joel and I got into a furious argument, interrupted (much to the relief of the rest of the class) after several heated exchanges by Seth's booming voice.

"Now, the spontaneous self, the inner self left alone, is a good thing," Seth began, staring pointedly at Joel, "and we will not go into a definition of the word 'good!' Left alone, the inner self keeps your body functioning and your eyesight keen; it keeps your balance perfect; it keeps you alive. It gives you a sense of joy and vitality and it fills you with a joy of All That Is, which, as most of you know, is my term for the word God!"

Boy! I thought, that guy's really getting it—and the first time he's in class, too! Ha! Much to my secret disappointment, however, I noticed that Joel wasn't too perturbed about it. I glanced at Ned. He seemed lost in another world.

"Left alone, then," Seth was saying, "you are a perfect creature—and you feel a oneness with nature. And when you walk down the street, you feel a unity between your fingertips and the leaftops and between your feet and the pavement beneath it. It is only when you meddle with the spontaneous self that difficulties arise—and these difficulties you may, if you prefer, call evil."

Joel nodded, thoughtfully.

"Evil arises, and we will not go into a definition of the word 'evil,' when—and precisely when—you do not realize that the inner self is the source of joy, vitality, and creativity!" Seth went on. "At that point, indeed, when doubts enter in, then you mistrust yourself and the inner self that forms your physical image. Then when you do not accept the spontaneous self, you decide you will accept certain feelings and deny others. And those that you deny, that you do not regard as acceptable, these grow up within you until they achieve a strong charge; and those repressed charges, individually and en masse, cause violence!

"And if you want to equate the word 'violence' with 'evil,' then that is the origin of it; and it is mistrust of the spontaneous self—the inner self—that is within you all.

"Now, you see, we have visitors, and I am sounding severe," Seth said with humor, still staring at Joel. "I must therefore tell you that, since I am far older than any of you and far deader than most, you realize and sense the vitality that flows through this image [Jane's]; and sensing it, realize that this same energy is available to each of you! It is your heritage—the heritage of joy and spontaneity and creativity—therefore, use it! Recognize it in yourself and do not mistrust it."

"Well," Joel said as Seth withdrew, "I guess I agree that repressing your feelings leads to an explosive anger, but it seems to me that, recognizing this, the individual should strive to look for the goodness in himself and cultivate it a little bit—given the world situation and all . . ."

Abruptly, Seth was back, his own expansive expressions and gestures moving Jane's body in humorous incongruity to her ankle-length dress and dangling earrings. "We will see more of you!" Seth pronounced to Joel in a low, Peter Lorre voice.

Joel raised his eyebrows, surprised.

"Now, listen to me," Seth continued in that grave, powerful tone. "You need not try so hard. If you trust the inner self, then you grow as a flower grows. The flower grows correctly, and it does not strive to grow, and it does not say to itself, 'I must grow two inches, so help me, by tomorrow night at twilight!' A flower *is*, and it allows itself to grow, and it is sure of its Is-ness and of the spirit of All That Is within it.

"Now, goodness is as natural as a flower that grows. If a flower stopped when the sun was shining down upon it, however, and if it began to consider and said, 'Wait! Should I grow to the left, or should I grow to the right? Is it good that the sun shines down on me, or is it too easy for me to grow in the light of the sun, and therefore should I attempt to grow instead in the darkness? Should I grow two inches to the right, or two inches to the left? I must strive to grow! I must develop an ego and an intellect, and I must try to reach that sun that is God and I must work hard because if I do not strive, I shall not achieve—and I must achieve!'

"But, beside our intellectual, conscientious flower is an idiot of a flower! And the idiot of a flower stands and feels the sun upon its face and opens up its leaves and says, 'This is the sun, and it is good within me; it is the spirit of growth, and I'll follow it and give it freedom; and I care not whether I grow to the right or to the left, for in perfect trust with the spirit within me, I know I shall grow correctly.'

"And so it grows, our idiot flower, and it grows from within. And it is perfect and it is strong, but beside it is our intellectual and spiritual flower. And *this* flower says, 'Again! Three o'clock in the afternoon, the shadows are coming and the shadows are evil, and this sun is fading, and the night is coming, and the night is evil; and I must consider how best I can confound these adversaries . . . and it is easy to fail and not use my abilities and not to grow!'

"And lo and behold, in the morning the sun rises, and what do we find? Our idiot flower in full bloom in the morning sun and our other flower with one leaf like this [Seth drooped his hand over the chair arm] and one leaf like this [his other arm stuck up in the air] and head down, still considering the nature of good and evil and not trusting the spirit of vitality which is within it; and therefore, not listening to the inner voice . . . but questioning at every point and at every hour: 'In which way shall I go? Shall I accept the sunlight or the rain? Or are these evil forces?' And telling itself over and over again that to grow is difficult and to die is easy. Telling itself over and over and over—in metaphysical terms, now—that to be good is difficult and to be evil is easy.

"And that is a deception!"

"The idiot flower," Joel asked skeptically, "that just stands there naturally and accepts its due—does it have a responsibility to try to enlighten his brother flower which seems to be caught in confusion?"

"It does indeed," Seth replied, "and it does by its example, for the other flower should look and say, 'How is it that my brother flower grows so beautifully in the sunlight?'

"Now, understand that I am speaking simply for an analogy," Seth said, "and I am not telling any of you that the intellect is wrong, or that you should not use it. Like any teacher, I am simply choosing an example. But the existence of our idiot flower is, in itself, an example, for I will tell you—in the simplest terms that I can tell you—that you can trust the inner spontaneous self. It is, in your terms, a spirit of All That Is. It knows how to grow. It grew you from a fetus to an adult, and it did so without your striving, and without your stopping it at every moment to say, 'Are you growing right? Is my left toe growing correctly or is it growing in the wrong direction?' If you would have had your say, the body never would have been formed correctly: you would have taken that much time to make up your minds . . ."

"Even though we feel the sense of spontaneity," Joel pursued, "do we have the option to react in view of it?"

"You go along with it!" Seth answered. "Unless you are a child, you will not enter the Kingdom of Heaven! Unless you are joyful, unless you live in trust of spirit, you are not whole. A little child shall lead them because the spontaneity of spirit knows All That Is . . . All That Is is not dignified! All That Is is not 'adult'! All That Is is not pompous! All That Is *is*, and in Is-ness comes . . . creativity. You can allow your intellect full freedom when it follows the spontaneity of your being.

"You follow the spontaneous self as long as you are conscious, in whatever life, or whatever existence. But to evolve spiritually, you must consciously join with it, joyously and with abandon.

"Now, my friend," Seth grinned at Joel, "Ruburt is not given to quoting from the Christian Bible or, indeed, of using Christian examples, but I will say this to you: There is a quote having to do with the lilies of the field.[1] Now when you do not trust in the spontaneous self you are like lilies in the field— our flower again—who suddenly begin to worry that they will not be fed, nor clothed, nor supported, nor sheltered; and that the nutriments from which they take their existence might be taken away from them. You are supposed to believe that you are supported and sustained . . . by God, in your terms: by a spirit of vitality, or All That Is. To the extent that you do not believe this, you cut yourself off.

"Now, that is my immediate answer to you this evening, my young man, but you can find your own answers . . . in your own spontaneous self and [in] listening to the voice of All That Is within you!"

Class had heard Seth's "idiot flower" analogy before, but this night seemed to fill it with new meaning, perhaps because of Joel's forceful input on good versus evil. Discussions continued until past midnight: analogies about the flowers were all very nice, but what about riots and wars? . . . Class joked and exchanged thoughts about the practical applications involved in being "idiot flowers": Did this mean to just go out and do any old damn thing you please and to hell with the consequences? Did "any old thing you please" automatically connote evil? Were "consequences" automatically bad?

The following week brought up another facet of the "consequences" of spontaneity. Joel reported to class that during his workday, he'd found an associate asleep at his desk in the middle of an important project. Joel confessed that he'd felt like kicking the sleeping man's butt, even though, rationally, he knew *that* wasn't the solution. How, Joel wondered, could you go about changing spontaneous feelings like that into "nonviolent" ones?

Seth came through with an opening succession of jokes and terrible puns, finally telling Joel not to deny the part of himself "that wanted to wring the other man's neck.

"You were so frightened of the thought that you immediately inhibited it!" Seth went on, humorously. "Now, let us consider that thought and *why* you were so terrified of it. You were terrified of it because you are terrified of the idea that evil is more powerful than good and that one stray violent thought of yours was more important and more powerful than the vitality of good . . . Your muscles tensed, your adrenaline production increased, [and] you wanted to wring his neck and you stood there and said, 'God bless you, my fine young fellow, may you live a long and happy life.'

"Now, telepathically, our fine young fellow knows exactly what you are feeling at the time!" Seth roared. "*You* are the one who is out of contact with your feelings and emotions at that point, however; for at this point of your 'spiritual progression,' you only imagine that you wish him good will . . . Originally, you were mad enough to kick him.

"You have some idea in your head that good is gentle and bad is violent and that no violence can be good, and this is because, in your mind, violence and destruction are the same thing. Now by this analogy, you see, the soft voice is the holy voice and the loud voice is the wicked voice and . . . a strong desire is the bad desire and a weak [desire] the good one, so that you become afraid of projecting ideas outward, or desires outward; for in the back of your mind you think that what is powerful is evil and what is weak is good and must be protected and coddled and prayed for and begged for.

"Instead, what I am telling you is that the universe is a good universe . . . your own nature is a good nature and you can trust it . . . Be aware of your own feelings [to Joel, in reference to the sleeping worker] . . . then, as far as is possible, communicate those feelings verbally in whatever way you choose. Use anger as a means of communication; often it will lead you to results that you do not think of and, in your terms, beneficial results."

During that week—and stemming, I believe, from Seth's words on spontaneity and the expression of anger—Ned had a vivid dream in which he found himself filled with an overpowering, directionless rage: as though he were literally exploding with hostility. In the dream, he was standing by a creek. Bending over, he saw a beautiful multicolored fish appear in the rippling waters. In a flash, Ned leaped into the creek and kicked the fish over and over and over until suddenly he was drained of all anger and hate. His dream self then wept with relief, and he woke up feeling refreshed and at ease with himself for the first time in weeks.

In class the next Tuesday, Ned described this fish dream with relish. "And I kicked the shit out of it!" he said, with vehemence. "Then, everything just—released, let go. It felt great! It was like—wow, like I realized that I could get rid of all the hassles inside . . . by just doing it . . ."

Joel had been listening to Ned's dream with a grave, disapproving look on his face. "One thing makes me uncomfortable about that," he said, interrupting Ned's dissertation. "If it's true that our thoughts form realities and our dreams go on without us, or if this was some helpless probable fish in a probable reality, then I just don't see how you could have kicked that poor fish. I mean, I don't think I would have wanted to kill the thing, because I would think you'd be responsible for life in all of its forms, wouldn't you? And here, you let loose on the fish and you kicked it and killed it, in violence."

You couldn't help but remember Joel's sleeping worker and his near miss with Joel's boot. But Ned, a tenderhearted person, particularly when it comes to animals, stared at Joel as if it were himself, and not his dream fish, being kicked. You could see Ned's good cheer deflate like a child's broken balloon.

"But I—" Ned stammered. I thought he was going to cry.

"Now!" Seth's voice cut in. "I come to the defense of Ned and the poor fish and of Ned, the poor fish!"

Ned smiled at Seth, obviously relieved.

"Our Ned chose a fish, subconsciously, for many reasons," Seth began. "First of all, the fish was a part of himself that he materialized within the dream state. It represented, to him, something quite different than the Christian fish [necklace] you [Joel] wear about your neck. The dream served several purposes. It allowed him to release aggression in a much *less* violent manner than he would have in the past. It also, however, allowed him to see the picture of his own aggression as it existed on a subconscious level of his mind. The aggression that he feared was not so great and big and powerful and black and hairy and threatening as he thought! Instead, it was a part of himself and very small—fish-size, you see, and easy to squash and kick!

"In this case, the fish was not a probable fish in another reality; it was a portion . . . of his own energy. Now, it would have been far more beneficial had he [Ned] been able to use that energy, keep it as part of himself, and transform it into a more constructive nature. However, the dream taught him that the violence within himself was not big and threatening and did not need to be feared. He could use it as a symbol to see how small it was in comparison to the whole inner self and how easy, therefore, to rid himself of it . . .

"Each individual life, all life, has its own built-in mechanisms against danger . . . You can become so afraid of violence that you overemphasize its effect; and, if you will excuse me, in doing so you are taking on the guise of the devil. It is the same thing, you see, as projecting upon a hypothetical devil all kinds of powers of destruction. You can do the same thing without realizing it by projecting into the idea of violence all powers, and then it seems to you that life has no ability to protect itself and that any stray thought of violence or disaster will immediately zoom home.

"Your poor little innocent flower: when it rains and thunders and storms come, does our little flower look up and say, 'Here comes that devil lightning and thunder'? It does not think that the thunder and the lightning and the wind and the rain are out to get it! It realizes that the strength and vitality of life is as much in lightning and thunder and the storm as in the sunshine, and it has the sense to realize that it *needs* the rain, even though the rain that comes down may rip off a couple of its leaves. You have much more protection than you realize!"

"Well," Joel said, "we appear quite vulnerable, though. I was thinking of the fish again. When you say the idiot flower may lose a leaf or two, but still have a great deal of protection, I was wondering—well, Ned's fish was only an image, but suppose I had a probable fish in some probable reality? What kind of protection would that fish have had against my violent acts?"

Seth regarded Joel for a long moment, and his voice turned somber. "Now, in the first place," he said, "there are several things you must understand. Some of these things you can misinterpret, and so I go lightly in class with them . . . but basically, you do violence to no one. Basically, you cannot hurt anything, but as long as you think that you can, then you must dwell within that reality.

"No one could hurt your friend's fish, even if it were a live one, in your terms. In your frame of reference, no thing, in your terms, is hurt without giving acceptance to the hurt; without attracting it, and without bringing it to itself; for within your frame of reference, you form your own reality. Not only human beings form their reality, but all consciousness forms its reality.

"This does not mean I am saying, kill, kill, kill," Seth admonished. "You do not understand the holy and sacred nature of life or energy and that you cannot misuse it. You may think you misuse it, but you are not allowed to misuse it. You are not allowed to destroy. While you live with these things, you must deal with them and bear their consequences. If you kill and believe that you kill, you will bear those consequences at this level of your development, but to think that you can destroy a consciousness would make the gods laugh. You cannot destroy one flower seed, much less a man!"

Joel didn't seem too convinced. Certainly class—and Seth—would bring up this issue of violence, aggression, and their consequences many times in the ensuing years. In 1973, for instance, Seth responded vigorously to a remark by Lauren DelMarie that "thoughts can kick people."

"And they [people] would kick them merrily back if you kicked them more often, [and] you would not need bombs—any of you!

"If you spontaneously let out your hostility when you felt it, you would not have this super charge that you felt you must throw out or be damned! It would not be so heavy on your head—or any of your heads! The problem is not what you think of as your negative thoughts, but your fear of them.

"Once you begin suppressing, you suppress all emotions to some degree, and set up barriers because you are afraid of the reality of yourself. If you cannot express anger, you cannot express love—not only that, you get the two confused!

"The only revolution is a revolution of thought. The only changes made in your history, and in your nation, will be made through the change of your thoughts, and not through violent action . . . You cannot change your world from without, for you form it from within."

But the class session on Ned's fish dream affected him dramatically. Afterwards, he said, he felt more "at home" with himself and could see his pent-up hostilities against "the Establishment" for what they were, as though the nameless "Them" existed out there in the same way that his fish had, in the dream-creeks of his own fears.

Two months after his fish dream, Ned was called up for his army induction physical—and flunked it flat. In that respect, at least, his terrors and conflicts were over—and it seems no coincidence that the battleground he created for himself with the draft authorities dissolved soon after his dream confrontation with fishy aggression. Of course, this wasn't the last time, by any means, that class drew its own battle lines on the issues of violence, peace, loyalty, and aggression.

In 1974, Jane assigned each of us to write an essay depicting how our beliefs affected other people and their reactions to us as individuals. A few short papers (dealing mostly with sexual attachments) were read and discussed, but it seemed like the same old hash. Was beauty a set of personal beliefs, or a set of cultural standards? Did the opposite sex really care if you were fat, if your beliefs were right? Or was that a cop-out? The whole debate was getting pretty boring.

Then Jed Martz stood up and brought the house down.

"I saw little justification for the U.S. involvement in Southeast Asia on any grounds—ethical, economic, practical, theoretical, or otherwise," Jed read from his belief paper (which I've quoted here in edited form). "I rejected President Eisenhower's Domino Theory (an ill-defined term). Due to these reasons I was not interested in doing my duty and serving my country in the Armed Forces. I also was not morally outraged enough to split to Canada or go to jail in protest . . . In my last term at college, I was called for a pre-induction physical. This was it—the big moment I'd dreaded for so long. I had to determine a plan of action. I thought of opting for a medical deferment since I'd had a double hernia and a pinched nerve in my back, but I knew I was in good health and that method wouldn't work. Then I decided I would have to play freaked out. I had never acted before and I knew I would have to be convincing. It was my strong belief that I was going to get out of the draft without having to leave the country or go to jail.

"I was called down at the same time as a friend of mine, Willie the Fireman. I stayed up all night and at five in the morning I dressed. I was unshaven. I put on sunglasses and a pink shirt and my flamingo-pink over-alls. I wore no shoes or socks and a torn coat. I applied to my clothing and my person generous helpings of the following: scotch, mud, ketchup, vinegar, rubbing alcohol, urine and various other unusual cosmetics. I took the train, and the other passengers took one look or sniff in my direction and departed for the other end of the car. The one item that had the most distinct odor was a skin-disease cream called Leucoderm. I wanted to buy out the company and patent the product as a guaranteed draft repellent . . . I got some weird stares from Willie's parents [when I got to his house]. 'Your friend's here, and he's wearing his pajamas and doesn't have any shoes,' they said.

"When we got to the draft-board waiting room, Willie said pay no attention when your name is called, but go up to the desk for our papers after everybody else. We got to a room full of desks, and I sat at three different ones . . . I took the pencils from all of the desks around so the others had no pencils, whereas I had nine of them . . . I filled out the medical history form with checks and crosses in all the negative and all the affirmative columns. I also scribbled on the page and wrote lefty so I couldn't see how they could make any sense out of it. I checked off such items as homosexual tendencies, bedwetting, recurrent hallucinations, drug abuse, etc. Then we were to take the forms to a room where we were to strip down to our underpants (which I conveniently hadn't worn) and we were given a little cellophane bag to carry our valuables in.

"I walked into the room, and as everyone else hung up their clothes and got in line, I stood there staring at the ceiling.

"After a while, someone came over and asked me what I was doing and I handed him the papers with the cellophane bag on top and stared at him. He told me to take my clothes off and I just stared at him in a petrified way and shook my head, no. They took me to a medical doctor who tried to persuade me to see the psychiatrist; I protested that I was deathly afraid of them. Finally I relented . . . The psychiatrist had long hair and a bushy mus-tache so I thought that he might be hip to me; but I stared at the floor and didn't look at him once and spoke in an almost inaudible voice. He looked at what I'd checked off: homosexual tendencies. 'Have you ever had sex with a male at any time?' he asked. I said, 'No, I want to, but I'm afraid.' He asked,

'Have you ever had hallucinations?' I said 'I've seen frogs—and colors.' 'Do you take drugs?' 'Sometimes.' 'Are you on drugs now?' 'No.' He was taken aback by that. He had difficulty believing that this was my normal behavior! Had I ever seen a psychiatrist? 'No, I'm afraid they want to hurt me.' Finally he gave me my papers after filling out a report; I read this while walking through the halls: 'withdrawn, incoherent, wearing dark glasses, describes vivid hallucinations.'

"I received a 4-F: not qualified for any military duty, period. I related these incidents to illustrate in a personal way how one can have beliefs that prove themselves successful in practical physical terms.

"Incidentally, I feel patriotic about this because I felt any military career would turn out (for me) along these lines for real."

Most class members, of course, had punctuated Jed's unperturbed reading with screaming whoops of laughter. Jed finished his essay and looked around the room quietly, not a hint of expression on his round, innocently bespeckled face.

"Oh, Jed," Florence MacIntyre said finally, her face contorted with disapproval. "How could you have degraded yourself so? *How could you have acted like that?*"

"Oh, come on!" someone shot back, but Jed just shrugged his shoulders, unoffended. "I didn't feel degraded," he said. "I felt that the draft and the war and all of that was more of a degradation, and I wasn't willing to do *that*."

"I just don't see how any intelligent person like yourself could lower himself to something like that," Florence stated. "How—I mean—don't you have any feelings of dignity? Or any feelings of loyalty to your country at all?"

"Yes, I think I do," Jed said. "That's why I did it." Others in the room were leaping to Jed's defense; few remarks were made (aloud) in agreement with Florence. Up boiled a heated argument. Voices rose to fever pitch. Faces on all sides turned red with anger. Everybody was shouting at once. Jane, for the most part, listened in silence.

"I thought Jed's attitude was pretty stinking," Harold Wiles remembers (although he didn't say much at the time). "I think he expended a lot more effort staying out of the service than he would if he'd gone in! All I remember was an underlying feeling of disgust for his methods and attitude and what he went through."

Predictably, as voices in the room got louder and louder, Seth whipped off Jane's glasses and shut off the whole brouhaha with his commanding "Now!"

With great precision, he placed Jane's new granny glasses on the coffee table. "This has been your night. And it is still your night," he began. "But when all the young men refuse to kill for the sake of peace, and when all the women forbid their men to kill for the sake of peace, and when you realize that no peace will come through killing, and that the end does not justify the means, and when you grow full and light with thoughts of peace, *then* there will be an end to war! But as long as any men go to war for the sake of peace, there will be war. And as long as any woman teaches her sons how to go to war because of love of peace, there will be war.

"You make your world. When you populate your world with ideas of peace, then peace will grow. When you think thoughts of aggression, you attract aggression and you draw it out from others in daily contact, and on the part of nations.

"When you do not understand yourselves, you project what you do not understand upon others—upon your friends and associates—and then you become afraid of what you do not understand, not understanding that it is your own fear. And you do the same thing as a nation with other nations. There is no way to ensure peace but for every man, *every man*, to lay down his arms."

"But his behavior was just crazy!" Florence interjected angrily.

"To do what he did does indeed appear crazy. Idiot behavior in the world that you know!" Seth replied. "But it is very sane behavior. Our friend here [Jed] was not able to leap the barrier. He could not make a creative achievement out of going to war. And I will tell you," Seth turned directly to Harold, who until then had said nothing, "were you his age, and in the same war, you would have done in your own way, the same thing! You would have turned it into a creative endeavor indeed, and you would have helped lead that generation!"

"I never did quite get what Seth meant by that remark," Harold said, seven years later.

"Well, if Jed were my son, I'd be completely ashamed of him," Florence said, adamantly. "I've brought my son up to understand what loyalty and dignity are, and to do his duty when necessary! To feel a sense of responsibility! I would never want him to act insane!"

"If sanity is to lead your sons to death, then I would rather be insane any day," Seth told her. "And this is not to pick out our Lady of Florence, either. For in your own ways, and in different circumstances, your reasoning is often the same [as Florence's]. And many of you still think that peace must be quiet and dignified, and excitement is to be found only where there is not peace . . . so think of the ways in which our Lady of Florence's thinking applies to your own, in other areas of your activity and thoughts.

"A point I want to make: It takes aggressive energy to send forth thoughts and feelings of peace. So your idea of aggression is completely wrong. Aggression is action, and the thoughts of peace radiated outward take aggression and joy and vitality . . . the thrust for peace is as natural as the thrust of a flower to grow up from the ground. Now, continue."

Jane came out of trance, and we started to repeat Seth's words to her, as best we could. "He said Jed was right when he acted crazy like that," one girl explained. "I guess he was telling us to be nonviolent."

Immediately, Seth reappeared. "Your very breath, in those terms, does a violence upon the air. A joyful violence!" Seth exchanged a round of smiles with Florence, who was quietly sipping wine, her face red and tense.

"You do not understand our Lady of Florence's position," Seth said, "and you use the same thinking yourselves in other areas, and it is this: Supposing our fine American boys decide not to fight. But supposing our fine Russian or Chinese boys do not come to the same decision. So you are leaving yourselves open—so you must meet any threat, or be weak! So," Seth gestured at Florence again, "I understand your position."

"You read my mind, Seth," Florence said. "I was just thinking, I hope Seth tells the enemy to put down their arms too."

"Now," Seth answered quietly, gravely, "the 'enemy' does not need a Seth any more than you do to tell them to lay down their arms. They need their own inner selves. *And if one side lays down its arms, the other side will realize there is no need for arms.*

"You cannot understand this now, and yet I tell you that your preoccupation with arms, as a country, is received by others, and your own thoughts are materialized and you create wars in your minds that then must be fought with your flesh and your blood. And no drop of blood flows . . . that does not first flow in your mind, and in all of your minds!

"And there is no other way to have peace but to believe in peace. As I speak here, others also speak in other countries, as they have in other times. And you have not listened! And in not listening, you continue to create the reality that you have. And, in creating that reality in the world that you know, and in time as you understand it, you return again and again—sons who have been slain on the battleground are born as women, who then bring up their fine sons to repeat once again the old history.

"So it shall be done to you as you do. And, as you think, so is your world. The reality that you have is a replica of your thoughts. If you do not like the world, you must change your thoughts, and no exterior manipulation will change the face of your experience one iota if you do not change your dreams and your thoughts!

"You create the mountains. You create your bodies. You create the seasons and the continents and the rivers. You create—" Seth glanced down at Renée Levine and Stewie Gould, "Renée's smile, and the hand upon which Stewie's head rests. And the war and the pests, *all of the pests*, that seem to haunt mankind—war, and poverty—you create those.

"It is your world. Then change it—now!"

While class was trying to fill Jane in on Seth's comments, the main doorway downstairs banged open and we could hear footsteps coming up from the hall. To our surprise, Dan MacIntyre, Florence's son, walked in the door and sat down next to his mother. Dan hadn't been to class in a long time, and it was getting close to 11 o'clock besides. As Dan listened to explanations of what had been said, he started to fidget nervously. Finally, he and his mother regarded one another, rather shyly.

Florence MacIntyre

"What's going on? What did you tell them?" Dan asked good-naturedly.

"Well, Florence, tell him," Jane said.

Florence cleared her throat. "I was just telling them how I've taught you to have a sense of responsibility and loyalty to your country, that's all," she said.

"What!?" Dan burst out, aghast. "You mean, about this crazy war? Are you serious? Forget it! I'd never go. No way!"

"Dan-iel!" Florence shouted in dismay, but instantly, Jane's glasses were waving in the air from a Sethian hand. "Let that be a lesson to you, in line with what I said earlier!" he said to her.

"I would still want him to have his dignity," Florence replied, her voice shaking.

"Of what kind?" Seth asked.

Florence looked down at her hands and didn't answer.

"A flower has dignity!" Seth continued, gently. "*You* have dignity! He [Daniel] has dignity! He has dignity no matter what he does, and he [Jed] had dignity when he pretended he was an idiot!"

Seth sat back in the chair and rocked back and forth, eyes closed, for several minutes before continuing. "As long as you believe in aggression and in force, in this country, you elect persons who believe in aggression and in force and who react to it, and so do the people in all the other nations," he said. "Unfortunately, you equate aggression with strength, so you are afraid to elect a peaceful man. And all the other countries feel the same, so they are afraid to put into power, by whatever means, peaceful men. So your world situation is the result of your individual beliefs, en masse.

"Now, when individually you believe in peace, and when you no longer believe that good is weak and evil is powerful, then on a country-wide basis, you will put people into power who believe in the active nature of peace. And, again, there is no other answer.

"I am, basically, as you are, independent of flesh. But in your terms, and in your terms alone, you have issue—physical issue, that must deal with the time and the place that you have created. And as long as you believe that you must fight for peace, you will lose your issue.

"In greater terms, you know quite well that you cannot annihilate a consciousness. And all of those who die in war know well that they will die in war ahead of time. But still, in physical terms, all of that must be worked out, for the very point of physical existence is that you realize that your thoughts become matter while you are here, and matter can be vulnerable. And so through direct experience you learn what happens when you let thoughts and feelings of aggression have full play. I have said this in my book [*The Nature of Personal Reality*].

"An artist may create a warscape, and you can look at it, and it may be a masterpiece. But you are multidimensional creators! And when you create a warscape, then brushstrokes suffer, for *you are* the brushstrokes. And the guns are real, and the wounds are real. But it is an excellent representation—an excellent multidimensional creative endeavor!

"If you do not like the landscape, then you change the brushstrokes. You wipe out the oil. You make a new painting.

"And now, I bid you a fond good night, blessings and all!"

As class was leaving Jane's living room, Florence walked over to Jed and told him, "It's not that I don't like you, because I do like you. It's just that I don't understand how you could have done all that."

"It's okay," Jed said; his expression hadn't changed from its mild complaisance throughout the evening. "I don't mind. But I don't really understand your objections either, I guess."

I'm not sure that Florence, Jed, Harold, Daniel, or any of us really understood the full implications of Seth's remarks that night, but the point of it was drilled into us again in one of Jane's final classes—an "un-class," really, held on a Saturday night in July of 1975. It was then that Seth suggested that we start telling ourselves that we lived in a "safe universe."

A safe universe? In this age of the Bomb, was there really, in practical terms, any such thing?

"Now, each of you, to some degree or another here, believe that the universe is not safe, and therefore you must set up your defenses against it," Seth said that summer evening. "Now, the one-line, official consciousness with which you are familiar says, 'The world is not safe. I cannot trust it. Nor can I trust the conditions of experience, or the conditions of my own existence. Nor can I trust myself. I can look at a squirrel and rejoice, but I cannot look at myself and rejoice, for lo, I am filled with iniquity, and I am, to some extent, evil, and I must hide myself. I am not only evil, as myself, but I come from a tainted and flawed race, and my father and my mother are tainted before me, and I send these tragic flaws before me into the future; and therefore I must need protect myself, and I must set up my defense in whatever way I can, to protect myself in a universe that I cannot trust, and to protect myself from a self that is evil and flawed.'

"You have an entire civilization and world set up about those beliefs I have just given you: that the universe is not safe; that you must defend yourselves from enemies that come from without, and worst of all, from enemies that are within. And so indeed do you feel uneasy, and set up your barriers, and run as fast as you can, in whatever way given you, from those enemies that are the result of a one-line official kind of consciousness.

"As long as you believe that you dwell in a universe that is a threat, you must defend yourself against it. As long as you believe that the self is flawed, and that your race is damned and evil, you must also defend yourself against yourself, and how can you then trust the voice of the psyche?

"And, when I say to you, 'Be spontaneous,' how dare you take that step, when to be spontaneous would obviously give rise to all the lust, and all the passion, and all the murder, and all the hatred, to you quite obviously inherent in the human heart? And so you say, 'I will try to be spontaneous, but how can I? I believe that *I* am good, but how can I be good when I come from a race that is evil?'

"You try to say, 'The universe is safe,' and then you watch the news on television, or you read your newspaper, and you say, 'What lie is this? How can the universe be safe when I read about wholesale murder, and war, and trickery, and greed? How can I be myself, for if I am myself, will I not unleash unto the world only more of the horror that I see about me; for surely human nature cannot change, and human nature is evil. Look what evil it has already worked upon the planet in which I have my existence; then tell me, Seth, be spontaneous. What do you ask of me, and how can I therefore in this context stand upon the authority of my own psyche and say, "I insist that I am good"?'

"The official line of consciousness forms a world about it, and you perceive and experience that world, and it will always show you the results of the beliefs that are inherent in the official line of consciousness. While you devote yourself to that official line of consciousness, the world will always appear the same: evil, disastrous, bound only for damnation, whether through nuclear destruction, or the greater judgment of a fundamental god.

"The one-line stage of consciousness was necessary for reasons that Ruburt has given [in *Psychic Politics* and *Adventures in Consciousness*]. But that stage contained within it its own impetus. It set up challenges that could not be solved at that stage of consciousness, and that would automatically lead you into other strands of awareness. Only then can those contradictions make sense. Only then can you say, individually—and listen, now—'*I live in a safe universe.*'

"You need not say, 'The universe is safe,' for at your present level that will only enrage you! You say, instead, 'I live in a safe universe,' and so you shall. And those defenses that you set up against threats will crumble, for they will not be needed. But you *are* safe, and you are innocent, and you can become aware of that innocence.

"When you . . . leave the official one-line kind of consciousness as your criteria for reality, you will take it with you as one picture, or as one view; perhaps as a landscape that you have seen somewhere—a beautiful one that you love! But it will not be the entire picture. You must step out of that picture, while loving it and holding it tenderly in your hands."

WARREN: "Seth?"

SETH: "My dear friend—one more time!"

WARREN: "All That Is knows of the portion
of himself that is us. Is there . . . "

SETH: "All That Is does indeed know himself,
or itself, and wakens to itself as you."

WARREN: "Is there a part that sent us out, similar to
All That Is, that knows each part of us that is?"

SETH: "There is indeed."

WARREN: "Is there any way that we can make
ourselves aware of the portion that sent us?"

SETH: "There is indeed."

WARREN: "What is it?"

SETH: "Know yourself."

Notes

CHAPTER 1
Who Said Truth Was Stranger Than Fiction?

1. This manuscript was completed and published as *How to Develop Your ESP Power* in 1966 (New York: Frederick Fell, Inc.). It was reissued in 1976 as *The Coming of Seth* (New York: Pocket Books).

2. From chapter 1, "We Meet Seth," of *The Seth Material.*

3. Jane's fantasy novels, *The Education of Oversoul Seven* and *The Further Education of Oversoul Seven*, published 1973 and 1979 (Englewood Cliffs, NJ: Prentice-Hall).

4. For a complete discussion of aspect psychology, see Jane's *Adventures in Consciousness.*

5. See chapter 8 in *The Seth Material* for a complete description of these tests that Jane, Rob, and Seth participated in for more than a year. The results of these tests remain a mystery to Jane and Rob; Dr. "Instream," as Jane called him, has since passed away.

6. Jane mentions this personality in chapter 5 of *Adventures in Consciousness.*

7. See chapter 1 of *The Nature of Personal Reality* for Rob's notes on the flood and its effect on the city of Elmira.

CHAPTER 2
The Cast of Class and How It Grew

1. The psychologists, psychiatrists, and other scientists who attended Jane's class are on record in Jane and Rob's files.

2. I believe that the Codicils, as presented in part 3 of Jane's *Psychic Politics*, represent the kind of consciousness that class was in the process of developing.

3. *archy & mehitabel*, by Don Marquis (New York: Doubleday, 1927,1930). Included in this collection of a cockroach's nightly essays on a newspaper-office typewriter are "mehitabel was once cleopatra"; "pete the parrot & shakespeare"; and "clarence the ghost." (Archy the cockroach could manage all typewriter keys except the uppercase shift lever.)

4. Gnosticism originated in pre-Christian times and is a system of religion and philosophy that believes in knowledge, or gnosis, as the means of salvation from the tyranny of matter, rather than faith or a search for "truth." Seth has more to say about Arturo in *CWS*, book 2.

5. For many years prior to World War II, Elmira was the Broadway tryout center for hopeful theater productions, and a well-known summer theater location; the nearby Corning Summer Theater has largely taken over this last role.

CHAPTER 3
Experiments

1. Published 1974 and 1976, respectively (Englewood Cliffs, NJ: Prentice-Hall).

2. Simply: alpha is one of four officially recognized brain wave patterns, measured in hertz units, or cycles per second. From the slowest to most rapid, they are: delta, the wave of dreamless sleep; theta, of creativity and dreams; alpha, of relaxed alertness and changing consciousness; and beta, typified by concentration and intense focus on the daily world.

In appendix 17 for session 711 of *The "Unknown" Reality*, volume 2, Seth says that the beta waves "seem to be the official pulse of your civilization, giving precedence to official reality." Appendix 17 of *"Unknown"* makes interesting reading for Seth's further comments on brain wave patterns. See *CWS*, book 2, appendix 1 for an alpha "monologue" of Seth's.

3. Again, see more of Theodore's automatic writing and meditation experiences in "The Great Hall" in *CWS*, book 2, appendix 2.

4. The "Instream" tests, described in chapter 8 of *The Seth Material*.

CHAPTER 4
Who Hasn't Got a Secret?

1. *Stranger in a Strange Land* by Robert A. Heinlein (New York: G. P. Putnam's Sons, 1961).

2. Ibid., p. 204.

3. Seth also complimented Florence, humorously, on her timing in missing the first of the secrets sessions: "Since you are a faithful member of this class, then it seems to me that you are using your abilities very well, for you know precisely when to stay away!"

4. Seth's analogy here was directed at me—for I had just told a secret I held with such fierce tenacity that I refused to reveal it again, when I wrote up this chapter in 1979. I'd had a baby on Martha's Vineyard in 1968, and given him up for adoption. By 1971, only a few close friends (including Jane) knew about this; my parents never knew at all (consciously, anyway). Not until 1993, long after my parents were gone, did I even muster the nerve to tell Sean that he had "a brother out there somewhere." Telling the secret in class felt terrible, humiliating beyond recourse (not that I'd had a baby, but that I'd left him behind), though Seth's words were oddly, if momentarily, soothing. Only years afterward could I see that this confession helped me begin to release the weight of abject shame I'd punished myself with for so long (having let the child go, I held onto this).

A few classes later, I asked Seth if I would "ever see that baby again," and Seth stared at me for a long, strange moment and replied, "Indeed. I am answering in the affirmative," and that was all. I never asked any other questions about it; this bit of ghostly hope seemed miraculously more than I deserved. I was too cowed by the impenetrable wall of silence adoption imposed in those days to imagine that anything other than a stroke of magic would reunite us. And though I didn't tell my secret in its pages, *Conversations with Seth* is seeded with what I thought were clues any child of mine would eventually discover, recognize, and find me thereby.

Well, magic can happen in straightforward ways. In April of 1993, Sean made exactly two phone calls and located a Massachusetts agency that willingly connected us with "that baby" a few days before his twenty-fifth birthday! Dave and Sean and I have gotten together several times since then, including a visit in 1998 to Dave's Beach Plum Lobster Farm in Ogunquit, Maine, where I also met his parents. Moreover, the remarkable similarities and coincidences between Dave and me display an ongoing communication (and not a little magic) among us all, on many levels, that I plan to write about someday in depth.

CHAPTER 5
Belief Box

1.   See chapter 8, *The Nature of Personal Reality*, for Rob's notes on the effects of the Flood of 1972.

Interestingly, by the way, my loose-leaf notebooks of Seth class sessions had been on the bottom shelf of my crowded bookcase when the flood waters hit; likewise, my dream notebooks were stacked in the bottom drawer of my nightstand. Although floodwater covered and ruined both the nightstand and all my books, neither the dream notebooks nor the class sessions were hurt—in fact, when I dug these out of their muddy shelf areas, I discovered that their pages weren't even wet, even though the covers on everything were filthy. Of course the class notebooks were tightly jammed in their shelf space, so sheer pressure might have kept the water out; but then, all my other books were soaked through and through. The spiral-page dream books, which were just placed on top of one another, were undamaged in a drawer full of mud!

2.   *The Nature of Personal Reality*, session 614. Specific, detailed methods for discovering and changing beliefs are what Seth's book is all about, however, and should be read for an in-depth understanding of this premise.

3.   Today, Richie holds a regular job, and says he at last understands "the fulfillment of work."

4.   Carl did eventually sail across the Atlantic and lived for a while in Greece—tiller bolts apparently intact.

5.   The Prix de Rome is a prize given annually in the fine arts (sculpture, music, painting, writing) by American judges. One winner from each category goes to Rome for a year and while there is provided with a free studio and living costs.

6.   Since the time that I wrote this passage in 1981, George has come to enjoy an international following. His sculptures grace many public buildings around the world (including Port Authority in New York and the Bank One Ball Park in Phoenix, Arizona). He has also appeared on *Good Morning America* and other such shows, patiently answering the inevitable question, "But is it art?" "Damn right," says George.

7.   See chapter 13 of *The Nature of Personal Reality* for a complete discussion of these beliefs as related to "states of grace," personal and mass beliefs, and the private and social experience.

CHAPTER 6
ESP Revisited

1.   In the latter part of the sixteenth century, a land grant from Queen Eliza-beth I gave Sir Walter Raleigh permission to establish a settlement in the New World at Roanoke Island, North Carolina. Raleigh's first expedition there in 1585 held out for a year against hostile Indian tribes before returning to England. Virginia Dare, first child of English parents in the New World, was born on August 18, 1587, seven days after the landing of Raleigh's second, 117-person, expedition. But upon the return of Raleigh's ships from England in the spring of 1590, all trace of the Roanoke settlement had vanished—except for the enigmatic word "Croatoan" carved in a tree. Recent excavations in the area have discovered outlines of buildings on the Roanoke settlement site, however.

I'm not a history buff, by any means, and neither is Jane; at the time we talked to Brad I had only the vaguest of memories about "the disappearing colony." I think it's safe to say that Jane has no conscious knowledge at all of this bit of historical lore. For this footnote, I had to look up the above facts in the 1977 *The World Almanac*.

2.   In 1979, at the age of eleven, Nadine's son won the New York State Piano Competition, sponsored by the Federation of Music Clubs, for eleven- to fifteen-year-olds.

3.   Some other examples of this phenomenon could include the familiar child-hood "imaginary playmate." See Seth's reference to Rob's childhood "fragment" com-panion, page 28 of *The Seth Material*, in which the young Robbie briefly material-ized a playmate while sitting on a swing in a playground near his home. "Occasion-ally a personality will astound itself by such an image production," Seth said of that incident. "Usually this type vanishes by the time the personality reaches adulthood. In childhood, however, such instances are frequent."

4.   Seth also comments on UFOs in *The "Unknown" Reality*, volume 2, ses-sions 713 and 743; also in appendix 20 for session 713. Among other remarks on the subject, Seth says, on page 385 of session 713, that "Some reported instances of UFOs happened in the past as far as the visitors were concerned, but appeared as images or realities in your present. This involves craft sightings only." But by far the most provocative statement on these matters, on page 654 of session 743, is this: "You cannot understand perceived events unless you understand who perceives them." This last remark of Seth's can certainly apply to this entire chapter on "ESP Revisited."

5.   Page 655 of *The "Unknown" Reality*, volume 2.

CHAPTER 7
The Sumari (and Others) Come Home

1.   See chapter 6 of *Adventures in Consciousness*, in which Jane describes her feelings of projecting through the landscape outside her apartment windows as one might fly through a hole ripped in tissue paper. It's interesting to note her similar sensations during the alteration of consciousness experience that produced "The Physical Universe as Idea Construction," her first "psychic" experience (described in *The Seth Material*, chapter 1). She'd been sitting in front of those bay windows that time, too.

2. See session 594 for September 13, 1971 in the appendix of *Seth Speaks*.

3. Chapter 7, page 78, *Adventures in Consciousness*.

4. In volume 2 of *The "Unknown" Reality*, Seth lists the following "families" of consciousness (and more fully describes their purposes and intent):

1. Gramada: to found social systems.
2. Sumafi: to transmit "originality" through teaching.
3. Tumold: to heal, regardless of individual occupation.
4. Vold: to reform the status quo.
5. Milumet: to mystically nourish mankind's psyche.
6. Zuli: to serve as physical, athletic models.
7. Borledim: to provide an Earth stock for the species through parenthood.
8. Ilda: to spread and exchange ideas.
9. Sumari: to provide the cultural, spiritual, and artistic heritage for the species.

I think it's also interesting that in 1970, a year before the Sumari development and five years before Seth's list of families of consciousness, I wrote a short story based on a woman who'd attended class a few times. She was from Scandinavia, had traveled extensively in a variety of modeling jobs, and was well-versed in a multitude of philosophies (Seth's included) and cultures. The name I chose for this character in my story was "Ilda."

5. This transcription is reproduced in chapter 15 in *Adventures in Consciousness*.

6. George was always a bit amused that his entity name is also the French word for cheese. However, in Jane's Sumari poem, "Songs of the Silver Brothers," in chapter 8, of *Adventures in Consciousness*, "Fromage" appears in another (and perhaps more appropriate) context:

For darambi	I speak
Tol arado fromabe	And syllables rearrange
Marjor astare	My worlds
Fromage	Fossilings
O borare	Rise wiggling like seeds
Gravunde	To growth in words

7. However, I'll reproduce the Sumari words to Faith Briggs's song here to show what these sounds were like:

Faith's Sumari Song

Zhay zay ra ba dee kay zay ba.
Zhay zay ra ba dee kay lay ba.
Zhay zay lay ba bee kay zee ra
ba ohm lay dee.

Ezhay zee la rom ba,
Ezhay zay vrom be zhay.

Ezhay zay va ba ca bee ba tee zay
la ma be a;

Hahza me a,
Hahza me a.

Hahzay ray bo key zay dee a,
me a zhay zay bo:

Zay zay lome,

Zhay zay lome-bah
Zay zay vrom-bah
Zhay zay vrom bah!

Bay zee ta.

CHAPTER 8
Reincarnation

1. In fact, on May 15, 1970, Ned and I recorded remarkably similar dreams from the night before. In mine, I was a woman in some kind of uniform, trying to help soldiers climb into a large, canvas-covered truck, while machine-gun fire sprayed all around. In Ned's, he found himself the driver of a large canvas-covered truck; while gunfire exploded all around, he waited for a woman in the back of the truck to signal him to drive away. Both dreams ended in a mad chase through a large city (referred to in both our dream records as "like Munich") toward "the border."

2. Ned later received a 4-F (unfit for military service) classification for physical reasons unknown at the time of this session.

3. See session 692 for April 24, 1974, in volume 1 of *The "Unknown" Reality*.

4. I don't think that this sort of dream life is at all unusual, by the way. Try asking your friends about their childhood dreams and see! Many people will recall some pretty fascinating dream events. Parents could also encourage their children to talk about their dreams, or keep records of them (an elementary school teacher in my town has her students record their dreams in class every morning as a writing exercise). Just on an everyday practical level, the benefits of such record keeping are obvious.

5. See chapter 12 of *The Seth Material*.

6. Interestingly, Lauren's New York friend Jed Martz recorded the following dream *before* Lauren had his mirror experience: "I was a Confederate Lieutenant in charge of a field unit," Jed says. "In my dream, Lauren had the same position in the unit next to mine. [It was] about a year later that Lauren . . . asked Seth about [his Confederate officer]. I definitely had the feeling that one of these officers was an incarnation of *mine.*"

7. Reincarnating "backwards" in time is one of the themes of Jane's *Oversoul Seven* novels. Twentieth-century Lydia, who dies in *The Education of Oversoul Seven*, is reborn as Tweety in seventeenth-century Sweden in *The Further Education of Oversoul Seven*. Jane wrote the second novel in 1979, after class had ended.

8. See chapter 2 of *Adventures in Consciousness*, which describes how Bette and Joel reacted as pioneer woman and Indian warrior.

9. This is one of Seth's earliest references to the counterpart theory, later developed in answer to Rob's Roman and Jamaican-woman visions in the fall of 1974, as explained in *The "Unknown" Reality*, and as explored in *CWS*, book 2, chapter 6.

CHAPTER 9
The Naked and the Dread

1. See appendix 9 of *The "Unknown" Reality*, volume 1, for Seth's comments on the historical development of our concept of male and female.

CHAPTER 10
The Experiment Continues

1. One question we often pondered about this was what would happen if Jane allowed Seth to drink his cherished brandy. Would she come out of trance and find herself inebriated? Jane never consented to this fascinating piece of research.

2. Recounted in *CWS*, book 2, chapter 5.

3. Jane also discusses this class in chapter 1 of *Adventures in Consciousness*, "The Class that Went Too Far."

4. Among other correlations, there's an interesting connection here between this image and a coinciding dream experience of my son's and mine, which is described in *CWS*, book 2, chapter 9. In our dreams, the predominant feature was the same kind of flat, geometrical "plain of perspective," and other geometrical forms.

5. Seth is referring here to a development away from the one-line form of consciousness, as discussed throughout *The "Unknown" Reality*.

6. This double dream is described in more detail in the notes for session 692 of *The "Unknown" Reality*, volume 1.

7. Once again, this remark correlates, in my mind, at least, with the information Seth gave to me on my UFO sighting and its possible meaning as a "message sent from a future self," as described in chapter 6 of this book.

CHAPTER 11
Health, Healing, and How We Walked Through Each Others' Bones

1. According to the dictionary, Hodgkin's disease, a form of lymphoma, is a malignant tumor of the lymph nodes, accompanied by enlargement of the spleen and often of the liver and kidneys, affecting the blood vessels.

2. "[As to the wig story]," Will Petrosky commented to me in 1999 via email, "your assumption in the book was that I reached over to pull her ribbon. Actually, I reached over to touch her ribbon, much as I saw Sumari do—only I was a clumsy oaf, and my gentle tug, which wasn't supposed to do anything, pulled off the wig."

3. Though Jane never had cancer, her death in 1984 was a result of complications from rheumatoid arthritis, which had plagued her for many years. The

complex multilayered reasons and beliefs behind Jane's symptoms are woven throughout her books, journals, poetry, and the Seth material itself. All of these are now
available for study in the Jane Roberts Archives at Yale University, New Haven, Con-
necticut, as well as in reprints and new editions of Jane's work, including her riveting
last Seth book, *The Way Toward Health*, delivered from her hospital bed before she
died.

Still, the rumor referred to here in *Conversations with Seth* was one of many,
often very odd bits of screwy hearsay, that apparently circulated about Jane among
people she and Rob never met. It came back to her in one way or another that she
was dead or dying, an alcoholic, confined to a mental institution, or living in a house
surrounded by a ten-foot electrified fence and a pack of guard dogs.

"The only one that really got me mad," Jane said back then, "is when I heard
the rumor that I'd repudiated Seth and become a born-again Christian!"

4. The "Mu" chant, like its sister "Om," are both word-sounds used by meditative sects and groups for a number of reasons, one of them being to utilize sound
and energy to maintain light trance states. Class used "Mu" to send energy, or sometimes just for fun—but whenever we held a "Mu" contest to see who could keep this
word going the longest, Jane always won!

CHAPTER 12
The War of the Idiot Flowers

1. From Matthew 6:28, 29 (King James version): "Consider the lilies of the
field, how they grow: they toil not, neither do they spin: And yet I say unto you,
That even Solomon in all his glory was not arrayed like one of these."

Index

Page numbers appearing in italics indicate
illustrations; page numbers followed
by "n" indicate endnotes.

Sullivan, Mildred, 53
Sumari, 12, 25, 27, 43, 125–43,
    157–58, 168, 195, 206
    families of consciousness, 132–
    33, 243n
    inner city, 197–201
Sumari circle, 137, 138–39
Sumari–Jane, 132, 135–36, 138–42
symbolism, 62–63

table-tipping, 52–55
television, 1
thoughts, 227–28
    intertwining of, 212–13
    reality as, 232

UFOs, 115–17, 242n
universe
    safe, 235–36
"Unknown" Reality, The (Roberts), 5,
    7, 13, 123, 152

Valerie, 129, 132
Vanessa, 129, 132
vegetarianism, 210
Vietnam War, 220, 228–29, 233
violence, 220–21, 224–28, 230–34

war, 148–49
    Vietnam. *See* Vietnam War
Watkins, Ned, 17, 75–77, 148–49,
    214, 221, 225–28
Watkins, Sean, 214, 215–16
Watkins, Sue, 12–13, 16, *18*,
    37–40, 132, 148–49, 155,
    168–69, 172–73, 180
    biographical background of, 7,
    16–19, 20, 240n
    Conversations with Seth, reasons
    for writing, 3–6
    earaches of, 214–16
    ESP experiences of, 112–14
    ESP powers and, 108–10
    Jane Roberts's classes and, 3, 20–
    24
    Jane Roberts's comments on, 7–
    13

as loner, 20
    out-of-body experiences of, 18–19
    poems of, 16, 88, 108
    reaction of, to nakedness, 175–76
    on reincarnation, 152–56
    Sumari and, 134–36
Wiles, Harold, 4, 8, 56, 83, 136, 141,
    162, 171–72, 172–73, 180, 230,
    231, 234
worship, 30–31

Zahorian, Bette, 27, 128, 129, 136,
    139–40, 141, 162, 194
Zale, Bernice, 38, 114–15, 128, 136
Zale, Donald, 114–15

About the Author

Susan M. Watkins is a former newspaper reporter, feature
writer, and columnist, and the author of five books, including
Speaking of Jane Roberts and *What a Coincidence!*
She lives in upstate New York.

If you enjoyed *Conversations with Seth*,
we know you'll enjoy these other
titles by **Moment Point Press** . . .

Susan M. Watkins

Conversations with Seth, Book 2
25th Anniversary Edition
(available spring 2006)

Speaking of Jane Roberts
*Remembering the Author
of the Seth Material*

What a Coincidence!
*Understanding Synchronicity
in Everyday Life*
(available fall 2005)

Jane Roberts

Adventures in Consciousness
Psychic Politics
The God of Jane

Kenneth Ring, Ph.D.

Lessons from the Light
*What We Can Learn from the
Near-Death Experience*

For more information about these
and all of our Moment Point titles, please
visit www.momentpoint.com